Faith and Evolution

A Grace-Filled Naturalism

ROGER HAIGHT, SJ

ORBIS  BOOKS
Maryknoll, New York 10545

ORBIS BOOKS
Maryknoll, New York 10545

Fathers and Brothers
MARYKNOLL™

Scripture quotations are from the New Revised Standard Version of the Bible, copyright © 1989 by the National Council of the Churches of Christ in the USA. All rights reserved.

Manufactured in the United States of America.

Manuscript editing and typesetting by Joan Weber Laflamme

Library of Congress Cataloging-in-Publication Data

Names: Haight, Roger, author.
Title: Faith and evolution: a grace-filled naturalism / Roger Haight, S.J.
Description: Maryknoll : Orbis Books, 2019. | Includes bibliographical references and index.
Identifiers: LCCN 2019013968 (print) | ISBN 9781626983410 (print)
Subjects: LCSH: Creationism. | Evolution (Biology)—Religious aspects—Christianity. | Religion and science.
Classification: LCC BS651 .H247 2019 (print) | LCC BS651 (ebook) | DDC 231.7/652—dc23
LC record available at https://lccn.loc.gov/2019013968
LC ebook record available at https://lccn.loc.gov/20 19980783

The Jesuits

Contents

Preface

I can find no clear, logical reason why I became interested in the topic of this book. I am not a scientist, despite an early interest in mathematics, and I did not become one in the course of this project. But in place of a logic, perhaps I can retrieve for myself as well as others the path that led me to this work. It has certainly sprung from two deeply held convictions, the importance of the doctrine of creation for Christian self-understanding and, negatively, the lack of a systematic theology that addresses educated professional people who have been influenced by the criticisms of religion that emanate from the secular world and, especially recently, from the sphere of science. Many do not have and are looking for the means for processing their faith in today's secular, evolutionary, and technological world.

I did not develop an interest in the doctrine of creation all at once. It has strong standing in Christian teaching because of its prominence in biblical literature. Biblical testimony for the most part uses anthropomorphic language, but very early in Christian theological tradition creation gained a philosophically reflective apparatus. In the writings of Thomas Aquinas, who continues to exert an influence on creation theology, biblical imagery and philosophical reflection combine in a remarkable synthesis. Neo-Thomist Edward Schillebeeckx had a systematically grounded theology of creation that still operated in his later historically conscious and exegetical theology. Many years ago Dorothy Jacko, in her doctoral thesis on later Schillebeeckx, showed that, when one viewed the later writing of Schillebeeckx synthetically, almost everything he said about salvation could be understood in terms of creation theology. The ultimate savior is the creator God.[1] The epistemology of the doctrine of creation and its subtlety make it a powerful intellectual concept in discussing the topic of God. It provides a natural port of entry for a discussion with the secular world and with science.

---

[1] Dorothy Jacko, "Salvation in the Context of Contemporary Secularized Historical Consciousness: The Later Theology of Edward Schillebeeckx," PhD diss. (University of St. Michael's College, Toronto School of Theology, 1987), 83–136. The "almost" in my judgment here deliberately leaves space for the saving role of Jesus Christ, which Schillebeeckx neither neglects nor slights.

The problem of the waning relevance of Christian teaching about the fundamental character of reality in its core doctrines relentlessly preoccupies practitioners of the discipline of theology. No single cause explains the massive downsizing of the churches in the Western world. And one cannot easily cast blame on any particular kind of theology; the discipline will always be as pluralistic as the members of the churches. But in recent years increasing criticism of religion, particularly Christianity in the West, has come from the world of the sciences. More generally, Christianity and religion have little or no influence in the secular academic world and the sphere of professional life. It may even be considered a negative element and positively shunned. If Christianity bears relevant truth about reality and human existence, there should be a way to communicate this to the professional, academic, and scientific worlds.

I do not intend this discussion to resolve these problems; they lie in the background. The question that guides this work is simpler: How should we understand Christian faith as it professes itself in its basic teachings about reality, its doctrines? Theologians address this question in many ways, but one path not usually traveled consists of consulting the science that has such an influence on the present-day imagination. In many ways science has replaced Christianity in the West as the authoritative voice in culture. The abstract word *science* represents all the disciplines and scientists who carefully probe every aspect of our material world. *Evolution,* too, is a massively abstract word. It covers various subdisciplines in biology that study the large history of evolution, or the specific history of a given species, or the various mechanisms that explain the process itself.[2] But the collective word of scientists has become the major interpreter of the nature of things; science's effort at being a nonsectarian voice makes it the arbiter of opinion; science rather than the church often provides the final consultation before the exercise of conscience in matters of moral choice. These privileges that Christianity once enjoyed have been lost along with the general intelligibility and plausibility of Christian language for a whole sector of people in the West. Can a conversation with science, especially with evolution, which has so deeply modified our understanding of the human, reveal more clearly the logic of Christian faith and its relationship to the method and understanding produced by the sciences?[3]

---

[2] See Francisco J. Ayala, "The Theory of Evolution: Recent Successes and Challenges, *Evolution and Creation,* ed. Ernan McMullin (Notre Dame, IN: University of Notre Dame Press, 1985), 59–90.

[3] I do not consult science for its philosophy of life or accept the thoroughgoing materialism that accompanies the views of some scientists. I accept the following critique of Thomas Nagle: "The intelligibility of the world is no accident. Mind, in this view, is doubly related to the natural order. Nature is such as to give rise to conscious beings with minds; and it is such as to be comprehensible to such beings. Ultimately, therefore, such beings should be comprehensible to themselves. And these are fundamental features of the universe, not products of contingent developments whose true explanation is given in terms that do not make

Is such a conversation with science even possible today? Christianity and science got along well together for centuries before science took a turn to close observation, critical measurement, and empirically based experimental modes of verification. By contrast, the churches tended to take refuge in authority—of the Bible, of tradition, or of church leaders. The fork in the road did not really lie in the conclusions, although these were often opposed, but in epistemology, method, and diverging cultures. But we should be able to say today that difference does not have to mean exclusion or separation. Proof of that lies in the fact that the conversation between scientists and theologians has continued in a vital way, but in committee rather than as public discourse, among experts on both sides, rather than including ordinary theologians who generally are not qualified to participate. Consequently, the dynamics of the conversation never make it into the public sphere: not in the pulpits, not in seminary classrooms, not even in the common language spoken by theologians. In popular opinion an abyss separates religion and science, and Christian theologians and scientists, and the method of communication between them frequently looks either like warfare or mutual dismissal.

Given this situation and an actual turn toward science, mainly by the disciplines of spirituality because of the scope of science's recent cosmic vision or the common ethical problem of ecological responsibility, this book asks what science can teach Christian theologians about our own self-understanding. It is not addressed to scientists, and one will learn very little actual science from its pages, because actual science transpires in the disciplines that treat particular problems with their own methods and languages. The book primarily addresses Christians who are affected by a scientific culture directly or indirectly, and who either do not know how to process their Christian faith in this context or call it into question altogether. For example, William Stoeger asks the following question of Christian faith: "How can we speak of divine causality within the world as we know it, without compromising scientific and philosophical principles—without using an interventionist model, for instance?" He then notes that our theological conceptions "will have to be re-articulated and modified as a result of this interaction."[4]

Much of the Christian literature that incorporates scientific data does not process how the languages fit together; they merge the conclusions of the disciplines

---

reference to mind" (*Mind and Cosmos: Why the Materialist Neo-Darwinian Conception of Nature Is Almost Certainly False* [New York: Oxford University Press, 2012], 19). In short, it makes no "sense" to explain the world in a way that "mind" and its ability to explain are not constituent factors of the explanation!

[4] William R. Stoeger, "Describing God's Action in the World in the Light of Scientific Knowledge of Reality," in *Chaos and Complexity: Scientific Perspectives on Divine Action*, ed. Robert J. Russell et al. (Vatican City: Center for Theology and Natural Sciences, 1995), 242, 246.

without accounting for their differences and points of contact. In this work I am concerned with the way scientists and theologians question reality. Generally, one does not really understand a complex proposition without knowing the method by which it was generated. This book tries to appropriate how it is that one person can live critically in the two domains of science and Christian revelation and at the same time give credible witness to the coherence of Christian faith.

The first two chapters begin to address these questions. Chapter 1 offers an analysis of the world in scientific terms. But the picture does not really describe the world as science presents it to us, which most people are aware of at some level. Rather, it presents the world in terms of a few principles and axioms that characterize scientific presuppositions. This gives us some small purchase on the mode of scientific thinking as inseparable but distinct from the conclusions it comes to. This sets up an overt contrast between the logic of scientific and theological learning in Chapter 2. Scientific and religious or theological seekers will find what they are looking for on the basis of different evidence and verification. This comparison and contrast provide a key that opens the constructive chapters that follow. The methods of science and theology are different, but they do not compete with one another. All theologians and scientists could learn something from the other and remain faithful to the canons of their own discipline.

The methodological principles set up the rest of the conversation, which consists of theological construction within the context of what may be considered a culture influenced by science. In other words, the effort at inculturation looks upon science, as distinct from some scientists, as descriptive of our world on the basis of empirical evidence. The book seeks the meaning of Christianity within the framework of the cultural terms provided by science. I begin with creation in Chapter 3 because its subject matter at least appears to overlap with the scientific description of the beginning of our universe. The extent to which that is and is not the case will be instructive for understanding the logic of each discipline in relation to the other. This chapter, in its turn, lays out some theological principles that govern the rest of the discussion. The theology of creation plays a major role in providing a comparative and contrastive link to scientific thinking and principles for theological inference.

In the beginning of Chapter 4 I set up a hypothesis that the rest of the chapter seeks to establish. It says that the answer to the question of how God acts in history is found in the classic notion of *creatio continua*, which also sheds light on other theological loci as well, specifically the languages of the Holy Spirit, grace, and incarnation. In other words, the distinction between the orders of creation and salvation or nature and grace unnecessarily cause many problems for theology and for public Christian rhetoric. The difficulty finds resolution in creation theology in terms of God's creating presence, intrinsically, to all that God creates all the time. That structure also accounts for the dynamic meaning of Spirit in the Bible, the operation of grace in the history of theology, and the logic of incarnation. One can preserve all the assertions of tradition without the mystifying notions of a supernatural order or interventions into the natural order by following the path laid out by creation theology. This one move at once clears away much of the friction between science and theology and at the same time renders theological language simpler, deeper, and more intelligible.

With the internalization of those theological principles, Chapter 5 investigates the content and role of the doctrine of original sin. On the face of it, evolution does not allow space for an original sin. But frequently the theological meaning of original sin has been transferred to refer to a general condition of the human race because of what we experience in ourselves and around us. We thus have a situation in which the original sin that explained the condition of corporate humanity has been superseded, and in its place one has a straightforward phenomenology of human existence. One does not need theology for that. What has happened to the etiological purpose of the doctrine to maintain that sin originates from human nature itself and not from God's creative intent? In response, the chapter turns to evolution to explain both the origin of sin and the distinctiveness of human existence in being called to higher reflective standards of behavior than those of our animal ancestors. The doctrine of original sin, as distinct from human sin itself, appears to be an unnecessary, vestigial, Augustinian appendage to Christian teaching that carries several negative effects.

In Chapter 6 and Chapter 7 I take up the distinguishing and centering mediation of Christian faith, Jesus Christ. These two chapters do not add up to a fully adequate Christology; that subject has too much historical depth and is far too complex for a brief discussion. But the limited space promotes an economy of topics to be considered and crispness in the analysis. I have chosen topics that are affected by evolution and particularly the shifts in theological categories that scientific culture invites. Chapter 6 discusses the teaching of Jesus of Nazareth about God, prefaced by a discussion of how one deals with the Gospels as historical sources. Then, in Chapter 7, within an evolutionary context, I offer a clear outline of the rationale of Christology. Constructively, this contains a realist account of the Easter experience and Jesus's resurrection, a conception of salvation on which Christology depends, and a theological account of the divinity of Jesus the Christ.

Finally, I use Chapter 8 to summarize the main ideas of the book and bring them to bear on eschatology, the Christian understanding of the end of time. This entails introducing the idea of eschatology and discussing what is going on when we presume to talk about an absolute future. We find that the language about our destiny bears a close analogy to and dependence upon the way we speak about creation. But eschatology also draws a large horizon for human life as it moves forward, our own lives included. After a brief explanation of the meaning of spirituality, the chapter concludes with an understanding of what Christians can hope for as construed by Christian theology. This does not consist of many specific things but of a substantially hopeful vision of our common existence that finds its basis in a realist understanding of the resurrection of Jesus. The conclusion of the work shows that creation, Jesus Christ, and the absolute future structure the vision.

These chapters add up to something like a sketch for a fully developed painting. The argument here lies in the form and the arrangement of the pieces; each of these and other issues need color, precision, and depth. Some of these issues have already been thoroughly discussed. But these chapters contribute to a holistic Christian vision for our intellectual culture and to a discussion that does not end.

I received a good deal of help and inspiration for this project from colleagues. Three scientists have reviewed my language about the worldview, the method, and the kinds of conclusions various scientific disciplines generate about ourselves and our world. George Coyne, SJ, the former director of the Vatican Observatory, Gabriele Gionti, SJ, who currently works at the Observatory in Castel Gandolfo, and Arthur Yaghjian, a theoretical physicist working in the Boston area, all reviewed my chapters dealing with science. I am grateful for the time they took to read my early chapters and for the suggestions they offered. Three theologians who are deeply engaged in the dialogue with science have also reviewed my writing and offered valuable commentary. John Haught is widely known for his many works interpreting science for the Christian imagination; Elizabeth Johnson uses Darwinian evolutionary language to open up Christian theology to an ethics and spirituality for ecological responsibility; and Stephen Pope has written a magisterial work on the relevance of scientific thinking for Christian ethics. These authors, who write from within the conversation among these disciplines, helped me to be careful in my necessarily abstract approach to the interchange. Three other theologians have assessed the coherence and appropriateness of my doctrinal theology. Terry Tilley carefully read the first draft of the text and offered expert critical advice at several junctures. Hal Sanks, SJ, and Otto Hentz, SJ, fellow fundamental and systematic theologians, helped me to be clearer and more precise on delicate issues. Two longtime friends, both expert in writing theology, helped me clarify my analysis at every stage. Lucretia Yaghjian, a scholar in English literature and expert in the writing of theology, and Patrick

Amer, an accomplished lawyer and himself a theological author, reviewed my writing and simplified my communication with the reader. I am also indebted to Orbis Books for publishing this work and, in particular, to Paul McMahon, who has carefully edited this work. He has smoothed many of the rough edges of the text and guided it to publication. I am grateful to be the recipient of such wide-ranging, careful, and cooperative assistance.

1

The Beautiful World
Revealed by Science

This chapter shows that science has introduced a set of cultural premises for appreciating spiritual and religious matters that requires new language and new conceptualizations. The meaning of beauty on the scale revealed by science combines unimaginable size, intricate precision, and creative openness. Entering this world exceeds the revelatory potential of a piece of art to a level that invites the human imagination into transcendence. Can it be a key to a new common theological language?

Not many theological works begin by speaking of science as revelatory, let alone as a purveyor of beauty. But consider for a moment being in a museum that contains your favorite work of art, perhaps van Gogh's stunning *Starry Night*, or his simple portrayal of a set of peasant shoes at the side of the door revealing to the viewer a long day's work in the field and a larger way of life of a whole culture. Science can do that on the grandest of scales. Its technical language is mathematics that only a few understand at the various levels science uses it. But the cumulative conception that it releases in so many distinct parts can introduce the insight, engagement, and feelings that are captured on the naive but intense level of Psalm 104. In the language of prayer, the Psalmist describes the universe as God's work: "You spread out the heavens like a tent" and "you fixed the earth on its foundations" where everything works together in harmonious relationship (Ps 104:2, 5). Other psalms tell of destruction and lament, but we begin with the vast and wondrous intricacy of our world.[1]

---

[1] John Haught thinks of beauty on the grand scale like this: "Beauty is the harmony of contrasts, the ordering of novelty, the unifying of multiplicity, the gathering of diversity into deeper relationship" (*The New Cosmic Story: Inside Our Awakening Universe* [New Haven, CT: Yale University Press, 2017], 140).

This chapter meditates on the world presented to us by science for our contemplation. Although science strives for objectivity, this interpretive account
mixes subjective reaction with principles or axioms drawn from the material
world. These principles help define a worldview that has been internalized
by Christians, as everyone else educated in the West with its emphasis on a
scientific outlook. Enumerating these big ideas only hints at the sophisticated
intellectual framework used in the work of scientists. Abstract concepts offer
the dry skeleton of a culture without its fleshy personality. It provides "talking points" that outline a conversation before discussion injects substance
and nuance into the many facets of the whole. The motive for collecting these
ideas lies less in raising up obstacles and challenges and more in opening up
a beautiful imaginative framework that provides opportunities for interpreting Christian faith in ways that show its relevance for people who, in various
degrees, have internalized a scientific worldview and feel at home in it. In
principle, this should be all of us.

Before describing some of the new windows on the world that science has
built into our self-enclosing walls, a comment on the use of the term *revelation*
will help prepare the way. Perhaps a better term would be *discovery;* science
continually discovers new and sometimes surprising dimensions of what we
thought we knew and presently take for granted. Occasionally, the timing of
the find rivals in importance the discovery itself. Copernicus laid out the theory
of heliocentrism with mathematical notation, but people finally took notice
when Galileo published his telescopic observations, which provided persuasive
evidence of heliocentrism. No one thinks of science in supernatural terms; as a
body of knowledge, it unfolds in time by accumulated ideas. Each new discovery
has a story behind it; as a discipline, science sometimes involves high drama.
We begin, then, by reminding ourselves of the narrative character of scientific
revelation as personified in a number of momentous contributions of piercing
and courageous intellects that put things together when the time was ripe.

Revelations of Science

Philosopher and theologian Bernard Lonergan built a theory of knowledge on
the basis of human nature being possessed by a "pure desire to know."[2] He
draws the idea from Thomas Aquinas, where actions require abilities to act and
the ability in humans to know is not merely a possibility but a drive. It goes
on all the time and in everyone. But occasionally it manifests itself with public

---

[2] Bernard J. F. Lonergan, *Insight: A Study of Human Understanding*, Collected Works vol.
3, ed. Frederick E. Crowe and Robert M. Doran (Toronto: University of Toronto, 1992), 372.

significance in individuals when data imaginatively suggest massive reorienting conceptions, and they "fall into place." Suddenly we are faced with what can be called a wholly new understanding of the world and ourselves in it, because the new conception supplies new form and stature to everything. The idea of rearranging the furniture of our mind describes but does not come close to the depth of new meaning conveyed. The stories of Copernicus and Galileo, of Newton, Darwin, and Einstein share these qualities.

Nicolaus Copernicus was born in 1473 to prominent Polish parents who provided him with an extensive education. As a teenager he learned and loved astronomy, and never lost interest even after he took up studies in canon law, mathematics, and medicine. He never sought ordination, but he lived close to the church and served for a time as secretary and physician to his uncle, the prince bishop of Warmia in northern Poland. After his uncle's death Copernicus worked for the church in several administrative capacities as physician and administrator, and he continued to record his astronomical observations.

Others in antiquity, Aristarchus, for example, theorized that the earth spins on its axis and that the center of the universe is the sun rather than the earth. But common sense observed that the sun rose and set, and Ptolemy's geocentric picture of the universe held sway: the moon, Mercury, Venus, the Sun, Mars, Jupiter, and Saturn revolved around the earth each day. And beyond that the whole vast sphere of the stars also turned. The universe revolved around our earth. Early on, the observations of Copernicus convinced him that Ptolemy's model was wrong. The earth's threefold movement demanded a new picture of the universe: its spin to account for the sun seeming to rise; its orbit around the sun to account for the sun's seeming to change its position; and its tilt to explain the seasons.

But Copernicus was cautious. Only in 1530 did he circulate a relatively short description of his views, without a mathematical apparatus, to his trusted friends in order to test the waters. Finally, nearing the end of his life, he wrote his master work, *On the Revolutions of the Heavenly Spheres*. It was published in 1543, the very year Copernicus died.

The phrase *Copernican Revolution* does not overstate what his work accomplished; its consequences ran deeper than smoothing out the anomalies of the Ptolemaic system. It dethroned human beings from the center of the universe, altered the relatively large visible sky, and awakened the imagination to an enormous depth perception.[3] Things were no longer the way they appeared. The idea announced the quiet but insistent message of science. "In the four-and-three-quarter centuries since Copernicus, science—'the engine of

---

[3] Dave Pruett, *Reason and Wonder: A Copernican Revolution in Science and Spirit* (Harrisonburg, VA: Alba Enterprises LCC, 2015), 28.

the Enlightenment'—has driven the expansion of human self-awareness, sup-planting religion as the locus of authority and wisdom in the Western world."[4]

But that did not happen all at once. Although astronomers read Copernicus's new vision of reality and some rejected it, others more positively disposed allowed it to lie relatively dormant. It took the Galileo case to set the question in dramatic terms. Galileo was born in 1564, twenty-one years after Copernicus died. He lived in the Copernican universe and gradually gained fame as a mathematician and experimental genius. The way he brought heliocentrism to the fore passed through optics.

In 1609, Galileo, at the age of forty-five became fascinated with the spyglass; he realized the scientific potential of the invention. After deciphering the mathematics of light's refraction through the lens, he built a more powerful spyglass and by the following year had converted a super version into a telescope. He then announced to the world in a popular work, "The Starry Message," that he had discovered four planets that disobeyed Ptolemy, did not orbit the earth but rather revolved around their host, Jupiter. But this picture contradicted the explicit description of how God, in answer to Joshua's prayer, stopped the sun and the moon in their path for a whole day so that Israel could defeat the Amorites (Josh 10:12–14). Suddenly, the whole Copernican universe confronted the inerrant word of scripture, and Galileo narrowly escaped with his life. He died under house arrest in January 1642. No story illustrates better the potential of an imaginative vision to both release and imprison the mind.[5]

Almost a year to the day after Galileo's death Isaac Newton was born in England to a single mother whose husband had died months before. He was raised by his maternal grandmother and well educated before going to the University of Cambridge in 1661 where he finished his bachelor's of arts degree in 1665.

During the summer of 1665 the university closed as a precaution against the plague that was ravaging Europe; this provided what Newton later recalled as miraculous years of private study. He reminisced about "the two plague years of 1665 and 1666, for in those days I was in the prime of my age for invention, and minded mathematics and philosophy [science] more than at any time since."[6] In this short period he discovered calculus, an achievement he shares with Leibniz; the law of gravitational attraction; and a particle theory of light drawn from work with prisms and light's refraction.

Newton returned to Cambridge in 1667 to continue his studies. Two years later he assumed the Lucasian Chair in mathematics after its holder, his retired mentor, proposed that Newton was an unparalleled intellect who should succeed

---

[4] Pruett, *Reason and Wonder*, 316.

[5] Galileo's contribution to science far exceeds his work in astronomy, but this story provokes important discussion and illustrates well a theological mindset of early modernity.

[6] Cited in Pruett, *Reason and Wonder*, 7.

him. At the age of twenty-six, Newton was elevated to a prestigious university position.

Unlike Copernicus and Darwin, who changed perceptions on a popular level, one does not associate Newton with a single revolutionary conception, unless it is classical mechanics. In *Mathematical Principles of Natural Philosophy* (1687) Newton laid out the basic field of physics for the next two centuries. Euclid's five axioms described space in terms of geometry; in parallel, Newton developed three laws of motion in space. We take them for granted: the law of inertia says that a body remains at rest or in motion in a straight line unless a force acts upon it; the momentum of an object results from a product of its mass and velocity; for every action, there is an equal reaction.[7] These laws still operate in "local" situations and have been able to supply the principles needed to place human beings on the moon and bring them back again.

But a still larger contribution to science can be found in Newton's prodigious overall accomplishment: the thoroughgoing denotation of his insights into the workings of nature in the quantitative language of mathematics. Rewriting observations into repeatable quantitative formulas seemed to deepen their truth by universalizing it. Formulas provided the human intellect with a new power to quantify and then analyze, decipher, and predict the workings of nature. Simple observations like *x* caused *y* become compounded and yield a map of vectors of force in a complex system. "Concepts like 'cause' appear nowhere in Newton's equations, nor in our more modern formulations of the laws of nature." The laws of physics prescind from clunky causal language: "events simply are arranged in a certain order, with no special responsibility attributed to one over any of the others."[8] Newton brought the human intellect to a new level of understanding reality and was celebrated as the archetype among the Illuminati. He died in 1727.

Of the scientists chronicled here, Charles Darwin probably has the widest name recognition because his views have been so contentious. Until very recently approximately 40 percent of people in the United States did not accept evolution. Astonishing as that seems for a nation built on principles of the Enlightenment, it seems to be shifting among young adults in contrast to a persistent creationism. In any case, the story of the interchange between data and Darwin's inquiring mind well illustrates the human quest for knowledge. Born in 1809, he grew up fascinated with living things. He set a course toward medicine at the University of Edinburgh, shifted to divinity at Cambridge University, but never lost his naturalist passion. The turning point of his life was his acceptance of

---

[7] Peter Atkins, *Galileo's Finger: The Ten Great Ideas of Science* (Oxford: Oxford University Press, 2003), 87.

[8] Sean Carroll, *The Big Picture: On the Origins of Life, Meaning, and the Universe Itself* (New York: Dutton, 2016), 63. I take this to mean a change in language and the functional formulation of interacting forces rather than a negation of causes being at work.

an invitation to accompany the captain of the HMS *Beagle* in its long scientific voyage to the coast of South America.

Darwin's meticulous observations, and the time he had to reflect upon them, released his constructive imagination. Several insights were telling, one of which concerned time. Darwin read the geographer Charles Lyell on fossils.[9] Once he recognized "deep" time, development appeared everywhere. Variation among closely related species gave him something to consider as well. For example, on the Galapagos Islands the finches had taken on different forms on each island. Darwin was also impressed by the theory of Thomas Robert Malthus that nature has created an imbalance between generativity and food supply and that nature compensates for the shortfall in nourishment and other hardships by overproduction within the species. This creates an inherently competitive dynamic of life: different species sharing the same food in the same place cannot coexist in peace. Moreover, the stronger and more adapted a species is to its environment, the larger the possibility that it will prevail. Darwin's theory thus rests on four observable sets of data that fit together in wonderful simplicity: an immense period of time, for species to compete for the resources of life, driven by an impulse to survive, which will be selected naturally by a developed inheritable strength that is most suited to the environment.

Darwin had the rudiments of his theory in hand by 1842, but, like Copernicus, uncertain of its reception, he hesitated to publish his findings and turned to other interests. But in 1857, he learned from Alfred Russel Wallace that he had developed a similar theory. Wallace's paper along with some writings of Darwin were published in 1858, but Darwin followed up and published his developed theory in *On the Origin of Species by Means of Natural Selection, or the Preservation of Favoured Races in the Struggle for Life* in November 1859. The book eventually wed Darwin's name to evolution and widened the gulf between the scientific and Christian worlds left by the Galileo case. As Francisco Ayala notes, "Darwin's revolutionary achievement is that he extended the Copernican revolution to the world of living things. The origin and adaptive nature of organisms could now be explained, like the phenomena of the inanimate world, as the result of natural laws manifested in natural processes."[10]

It is not so difficult for Christians to imagine the jolt to self-understanding that evolution proposes to creationism: the "instant" creation of our world as it is in a relatively recent past. Many people still have to work out the adjustment. After Darwin, the work of Mendel (1822–84) on heredity and genes further

---

[9] "As Copernicus liberated the universe from its narrow Ptolemaic spatial confines, so Lyell and Darwin liberated the earth from its narrow temporal confines" (Pruett, *Reason and Wonder*, 157).

[10] Francisco J. Ayala, "Darwin's Devolution: Design without a Designer," in *Evolutionary and Molecular Biology: Scientific Perspectives on Divine Action*, ed. R. J. Russell, W. R. Stoeger, and F. J. Ayala (Vatican City: Vatican Observatory Publications, 1998), 103, see also 109.

refined evolutionary theory. We now live in the world of the genome after the discovery of the double helix of life by Watson and Crick in 1953. The story of how scientists crept ever closer to this formula of life over approximately one hundred years constitutes intense drama.[11]

Let us now consider briefly the post-Newtonian world of physics defined by Albert Einstein and quantum mechanics.[12] As in the cases of Copernicus and Darwin, after Einstein we have to say again, "Nothing is as it appears." Einstein was born in 1879, finished his early education in Germany, and then continued higher studies in mathematics and physics in Switzerland. After graduation he did not find an academic position but worked as a clerk in a Swiss patent office. In 1905, he had his own miracle year when he published four scientific articles that would revolutionize the discipline of physics. Threatened in 1933 by Hitler's National Socialism, Einstein moved to Princeton and worked at the Institute for Advanced Study until his death. Three familiar scientific categories permanently bear Einstein's name: special relativity, the convertibility of matter and energy, and general relativity. But these mathematically established ideas are difficult to visualize.

Special relativity seems counterintuitive in that it presupposes that the laws governing the physical universe depend upon the relative motion of the observer and the observed. Consequently, just as everything appears differently relative to the motions of the perceiver and the perceived, so too everything exists and behaves in a universe of interrelated bodies that are in motion. In this "picture" of the universe, the speed of light is constant; it has the same value in every frame of reference. But the physical world does not exist within distinct containers of space and time: space-time refers to a four dimensional continuum that differs from the distinct space and time of Newtonian mechanics. Motion, duration, the positions of things relative to others, and their mutual influence on each other are qualities of being which do not appear as such to perception.

The convertibility of mass and energy was also unimaginable until the explosion of the atomic bomb. Expressed in the neat formula $E=mc2$, where c represents the velocity of light, the formula synthesizes the fact that a body's mass is like frozen energy, and that energy can be released in the transformation of the atomic structure of mass.

General relativity, too, defies imagination. "Like a rope of great strength, General Relativity braids together three strands: the gravitational theory of Newton; the non-Euclidean geometry of Bernhard Riemann; and the special theory of relativity of Einstein himself."[13] This yields a picture of the universe

---

[11] As it is told by Siddhartha Mukherjee, *The Gene: An Intimate History* (New York: Scribner, 2016), 1–200.

[12] We thus jump over James Clerk Maxwell (1831–79), whose unifying work on electricity, magnetic fields, and light provided the revolutionary steppingstones for the work of Einstein.

[13] Pruett, *Reason and Wonder*, 111–12.

where everything, whether galaxies, stars, or atoms, is flowing in a space-time-gravity process of motion. All reality sails along curved and twisting geodesics or trajectories, and everything bears some influence on everything else. This describes what is going on within those distant objects in space that look like clouds; it also describes on an infinitesimal scale the world within the atom.

The world of quantum field theory does not build on Einstein as on a foundation but adds a complexity that Einstein actually resisted. The focus of attention shifts from the macroscopic world of the universe to the microscopic world of the atom. Quantum mechanics refers to atomic structure and the interaction of subatomic particles: protons, neutrons, electrons, and others, together with the various forces that constitute the field of their emergence. In contrast to the mechanical world of Newtonian physics, where the description of particles and waves is mathematically exact, atomic structure displays an element of probabilistic uncertainty that has to do with behavior that displays both particle-like and wave-like movement. In the world of quanta, "waves behave like particles and particles behave like waves."[14] As physicist Sean Carroll states: "Electrons are not gently spiraling inward but spontaneously leaping from one allowed orbit to another, emitting a packet of light to make up the difference between them. The electron is doing 'quantum jumps.'"[15]

Quantum mechanics represents a revolution analogous to those initiated by Copernicus and Darwin; it radically rearranges the fundamental elements in our vision of reality. It explains non-intuitively everything we take to be ordinary experience. Quoting Carroll again: "Not only does the deepest layer of reality not consist of things like 'oceans' and 'mountains'; it doesn't even consist of things like 'electrons' and 'photons.' It's just the quantum wave function. Everything else is a convenient way of talking."[16] This seems somewhat extreme in its minimalism, but it illustrates a tendency in science to explain what is by reducing complex phenomena to their material antecedents. The next chapter examines the powers and limits of the disciplines of science and theology and the relationship between them. What is known by science and by theology? Can they affect each other? But before going there we turn to an attempt at a synthetic

---

[14] Atkins, *Galileo's Finger*, 201.

[15] Carroll, *The Big Picture*, 161–62.

[16] Carroll, *The Big Picture*, 171. "It's the quantum field theory of the quarks, electrons, neutrinos, all the families of fermions, electromagnetism, gravity, the nuclear forces, and the Higgs [field]" (176). All that we experience is accounted for by the theory of how these elements interact. "If you want to describe what goes on in rocks and puddles, pineapples and armadillos—that's all you need. . . . Everything pulls on everything else. All of the real structure and complexity we see in the world come from electrons (and the fact that they can't lie on top of each other) interacting with nuclei and with other electrons. . . . But the vast majority of life is gravity and electromagnetism pushing around electrons and nuclei" (177). So all-pervasive is quantum mechanics in the contemporary physicist's imagination.

description of the content of the wisdom reflected in the many disciplines that make up the world of science.

Principles about Our World Drawn from Science

The first part of this chapter demonstrated that science is a human endeavor that unfolds in history. Through study and reflection we gradually learn more about our world and ourselves in it. This second part portrays in abstract terms a sketch of the world discovered by science. This "picture" forms the backdrop for understanding our faith today. When in various subtle ways this worldview becomes internalized in our life, it influences the interpretation of where and how our faith commitments fit into our lives and self-understanding. In this work, for example, a scientific view of the world calls up a new importance of the doctrine of creation and demands a new emphasis on the symbol of the Spirit of God. The same salvation from God mediated through Jesus Christ lies at the center of Christian faith, but the theological understanding of the traditional pieces of Christian faith's vision has to be reconfigured to fit this present-day culture just as the language in place was embedded in and drawn from a distant culture. In other words, the picture of the world that science lays out for us bears importance for the theological reconstruction of subsequent chapters.

One cannot possibly portray adequately the world as seen by "science." The idea itself displays confusion because the term *scientific* is a descriptor that applies to many different disciplines that analyze nature. They may share much on an abstract level of intent, formal canons of evidence and procedure, but the various subject matters and the content drawn from them, when they are compared, show differences that prevent easy generalizations. But we can build on analogies, and we can create an impressionistic account of the accepted content of the sciences that influences public thinking the way other cultural modes of thought have been internalized to shape our views. As Newton built a vision of reality around three laws of motion, we will imagine the contours of the world that science presents to people at large with five discrete but interrelated principles.

1. Our universe is unimaginably large.

As today's science measures it, the size of our universe dwarfs the image of every dreamer who ever stared up into a clear night sky. And its character incorporates a tidal wave of data being amassed yearly. Some data add up to true discoveries that are counterintuitive and, more than others, suffuse human existence with cause to wonder. They give rise to questions about human existence that form a framework for further reflection. Everyone has always known that the universe is very large, but in comparison with what we know about the universe, Aristotle's and Calvin's were small and cozy. As a species, the human race arrived very late in the existence of our universe, and the size of our planet has shrunk considerably in the overall picture.

The age of our universe is estimated today at approximately 13.8 billion years. People have become used to the idea of a billion through economics, where on national levels we speak regularly of trillions. But the size of the universe truly challenges the imagination. Mathematical physics has allowed measurement of the speed of light and the ability to determine the difference between light sources approaching and receding from outer space. Light from space thus allows us to peer into the past from when it was first emitted and only now reaches us. Tracing light backward to a source correlates with an expanding universe beginning with what was called, at first disparagingly, a Big Bang. We will say more about the beginning and the origin of our universe in the discussion of creation. But looking forward from the extrapolated time our universe began, it has been expanding on all its "edges" for over 13.8 billion years at a rate of around 151,000 miles per hour.

Science estimates the size of the universe through mathematical formulas. But the dimensions of the universe, even when translated into metaphor and analogy, cannot be assimilated by the imagination. Even the meaning of words is affected. A theologian affirms the *infinite* as a sphere on the other side of the boundary of finitude in order to project a formless mode of being by the negation of any limit. A scientist tends to mean "endless finitude." If the universe can expand infinitely, what is there beyond the boundary of the universe that allows it to expand except endless possibility? Not space, because the universe creates space, and space-time qualifies the universe as an intrinsic parameter. The picture science offers also comes with a possibility of the existence of other universes, of intelligent life in other parts of this one, and of the "programmed" death of this planet. Speaking technically, the theological difference between finite and infinite remains the same in a small or large universe. But "concretely," the framework that science proffers has been decentering our planet and the human by steady increment since Copernicus. Consideration of the size of the universe almost spontaneously gives rise to a primal spiritual sensibility, because gazing into the open heavens mediates a sense of magnitude that humbles and, compared with a local sense of achievement, seems diminishing.[17] The age and size of the world are *awesome* in the original sense of that term. The universe as science depicts it encompasses us and elicits an engaged affective response. We will try to

---

[17] Yet when one thinks in terms of quality or kind of being, reflective, intelligent being in no way seems slighted by size and quantity. The human finds and internalizes the size of his or her own environment and is expanded by it.

show how the distinctive form of the wondrous beauty of this picture helps construct a new form of faith.

The ideas of energy, entropy, creativity, and complexity further qualify our universe. They come from another scientific way of appreciating our universe and our planet. Thermodynamics studies how heat generates energy and, more generally, how energy itself operates. Here *energy* has an abstract meaning of "potential to do work," and it comes in many forms: as rise in temperature, as radiation from the sun, as electromagnetism, or as water falling over a dam. The analysis of how a steam engine works offers a concrete analogy of universal mechanisms. One can imagine our planetary system as a giant machine that runs on energy from the sun.

Entropy, too, bears a subtle meaning because it measures a negative quality of energy, the degree of its exhaustion or dissipation. The first law of thermodynamics states that the energy of the universe is constant, but the second law holds that, in the production of work, energy runs down, and particular systems of energy collapse into disorder and a powerless equilibrium. Doing work entails spending energy and thus higher entropy. In the big picture the expanding universe is also running down. As scientist Peter Atkins notes, all change bears an "unstoppable degradation of the universe as energy and matter spread in disorder."[18]

But work is often constructive, as in evolutionary development and the birth of new complexity in molecules, which combine into lifeforms, consciousness, and freedom. The very process of evolution runs counter to entropy as energy produces work that generates new and more complex forms of being. Although the constant drift is toward degradation of energy, "the consequence of that drift might be to ratchet up a structure somewhere else."[19] The universe, then, contains an intrinsic tension between entropic forces of dissipation and disorder over against negentropic forces of creativity manifest in the construction of new ordered forms of local being. The endgame is the destruction of all life; the death of human life on this planet is assured, and various scenarios predict how this will happen. But a truly marvelous picture arises out of the very entropy described by science. It presents, for our reflection, the fact that "all the kingdoms of creation have been hoisted out of inorganic matter as the universe has sunk ever more into chaos. The spring of change is aimless, purposeless corruption, yet the consequences of interconnected change are the amazingly delightful and intricate efflorescences of matter we call grass, slugs, and people."[20]

What can be said of the origins and place of the human in the universe? This question seems to be entailed in the contours of the vision that science represents. But it remains a thoroughly ambiguous question because of the different levels at which it can be addressed and the different responses that can

---

[18] Atkins, *Galileo's Finger*, 124.
[19] Atkins, *Galileo's Finger*.
[20] Atkins, *Galileo's Finger*, 125–26.

be given. The next chapter explores the difference between a scientific and a theological approach to the workings of our world. Science and theology will not have the same answer to the question of the place of the human in it. But at this stage of the discussion it is important to see that this first principle—*our world is unimaginably large*—has been formulated because we are constantly being reminded of it in different ways that affect our worldview. For a scientific imagination it functions as a reflective premise that is always in play. Our theological imaginations may not have expanded proportionately.

Another reason for formulating this principle stems from a theological sensibility. Theology has to become conscious that the size of the universe gives rise to real questions. They were not asked by theology in the same way before the Copernican revolution when, in a Christian quarter, the answer was taken for granted. But real questions today force Christian theologians into an apologetic mode of reflection in which they have to do some explaining, to themselves first of all. This means that theology cannot simply speak over the scientific account of the human within the universe as we find it but must provide a theological interpretation that coherently draws the world represented by science into a new theological synthesis. That prospect should be as exciting as the new scientific discovery of the universe itself.[21]

2. Everything in our universe exists as constantly dynamic motion and change.

In the scientific account, constant motion and change constitute the universe and the world in which we live. Several areas of study feed into that conclusion. It appears within distinct regions of investigation: thermodynamics, macrophysics, microphysics, biology, and so on. It offers a challenge to theological tradition that consistently over millennia has measured the truth of ideas on the basis of a stable tradition over against change or novelty. Irenaeus of Lyon, for example, defended the truth of theology against Gnostic teachers with the criterion that early formulas preserved a revealed universal truth fresh from its source over against new local ideas. We may be glad he did in particular cases for historical reasons. But cosmic emergence and evolution show that eternal metaphysical patterns of being and essences are not stable. The idea of eternal truths obscures the way earthly ideas should change in the measure that reality itself changes. Let us look at what science proposes on both a macroscopic and a microscopic level.

On the macroscopic level, educated people today have an appreciation of historical change and cultural evolution. But the experience of change has been

---

[21] John Haught shows how the size and age of the universe and its ongoing movement through time decenter the human, reinforce historical consciousness with a cosmic backdrop, and underline the place and role of the future toward which evolutionary creation may be heading. This should have some influence on theology. See *Christianity and Science: Toward a Theology of Nature* (Maryknoll, NY: Orbis Books, 2007), 127–30.

balanced by analogy and interpretation that keeps adjusting past formulas to a changing present. What science offers the imagination goes deeper. The descriptions of the processes of change come close to establishing constant "becoming" as the substructure of reality. This can be seen in the large field provided by the conceptions of space-time and relativity.

I have alluded to how the notion of time in science differs from ordinary perception and usage. Time may refer a marker of the present moment: What time is it? Time in another broader sense of an interval is the measurement of periodic motions: the earth about the sun, crystal vibrations, or radioactive decay of elements. More abstractly, it may indicate an independent envelope of duration in which particular beings are inserted. That would look like an objective correlate to a subjective point of view: time is a Kantian quality or an a priori form of perception. Psychologically, we automatically situate things in the categories of time and space. In science, by contrast, time tends to mean the duration of being, neither a subjective or objective entity but a quality of material reality. As the duration of all that is, time incorporates motion into itself; they are correlative aspects of everything in the world. Time's entanglement with the motion of things means that being is always also becoming. And constant change eliminates static being. Kinds of being, essences, come and go; they are temporary. Thus, the fact that everything exists as temporal corresponds with a condition in which everything is moving or in process.[22] Various forms of philosophy are built on this premise. For their part, philosophies built on the premise of unchanging forms of being have to adjust for the movement or changing character of all material reality in order to highlight this actual condition of temporal becoming.[23]

Much more could be said here about different rates and intersections of time-scales. For example, tracing the course of emergent reality presents stages of the time and change that defined reality; it names and analyzes the processes of change. Evolution refers especially to the becoming of living things and gives a finer description of the changes of species as they pass through time. Evolution occurs differently and at different rates across the history of our planet.

---

[22] See Michael Ruse, "Nature as Promise," *The Evolution-Creation Struggle* (Cambridge, MA: Harvard University Press, 2005), 214–35. This means the distinction between nature and history should be abandoned. "Nature is also historical; it is just as true that the future will not be like the past" (Holmes Rolston, III, *Genes, Genesis, and God: Values and Their Origins in Natural and Human History [The Gifford Lectures, University of Edinburgh, 1997–1998]* [Cambridge: Cambridge University Press, 1999], 208).

[23] The narrative of the universe tells of ascending complexities: evolution occurs "cosmologically, inorganically, geologically, biologically, socially and culturally." One can also think in terms of the layers of complexity that have been achieved: "atom—molecule—macromolecule—subcellular organelle—cell—multicellular functioning organ—whole living organism—populations of living organisms—ecosystems—the biosphere." Arthur Peacocke, *Theology for a Scientific Age: Being and Becoming—Natural and Divine* (Oxford: Basil Blackwell, 1990), 62, 38.

It participates in a broader movement of emergence that constitutes a cosmic history that is also ours: the history of the origin of the universe, the formation of galaxies and stars, distinct elements, our planet, life, myriads of species, prehistoric human types, Homo sapiens, our recent history, and the elements of a personal lifecycle. If we are to have a Christian interpretation of reality, it must factor in the temporal duration of our universe, the phases of life on our planet, and the new sense of the speed of our current cultural evolution as a species. All of these seemingly distinct stories constitute our own. We will explore further the implications of time as it is manifested in the evolution of life later. But we may notice, here, the continuity of the processes by which the elements of the physical world emerged and the variety of species evolved. Science proposes that a smooth, continuous, or integral transition, as distinct from the conflictual dimensions of history, marks the transition across different kinds of being. It imagines no need or role from agency outside of the universe to account for its development.[24]

This conviction about the autonomy and integrity of the material universe that does not look for interruptions from outside itself provides a good example of the strategy of this work. It encourages turning to traditions that find God dwelling within creation rather than depicting God operating anthropomorphically from outside. It will occasion a new relevance for a theology of God as Spirit working as creator and savior from within. It will affirm but reconfigure the notion of incarnation to connect God with the working of creative emergence and evolution as well as in Jesus's life and ministry. The point of presenting these scientific constructions lies in the way they can stimulate new ways of seeing the relevance of Christian faith to this very world.

Turning to the microscopic level, many physicists focus not on the heavens or the evolution of lifeforms, but on the atom in order to unravel the dynamic character of the material world. Study of atomic structure reveals a far busier space than the familiar model of Rutherford's hydrogen atom—a single electron revolving around its nucleus. The nucleus of a typical atom contains about 99 percent of the mass but is only about 1/100,000 the size of the atom: matter is virtually empty. Today, one has to consider the atom less as an object and more as a space defined by the movements of several subatomic particles and electromagnetic forces in their coordinated and reciprocally related movements. It is as if an atom were a unit of pure movement that entails particles and forces that embody the motion. Once again, things are most definitely not

---

[24] "Once there was no smelling, swimming, hiding, defending a territory, taking risks, making mistakes, or outsmarting a competitor. All these things appear gradually, also without precedent if one looks further along their developmental lines. In each quantum jump there is a little more of what was not there before, and if one integrates the differentials one gets something in kind where before there was nothing of that kind. In this sense the evolutionary story regularly produces more out of less" (Rolston, *Genes, Genesis and God,* 144).

as they seem. The very building blocks of material reality are units or subjects of motion and not static material so-called solids. This analytical description of matter lies buried in Einstein's formula for the convertibility of mass and energy. His mathematical and physical intuition laid out a formula for understanding the way in which the material world really consists of the activity of energy. In sum, matter is structured energy.

Stepping back from the dynamism that defines an atom, the energy contained within material things bears further reflection. The movement of subatomic particles, forming a system within a so-called atom, as if it were an object or a container, are so dynamic and, within limits, "jumpy," that they cannot be exactly determined or pinned down by measurement. At best, they can be pinned down mathematically by probabilities. This fairly objective description of microscopic reality yields a vague image of the constitution of reality itself. We need some kind of tensive abstract phrase, like *controlled dynamism* or *structured motion,* to convey the fundamental units of material reality. It is true that this underlying physical structure has no direct bearing or influence upon the way conscious human beings deal with the world. Only experiment and analysis reveal the physical and chemical substructure buried beneath conscious life. But the structure does make a difference to how we understand reality. In fact, it demonstrates that the various forms of stability that anchor our self-understanding are constructions that conceal as much as they reveal.

Earlier, we considered evolution in the context of a discussion of time correlative with motion and change. Evolution takes off dramatically with the emergence of life where change can be readily appreciated in the development of new species. Here, we underline another aspect of time's duration, the continuity of past, present, and future resulting in the interrelated character of reality.

The reality that evolved across time is "inclusive" because it continuously draws the past into a present that sets the stage for the future. Darwin drew a picture of this inclusion in his tree of the ascent of life.[25] This picture or graph abstractly outlines a unity of life across a spectrum of determinate lifeforms on the planet. As a species and as individuals the human being connects with every other form of being and, together with them, exists as part of the single movement of life on earth. When this continuity is extrapolated back into the universe, indications show that the basic elements we find on earth are constant throughout the universe. The picture stimulates a reverence for the complexity of the world and a sense of connectedness with all that is. Each person makes up a little part of the same physical universe. This common participation helps form a basis for a sense of moral responsibility.

---

[25] Charles Darwin, *The Origin of Species by Means of Natural Selection* (New York: Barns and Noble Classics, 2004; original 1859), 102–3.

Humanity is the cosmos conscious of itself. This philosophical truism may surprise an everyday perspective on the world. Spontaneously, we perceive ourselves as other than the world and gaze out on a reality distinct from us rather than think of ourselves as being another form of it. The maxim also draws out further the significance of evolution's continuity. Human beings do not exist above or outside the physical world. As part of it, it lives in us; it is us, and we are it. "No part of the universe can be understood except in its dynamical and evolutionary relationship to all other parts of the universe. . . . The best of scientific knowledge tells us that all of the diverse objects in nature have had a common origin and have shared in and come from a common evolutionary process."[26] We are the evolutionary process itself that is becoming more aware of itself in us. In our lives as individuals, more evidently in large groups but also in the species as a whole, evolution has taken a turn toward conscious activity.[27] This development may not seem apparent because, until recently, no center of consciousness has given the species an objective sense of common purpose. In some measure we are reacting together to an endangered habitat. The recognition of this problem also opens up a large unknown immediate future for humanity.

In sum, time, the duration of motion, and material becoming itself are folded together to make all physical reality interconnected; everything is interrelated through temporal process. Science does not theorize about being as a whole; it unfolds piecemeal across many distinct disciplines and the facets of the world that each one engages. But in its sharp descriptions of the basic motions and behaviors of various aspects of reality, science lays down some fundamental contours for philosophical and theological self-understanding.

If *being* bears the essential character of *becoming,* is there a platform of stability in the universe? The principle of indeterminacy, which characterizes the elementary units of finite reality as we know it, has been described as "being lost"; that is, "you either know where you are, but not where you are going, or you know where you are going, but nothing about where you are."[28] Indeterminacy, as the inherent characteristic of the basic elements of the material world, has echoes in self-perception. Where does one look for an anchor in a sea of motion? This is an ongoing question in any dialogue with science because science does not, and cannot, offer an answer in any ultimate sense. In the next

---

[26] George V. Coyne, "From Matter to Emergence: Scientific and Theological Views on the Nature of Life," in *Theology and Science: Discussions about Faith and Facts*, ed. Joseph Seckbach (Singapore: World Scientific Publishing, 2018), 246–47. In another place Coyne asks: "Why did it take so long to make even an amoeba? . . . We did not have the chemistry to make even an amoeba until we had had three generations of stars" ("Destiny of Life and Religious Attitudes," in *Life as We Know It*, ed. Joseph. Seckbach [Dordrecht: Springer Science, 2005], 524). The elements of which we are constructed were baked in the furnaces of the stars.

[27] Although science does not support the personification of evolution, a valid point is being reiterated here: human beings form part of evolving life.

[28] Atkins, *Galileo's Finger*, 220.

chapter we discuss how an interchange between a scientific and a theological imagination might be conducted. And in the chapters that follow this question will be answered with more specificity in relation to particular theological interpretations. Through a theology of creation and the ideas of divine Presence and Spirit, theology can draw the dynamics of reality revealed by science into a larger synthesis.

3. Everything in motion is governed by layers of law and system conditioned by randomness.

A variety of issues swirl around terms like *the laws of nature* and *randomness, determinism* and *chaos theory, necessity* and *contingency*. All of these terms have referents in a variety of specific contexts or spheres of operation. Can we gain some precision in the use of these terms on an abstract level that may function to clarify the discussion at all levels? A large understanding of how these terms relate to one another will be helpful for sifting through a number of different problems. The line of the discussion that begins with a scientific notion of a law of nature and moves through randomness to the emergent complexity of lifeforms manifested in evolution leads inevitably to the deep question of whether the whole of reality can be considered suffused with some form of directed purpose (teleology). Scientific method cannot resolve that issue, but it certainly raises it as a human question.

Laws of nature are ably discussed by astrophysicist and cosmologist William Stoeger. He studied the question of the status of physical laws from the perspective of how, as formulas, they are generated or determined by the disciplines of science.[29] A summary of his conception of the *laws of nature* can be laid out in a few abstract but telling propositions. The most important quality of the laws of nature stems from how they are constructed rather than discovered.[30] The scientist infers laws of nature by describing the regular, repeatable behavior of physical reality. What are the laws of nature? Objectively, they refer to "the regularities, processes, structures and relationships which we find in reality."[31]

---

[29] William R. Stoeger, "Contemporary Physics and the Ontological Status of the Laws of Nature," in *Quantum Cosmology and the Laws of Nature: Scientific Perspectives on Divine Action,* ed. Robert John Russell, Nancey Murphy, and C. J. Isham (Vatican City: Vatican Observatory; Berkeley, CA: Center for Theology and the Natural Sciences, 1993), 209–34.

[30] Notice the epistemological entry into this question. It treats science, first of all, as a way of knowing. This perspective plays a defining role in this book.

[31] William R. Stoeger, "Conceiving Divine Action in a Dynamic Universe,"in *Scientific Perspectives on Divine Action: Twenty Years of Challenge and Progress,* ed. Robert John Russell, Nancey Murphy, and William R. Stoeger (Berkeley, CA: The Center for Theology and the Natural Sciences; Vatican City: Vatican Observatory Publications, 2008), 237. These may be divided into those we know and those that potentially are there but not known. Stoeger makes the same point in "The Mind-Brain Problem, the Laws of Nature, and Constitutive

As formulas, they do not exist independently of actual motion; they do not, like platonic ideas or blueprints, preexist the actual behaviors they describe. They do not prescribe an a priori necessity, because they frequently change or are adjusted in different new circumstances. An "absolute" law only remains so until something new is revealed in nature's behavior such that new laws are required.

The laws of nature, because they describe and do not determine nature's behavior, do not cause things to happen.[32] And they do not encompass all reality but only extend as far as the evidence and our perception of it allow. The evidence of patterns of behavior provides the material for science to construct the law. Stoeger strongly cautions against the confusion that the law is a reality instead of an approximate description of reality always set within context and circumstance.[33]

Since empirical evidence guides scientists' formation of laws, it becomes apparent that a strict determinism defined a priori by the laws of nature is untenable in principle. The idea presupposes an absolute character to a law that it does not possess and cannot possess. Because reality evolves, human intelligence does not possess exhaustive knowledge of the world and thus changes, and no one-to-one correspondence between the description and actuality exists. Actuality and further possibility always exceed what can be described by a law.[34] On the one hand, the laws of nature reflect the real, and they point to patterns that guide the process of evolution in distinct reliable ways. On the other hand,

---

Relationships," in *Neuroscience and the Person: Scientific Perspectives on Divine Action,* ed. Robert John Russell et al. (Vatican City: Vatican Observatory; Berkeley, CA: Center for Theology and the Natural Sciences, 1999), 130.

[32] Modern science uses the language of causality sparingly. It still has its uses, but generally science appeals to a different grid of understanding. The universe is in motion. The basic notions of space-time, quantum fields, equations of motion, and interactions do not need a push or a pull. The shift in language, therefore, does not eliminate causality but rather works within a framework of motion and aims at formulating the dimensions of motion in repeatable equations. See Carroll, *The Big Picture,* 28–29, 63.

[33] "It is an illusion to believe that these incredibly rich representations of the phenomena are unconstructed isomorphisms we merely *discover* in the world. Instead they are *constructed*—painstakingly so—and there is no evidence that they are isomorphic with structures in the real world as it is in itself" (Stoeger, "Contemporary Physics and the Ontological Status of the Laws of Nature," 216). This is especially true in the sphere of biology. We said earlier that Newton's use of mathematics as the language of science tended to objectify and universalize its findings but never so that it detaches law from circumstance. For example, water consistently boils at a definite temperature, but a different one at different altitudes.

[34] Sometimes there is slippage in the usage of *determinism* to mean "continuity" and "consistency": it is true that everything that happens flows continuously and consistently from its immediate past, but evolution bears witness as well to randomness and increment in quality of being. Prediction of the long-term future from the present remains conditional and by degrees ambiguous.

the laws of nature are not metaphysically absolute but probabilistic statistically analyzed patterns that appear invariant until they change.

Laws are conditioned by randomness. This formula conveys a sense of a massive stream of becoming that is "open" but shaped by past consistencies that can be relied on. And yet "random" or "contingent" and unaccountable events modify the flow of expected behavior. Randomness can be understood as "the convergence of previously unrelated causal chains," or it may stem from "quantum events and hence [be] essentially unpredictable."[35] Later it will appear that this tension between law and randomness points less to a description of potential chaos and more to a dynamic formula for production of the new. Because being always involves time's motion, and action always releases complex forces within multidimensional environments, every action possesses and produces a certain newness. Slight variation and novelty over long periods of time add up. Each new species along the tree of life bears witness to incremental change.

Given the tension between law and randomness, some scientists favor regular pattern and others stress an open future. Consider, for example, how the language of Sean Carroll veers toward determinism: "Indeed, the entirety of both the past and future history are utterly determined by the present." "The universe . . . marches forward, instant to instant, under the grip of unbreakable physical laws." Carroll is resolute in insisting that "the past and future are determined by the present state of the system." "If this certain thing happens, we know this other thing will necessarily follow thereafter, with the sequence described by the laws of physics."[36]

By contrast, the language of Stoeger integrates the idea of randomness neatly into language that insists on laws and system; he sees randomness and systemic openness producing creative tension. This is particularly true in biological evolution. Chance, randomness, and contingency, he says, "are frequent and important in biological evolution, rendering its actual course indeterminate or unpredictable in exact outcome from any particular stage."[37] Random events

---

[35] Ernan McMullin, "Evolutionary Contingency and Cosmic Purpose," in *Finding God in All Things*, ed. Michael J. Himes and Stephen J. Pope (New York: Crossroad, 1996), 144.

[36] Carroll, *The Big Picture*, 32–34. These views express the idea of continuity rather than strict determinism since he "fudges" on predictability. But does unpredictability stem from lack of knowledge or intrinsic indeterminacy? All evidence to date indicates that indeterminacy is a fundamental property of microscopic physical phenomena and thus of all long-term behavior.

[37] William R. Stoeger, "The Immanent Directionality of the Evolutionary Process, and Its Relationship to Teleology," in *Evolutionary and Molecular Biology: Scientific Perspectives on Divine Action*, ed. Robert John Russell et al. (Vatican City: Center for Theology and the Natural Sciences, 1998), 179–80. "There are reliable and relatively permanent underlying regularities and patterns of behavior in material reality which enable and effect that development without fully determining it. They are complemented by a certain amount of randomness and uncertainty at different levels, upon which the inherent regularities and processes can

have short-term and sometimes long-term effects that can be understood within the sphere of the laws of nature. Thus, the phrase *pure chance* is ambiguous; and the idea that "evolution proceeds by purely chance events, is much less than a precise description of this source of unpredictability in biological evolution."[38] In sum, there does not appear to be any problem in regarding the dynamic reality of the universe as structured by a tension between clear, strong patterns of behavior and catalytic variations stemming from vectors of force that are unforeseen and even truly random. The question of direction and purpose directly affects a Christian sensibility, so that this question will return. We will see that natural process itself points to openness and direction toward a range of possibilities.

The terms *emergence* and *complexity* evoke problems in constructing a bigger picture of reality. Looking forward, a number of areas of tension come to the surface: law and randomness together generate newness, but is the whole system of the universe open or moving in a certain direction? Several options present themselves. On the one hand, determinists may or may not perceive a direction in the process; on the other hand, some who regard process as open ended may still see a direction in it that is well short of a determined goal. Still others may maintain that such a perception is purely a posteriori, looking backward after the fact and not intrinsically programmed. Wherever you are, the past got you there.

These issues can be described in terms of emergence and complexity. *Emergence,* the arrival of new and unpredictable organizational principles, refers to the increment in the character of reality developing from within the material world during the course of temporal development. For example, one can chart the transitions across thresholds from protons and neutrons, to atoms with nuclei, to stars, to the self-sustaining chemical reactions that constitute life, to multicellularity, consciousness, self-consciousness, and culture. Emergence refers to layers or levels of reality that fit with each other and form new systems.[39] When scientists look at the trajectory of evolution, beginning with the formation of basic elements, some see purely random and directionless development, like a stray dog following its nose. Others see within the process a drift or a direction toward *complex* and higher forms of life. As indicated earlier, one has to be careful not to personify evolution as an intentional process in its particulars. Evolution is not a person; evolution does not choose. Evolution is blind. But the massive progression suggests "a creative upflow of life transmitted across a

---

operate to produce variety and trigger diversification" (William R. Stoeger, "Faith Reflects on the Evolving Universe," *Finding God in All Things*, 170–71).

[38] Stoeger, "The Immanent Directionality of the Evolutionary Process, and Its Relationship to Teleology," 180.

[39] Carroll, *The Big Picture*, 102–4.

long continuing turnover of kinds, across a long history that includes struggling toward more diverse and more complex forms of life."[40]

On this issue Stoeger seems to have taken a moderate position, which he states as follows: "Though [evolution's] actual course is indeterminate, its general course towards complexity, self-organization, and even the emergence of self-replicating molecules and systems, given the hierarchies of global and local conditions which are given, can be interpreted as inevitable in the universe in which we live."[41]

Is reality governed by direction to a goal? This question lurks behind all of the reflections on the directionality of evolution. Direction is one thing; purpose is quite another, depending on the scope of meaning that one assigns it. On the one hand, for Christian faith, going back to its origins in its parent Judaism, belief in a personal God included a strong anthropomorphic sense of purpose—a personal God was in charge. When evolution seems to deny the purposefulness of the Creator, it becomes hostile not only to the stated beliefs of Christians but to personal faith. For God supplies the basis of the coherence of reality, and radical randomness seems to undercut meaning itself. On the other hand, there are other ways of thinking about God's providence. "Thus, in theology's conversations with contemporary science, it is more helpful to think of God as the infinitely generous ground of new possibilities for world-becoming than as a 'designer' or 'planner' who has mapped out the world in every detail from some indefinitely remote point in the past."[42]

Several reflections from the history of science, philosophy, and theology provide distinctions that put a finer point on this absolutely basic question raised by the dynamics of a scientific worldview. Sometimes *purpose* means "intended activity," as in a person doing something in order to attain a goal. Sometimes *purpose* has a functional meaning of "elements fitting together because each serves a purpose."[43] Beyond that, some discussions of teleology or purposeful direction toward a goal compound the issue of God's purpose with the questions of theodicy that flow from the experience of so much evil in the world. Did God

---

[40] Rolston, *Genes, Genesis, and God,* 34.

[41] Stoeger, "The Immanent Directionality of the Evolutionary Process, and Its Relationship to Teleology," 180. More strongly, he says: "What we refer to as chance, or contingent, events do not disrupt the directionality of evolution. They contribute strongly to it. As I have stressed above, directionality is coded into the concrete totality of physical reality, and that includes these 'unforeseen' accidents or chance events—whether they be of ultimately classical or quantum provenance. The fact that they cannot always be predicted with certainty does not disqualify their contributions to directionality" (173).

[42] John F. Haught, *God after Darwin: A Theology of Evolution* (Boulder, CO: Westview Press, 2000), 119. Patrick H. Byrne discusses design, randomness and purpose in an evolutionary world from a Lonerganian perspective ("Evolution, Randomness, and Divine Purpose: A Reply to Cardinal Schönborn," *Theological Studies* 67 [2006], 653–65).

[43] McMullin, "Evolutionary Contingency and Cosmic Purpose," 148–51.

plan all this conflict and suffering? What is at stake, here, transcends objective description of the world and cannot be discussed out of context. Purpose will become important in our later discussion of where faith meets science.[44]

Robert Wright offers a tight argument for seeing purpose in natural selection that transcends directionality. The test for purposefulness is threefold: "[a] persistence toward the hypothesized goal [b] under varying conditions [c] by processing information." The process of natural selection fulfills the three conditions: (1) the *goal* is the creation of organic complexity: "broadening the diversity of species, raising the average complexity of species, expanding the outer limit of complexity, and expanding the outer limit of behavioral flexibility—that is, intelligence"; (2)The evidence of the consistency of this drive in the face of *different obstacles* is plentiful; and (3) it does this by *processing information*, at various levels of sophistication. For example, "Trial and error is a system of information processing—even if . . . the trials are randomly generated." The movement of natural selection is like a "groping." "It assimilates the feedback into amendments of design that allow it to keep generating complexity amid varying conditions." If natural selection "exhibits flexible directionality via information processing" why would one not call it teleological?[45] When this discussion gets overly subtle, Wright shows that it becomes important to check back into the large vision that is being articulated.

4. The intrinsic character of life is marked by conflict, predatory violence, suffering, and death.

With this thesis we shift attention from the general character of reality as dynamic motion to note how this takes form in the sphere of life, especially in terms of the structure of evolution. A description of the character of life has direct bearing on the human. One cannot understand humanity without passing through evolution because of the continuity and integrity of reality in space-time. This condensed description of human existence from the perspective of evolution raises the question of the sources of evil and moral depravity that form the subject of Chapter 5. We do not include features such as mutuality,

---

[44] Ian G. Barbour offers a brief response to the question of randomness and divine purpose: "There can be purpose without an exact predetermined plan" (*When Science Meets Religion* [San Francisco: HarperSanFrancisco, 2000], 63). Stephen Pope offers a clear analysis of Stoeger's position on what can be said of directionality and purpose in evolution from the perspectives of science and faith in "Does Evolution Have a Purpose? The Theological Significance of William Stoeger's Account of 'Nested Directionality,'" *Theological Studies* 78 (2017), 462–82. See also Stephen Pope, *Human Evolution and Christian Ethics* (New York: Cambridge University Press, 2007), 119–23.

[45] Robert Wright, *Nonzero: The Logic of Human Destiny* (New York: Vintage Books, 2000), 313–15.

altruistic alliances, friendship, and empathy, because they do not challenge faith's vision in the same way.

Science defines life in terms of complex sets of molecules that are self-sustaining by some form of metabolism and an ability to reproduce. Evolutionary life includes flexibility, an ability to mutate in response to environment.[46] Life began on our planet as single-celled organisms such as bacteria as long ago as four billion years. That is remarkably early if earth was still being formed 4.5 billion years ago. We have seen that the convertibility of mass and energy and the very structure of the atom show that reality in its building blocks consists of dynamic energy. The constructive side of that dynamism appears to us most readily in the evolution of life. Darwin's tree of life graphically communicates how the ascent to the human brings its past with it so that everything relates to everything else.

What does the human look like from the perspective of the evolutionary life sciences? We get a composite picture from a psychologist, a biologist, and a paleobiologist who is a professor of anatomy.

The first step in an evolutionary description of life shows how deeply we are shaped by heredity. Evolutionary psychologist Steven Pinker argues forcefully against the common idea that each human being comes into this world like a blank slate to learn all the things that will shape the person. Science, especially through evolution and heredity, has simply destroyed this idea. Pinker summarizes the approach of the evolutionary biologist and psychologist: "Evolution is central to the understanding of life, including human life. Like all living things, we are outcomes of natural selection; we got here because we inherited traits that allowed our ancestors to survive, find mates, and reproduce. This momentous fact explains our deepest strivings."[47]

Pinker's theory of human nature expresses the views of many evolutionary biologists and psychologists. Human nature, including the human mind, "is equipped with a battery of emotions, drives, and faculties for reasoning and communicating, and . . . they have a common logic across cultures, are difficult to erase or redesign from scratch, were shaped by natural selection acting over the course of human evolution, and owe some of their basic design (and some of their variation) to information in the genome."[48] This language shows how completely an evolutionary perspective enfolds the discipline of psychology.

The widely known biologist Edward O. Wilson believes that human nature can be completely deciphered by evolutionary science. He displays this premise in his explanation of human aggressiveness. "Are human beings innately

---

[46] Stoeger, "The Immanent Directionality of the Evolutionary Process, and Its Relationship to Teleology," 174–75.

[47] Steven Pinker, *The Blank Slate: The Modern Denial of Human Nature* (London: Penguin Books, 2002), 52.

[48] Pinker, *The Blank Slate*, 73.

aggressive?" he asks. "The answer is yes. . . . Only by redefining the words 'innateness' and 'aggression' to the point of uselessness might we correctly say that human aggressiveness is not innate."[49] Wilson wants to communicate that aggressive tendencies do not add up to a flaw in human nature and are not a pathological symptom but are an inherent part of human nature. Human beings obey rules learned over hundreds of thousands of years in spontaneously dividing friends and aliens, fearing strangers, and responding to hostility by aggression. Evolution acts like a very old parent shaping human nature across time.

Like Pinker and Wilson, Daryl Domning also finds a fundamental organic and even inorganic inward turning in all beings: all of us have within us an instinct for self-preservation that "tends to suck into itself" what it needs to survive. All individuals "will compete with one another for that material and energy wherever those are in limited supply." "Life must always sustain it*self* by acquiring materials and energy, if necessary at the expense of other life, through competition and self-interested cooperation. This behavior is *necessarily* reinforced by natural selection: if you don't do it, you don't long survive, much less evolve. This is how life and evolution *have to* work, in any material world—including the one that the Creator pronounced 'very good' (Gen 1:31)."[50]

These views should not be regarded as extreme. They reflect a consensus across disciplines dealing with human nature as it has emerged through the evolutionary process.

Natural selection and its competitive character involve basic issues of life and death. We can turn to Darwin himself for a description of how humanity has evolved within such an ultimate context.[51] Most people at least vaguely know how the mechanism of evolution works. It presupposes the dynamism of life. Generation gives rise to variation, and variation continually adapts to environment through selection of sexual partners that favor reproduction and diversification in progeny. Darwin described the process as a struggle for existence, especially in times of shortage of the resources for life. The struggle for existence yields preservation by inheritance of the variations that better adapt a species to its environment. Natural selection provides the way nature promotes survival, as "every slight modification, which in the course of ages chanced to arise, and which in any way favored the individuals of any of the species, by

---

[49] Edward O. Wilson, "Aggression," *On Human Nature* (Cambridge, MA: Harvard University Press, 1978), 77.

[50] Daryl Domning, "Sin, Suffering, and Salvation: What Does Evolution Have to Say about Them?" *The Atom and Eve Project: Using Science in Pastoral Ministry* (Washington Theological Union, Nov. 10, 2012), 7, http://washtheocon.org/resources/using-science-pastoral-ministry/. We will return to these ideas in Chapter 5 when we take up the theological notion of sin.

[51] It is true that Darwin wrote over a century and a half ago and much has been learned since then. But Darwin got most of it right, and he presents his vision in straightforward descriptive terms.

better adapting them to their altered conditions, would tend to be preserved; and natural selection would thus have free scope for the work of improvement."[52] The success at survival by one species entails the extinction of the species that did not adapt sufficiently; life contains "a constant tendency in the improved descendants of any one species to supplant and exterminate in each stage of descent their predecessors and their original parent."[53]

In Darwin's original conception both the struggle for existence and natural selection presuppose the interdependence of one being with another, of groups dependent on groups, and species on species. Natural selection describes the structure of how each organic being and species "comes into competition for food or residence, or from which it has to escape, or on which it preys."[54] As everyone who watches shows about nature knows, the struggle for existence entails conflict, violence, and predatory behavior; it results in suffering in higher species and death to all of them. The continuity and consistency of natural process, of natural selection, and the path to the appearance of the human lead to a view in which humanity's proclivity to conflict, violence, predation, and the infliction of suffering on one another appears to be constitutive of human nature. Much more has to be said here, but this picture cannot be dismissed out of hand.

Given this scenario, how does one balance the unity of life and the individuality of the person? In the course of the development of Western culture, not to mention so many other ancient cultures, people have internalized different conceptions of the human: Animal rationalis, Homo religiosus, Homo ludens, Homo faber, and so on. So, too, we can regard the processes of evolution from various perspectives. Imagining the wide horizon of the development of life has to fill one with an awe not far from that expressed in Psalm 104 that glories in the panorama of life's interrelations, whether or not one is a believer. From the intricacy of each distinctive increment in life's form, to the impersonal competition of living things for survival that so intrigue the viewer of the documentaries of nature, the magnitude of the whole project is staggering. The Grand Canyon and the depth of the sky on a clear, dark night seem ordinary compared with the journey of life. But when we shift perspective to the single human person, and analogously to the higher animal that suffers, the enterprise becomes morally ambivalent. Life is great for the big cat who has feasted on a Thomson's gazelle, but not so much for the gazelle. And not so much for each child lost in a war between human groups programmed to compete for resources and dignity. This situation raises fundamental questions about the "nature" of human existence and the sources of morality and, of course, immorality.

---

[52] Darwin, *The Origin of Species by Means of Natural Selection,* 75.
[53] Darwin, *The Origin of Species by Means of Natural Selection,* 107.
[54] Darwin, *The Origin of Species by Means of Natural Selection,* 72.

The question of meaning lies buried in the workings of nature.[55] Where are we to look for an unrestrictedly positive ground of meaning? In the previous section the intrinsic character of reality as dynamic motion led to the question of whether one can discern direction, not to mention purpose, at work within the process. The question represents the human mind trying to understand the world and the place of human existence in it. That imperative imposes itself again in a new negative form when we have to defend the idea of God in a world of conflict and suffering. How do we account for so much violence and sin within the human community without blaming God the creator? The question of theodicy accompanies us wherever we go: Can the idea of a benevolent God be defended if the world is a divine creation into which conflict, violence, predation, and suffering are systemically built?

Two difficulties accompany an evolutionary framework for understanding the world and life, especially human life, within it. The first lies in the difference between an objective description or explanation of processes and subjective experiences. We just noted how a recognition of the grandeur of the evolutionary process does not always match an individual's experience of life. From the objective perspective of objective discovery, evolution appears to knit many different elements and forces together in intricate detail. Science picks this up and offers objective explanation in terms of functional operation. But the beauty of objective explanation may have little affective bearing on particular human experiences. Part of the intrinsic tension between science and Christian theology lies in the impersonal character of scientific analysis and, by contrast, the existential engagement of faith's experience and discourse. Science does not have room for existential language, and occasionally some scientists seem to dismiss it as materially insignificant. The distinction between objective explanation and existential encounter runs throughout this book.

The second polarity lies within human experience. This consists of an assessment of human life itself: Is life worth living? Without turning to science, some forms of human life seem more worth living than others. Two formulas, representing polar extremes, sum up human experience: (1) the cycle of human life is miraculously beautiful, although tinged with suffering and leading to death, but this is natural; and (2) human life is filled with pain from beginning to end, with a few bright moments of happiness. Both views deftly describe the experience of many people at the ends of a spectrum of different encounters of life. But the negative form of human experience most incisively raises the questions of meaning, coherence, and value. No issue cuts more deeply into the religious imagination. Everyone asks the questions of the coherence

---

[55] *Meaning* refers to intellectual coherence within some context; one has meaning when one grasps a unity of intelligibility that can be shared with others.

and value of human life because they engage the self. We have to submit the beauty of the world to cross-examination.

5. Science consistently reveals new dimensions of the universe.

This last section anticipates, in some respects, the discussion in the chapter that follows on the relation of the methods of science and Christian theology. Theology should be attentive to the results of scientific investigation as it reveals the inner structures of the world and ourselves. There will be plenty of space available in following chapters to discuss the blind spots of science and the blindness of some scientists, not to mention the same deficits among theologians. The point here is to show that science should not be regarded as an enemy of theology but as a friend and ally.

Science reveals ourselves to ourselves. At several junctures the brief history at the head of this chapter makes it dramatically clear that science describes constituent particulars, regularities, and processes of nature in a way that ordinary experience could never have revealed. People often confine this aspect of scientific inquiry to the nonhuman world, but insofar as human beings are also part of the natural world, science also includes us under its microscope. Dimensions of human experience that ordinarily go unnoticed are revealed in new and unfamiliar ways when subjected to scientific analysis, understanding, and methods of confirmation.

The dimensions of that revelation are too many to count, but this chapter alludes to their scope. Copernicus, Kepler, and Galileo transformed the way human beings envisaged the cosmos and understood themselves. So radical was Darwin's reconstruction of life and human existence in it that many people still cannot accept it. Our descent and inheritance from the animal kingdom fundamentally alters how we understand our personal behaviors and our social relationships.[56] Our understanding of microscopic physics requires fundamental revaluations of the "new" versus clinging to the past. Human beings resist the passage of time and change; science shows that the foundational ground of reality consists of process or becoming. Basic issues of spirituality, calculated in terms of personal orientation, are decided at the level of these primal axioms.

There are many questions that science cannot answer, and when it tries to answer them on science's terms, it gets them wrong. Why is there anything at all? is the standard question from which science must retreat. Does God exist? How does God relate to the world and to human beings? How do we answer

---

[56] From the very first chapter of *The Origin of Species by Means of Natural Selection* Darwin communicates a new way of looking at things; that is, species, basic "kinds" or "natures" of living things, are changed from within, not by an external agent creating each new species. To understand and explain reality, we have to begin from below and observe what happens. A contrast with Plato here shows the difference this new mindset makes.

these questions? The scientist says: "There is nothing to the painting other than those atoms. Van Gogh didn't infuse it with any form of spiritual energy; he put the paint onto the canvas."[57] Carroll makes a limited point, but more needs to be said about any work of art—and surely about the status of the massive picture of the universe that has been constructed by the imaginative creativity of the scientific community. What is the value of that work? Scientific discovery has enhanced what humans take to be the beauty and integrity of our universe and of life on our planet. Yet these qualities are part of a habitat that we take for granted, not to mention abuse. That world, however, does not exist out there and over against us; we are that world now conscious of itself. Theology has to appropriate our being part of the material world and be driven by the humanistic premises of wonder and gratitude for the created reality that is *re*-presented back to us by the sciences.

Science explains reality by mapping the consistency of its inner mechanisms. We do not need to dwell on this point here; it will emerge again. But it needs to be stated as a premise for reflection. Science does not just take a look; it makes observations, remembers them, records them, relates them to others, compares and measures the differences, and then does it again and invites others to do the same before drawing conclusions. The conclusions of science are forced upon it by the consistent repetition of the data themselves. We said that the "laws of nature" are not absolute, but they are taken to be universal until they are shown to be inadequate, and the inadequacies often foster a new version of the "universal" imposed by mathematical probability. In many ways this offends a classical understanding of unchanging reality, but the influence of science is creating a culture that takes it for granted.

Science lays down conditions for plausible answers to spiritual questions. This proposal states in blunt terms a point that is delicate and requires sensitivity to the religious imagination. The case can be made today gently but forcefully by looking at the Galileo affair as an allegory. That classic standoff between two sources of authority represents the beginning of the loss of the authority of the churches and an increased confidence in science within Western culture. This did not happen all at once; the process extends into the present. It places two sources of truth in direct confrontation with each other. Which is right, science or the Bible?[58] In the course of unprecedented intellectual progress the churches appear unprepared, defensive, resistant, and condemnatory before finally capitulating. As Whitehead stated: "The result of the continued repetition

---

[57] Carroll, *The Big Picture*, 95.

[58] In reality, nothing was so simple, because each conclusion was set in an epistemological culture and was mediated by all sorts of hermeneutical factors. But in the symbolically real terms of cultural communication, the impact was and is today often felt as confrontation between two distinct sources of knowledge that are often hostile to each other. This situation calls for criticism and revaluation.

of this undignified retreat, during many generations, has at last almost entirely destroyed the intellectual authority of religious thinkers."[59]

From today's perspective the church's problem with Galileo easily dissolves within an elementary critical theological imagination. The teaching and authority of the Bible work in a different way from that of science; they do not appeal to the same sources of authority or receptors of evidence. The picture of stopping the sun is figurative speech; it symbolizes God's presence and support and so on. The religious thinker today does not ask whether the earth stopped spinning. Rather, the theologian enters "inside" scientific language and respects its authenticity on the basis of the canons of investigation. Theology then suggests a distinct form of theological language that either models itself on scientific method or simply leaves the sphere of the scientific imagination intact and places its views alongside and independent of science.

Science operates on the assumption that everything subject to repeatable physical measurements can be explained in principle, except questions that transcend the empirical sphere such as why anything is, that is, the reason that it is at all. A scientifically conscious culture treats everything as if it had a historically antecedent cause. It assumes that cultural matrices are so complex that there cannot be one exclusive way of understanding anything, but that any valid position could be contextually explained or justified on the basis of principle and evidence. When we apply this formula to the way we understand generally, it provides a complex framework and an opportunity for a new understanding of Christianity that will address people who participate in this scientific culture in various degrees. Analogous to Hellenization, medieval Aristotelization, early modern and reforming evangelicalization, and various forms of modernization in theology, such an inculturation would retrieve and restate in a new idiom the authentic and consistent faith of the Christian tradition.

In the context of our discussion, the theologian has to ask what God is and what God does. These questions will not be answered here. Rather, I pose them as the outcome of this first discussion, which presents us with an element of challenge. How does the theologian address a scientifically informed culture that possesses an imagination conditioned to respect empirical evidence and outcome? As far as science can determine, God does not do anything! That's the problem. Whatever God does, it seems intrinsically unobservable. Can the empirical demands of science be admitted by a Christian theologian in a way that recognizes the authority of scientific investigation and at the same time builds an understanding of reality that respects a tradition of faith?

✦ ✦ ✦

---

[59] Alfred North Whitehead, *Science and the Modern World* (New York: The Free Press, 1925), 188.

The Preface outlined the aims of this discussion. We are not trying to affect the spiritual commitments of scientists but to allow science, particularly evolutionary science, to have its rightful impact on theological construction. This it does in two distinct ways: as method and as discovered content. We will try to enter into a scientific imagination and allow the way it reasons to affect theological reasoning. And we will allow the conclusions of a scientific consensus about the operation of nature to influence Christian theological conceptualization and language about its teachings or doctrines.

The answers to the questions, in the end, will be theological, but they will be coherent with what we know about the world from science. They will characterize God's action in the world in a concept that does not contradict the universal laws of science but points to the transcendence of God and God's presence and activity in the world.

2

Understanding Reality
through Science and Faith

How do the disciplines of science and theology relate to each other? This chapter describes broadly the premises and logic for scientific and theological discourse. In this way, it sets out the epistemological field and introduces the suppositions of the work.

There are different ways of looking at things. When those "ways" represent academic disciplines, each one searching to understand as accurately as possible the nature of the reality we share, it raises the stakes of the differences. The terms *science* and *faith* entail differences from each other that have been maximized or minimized according to historical and cultural circumstance. This chapter takes up the relationship between these practices and commitments today in order to clarify the epistemological field of this book. It describes science and theology abstractly as ways of knowing in order to compare and contrast them; it intends to show how they can relate to each other constructively. In some ways this discussion lays out the suppositions of the whole work. In the end, we focus on theology rather than faith or religion because theology, while rooted in faith, more properly refers to a critical intellectual discipline.

Reflection on the relationship between science and theology frequently leads to typologies that summarize various conceptions of how these two spheres of study relate to each other. Ian Barbour charts four positions: (1) *Conflict:* they are hostile to each other, and both sides maintain incompatibility. (2) *Independence:* these are two separable spheres of questions and domains of intelligibility and language. They do not interfere with each other. (3) *Intersection:* dialogue defines the relationship, because at several points the two discourses share the same subject matter, for example, the world, its grounding, and the human. They talk with each other. (4) *Integration:* conflation names possible places where these two spheres of experience and knowledge overlap and can be seen

31

as mutually influencing each other.[1] Such types show the breadth of positions on these matters. But because of the overly abstract nature of typologies, we follow another point of entry into the discussion by turning to a description of the kind of knowing that lies at the basis of these fields of study.

Both of the terms, *science* and *faith,* have two distinct senses or meanings. They refer subjectively to the kind of knowing that is going on and objectively to the body of knowledge generated by them and gathered into a collection of data and conclusions, or systems of understanding. They both consist of ways of appreciating and making judgments about reality that can be analyzed into methods and procedures for interpreting data, and these methods yield more or less objective contents. To emphasize the point, science can refer to an activity or to the objective truths it produces or discovers, and the same can be said of faith, even though both terms lack a verb form. In the light of this distinction, the direct comparison between the judgments of science and theology as bodies of knowledge, as if they had the same objective standing, will end up in confusion. For example, one cannot notice that "science holds X about Z" while "faith contradicts science and holds Y about Z" and then proceed to measure them over against each other without further noticing that the evidence and reasoning on which each statement rests differ considerably.

Given this distinction, this chapter focuses attention on the kinds of knowing represented in the disciplines of science and theology. The emphasis falls on the difference of theology from a scientific way of knowing.[2] Only then can we examine where these disciplines overlap and how they may influence each other. But at this point I stress the distinction of theology from scientific knowledge for two reasons. First, the distinction sets up the basis for the autonomy of religion, faith, and theology. When science as objective content seems to impinge directly and positively on the content of theological reflection, this should alert one to the possibility that something may be wrong in the presumed scope of either science or theology. An impasse between science and theology may be caused by one or both of the parties not respecting the distinctive epistemologi-

---

[1] Ian G. Barbour, *When Science Meets Religion* (San Francisco: HarperSanFrancisco, 2000), 2–4. Different authors present slightly different typologies conceived from distinct points of view.

[2] William Stoeger enumerates ten differences between science and theology: different objects attended to; assumptions and starting points; the kinds of evidence required; the methods; the criteria for validation; the results and their application; the communities of discourse that are engaged; the character of their social and cultural impact; the horizons of knowledge, meaning, and value; and tightly defined spheres of the empirical v. transcendent spheres of meaning ("Relating the Natural Sciences to Theology: Levels of Creative Mutual Interaction," *God's Action in Nature: Essays in Honor of Robert John Russell* [Burlington, VT: Ashgate, 2006], 27–28).

cal character and warrants of their own or the other's intellectual discipline. Second, by implication, this autonomy allows the religious imagination of theology fully to respect the sciences as autonomous in their own spheres and vice versa. On the one hand, then, science cannot imperil authentic religion or theology. But, on the other hand, for this to be the case, theology has to accept the intrinsic limitations of religious knowledge and the autonomy of science. These ground rules enable reflection on how these disciplines can interact and perhaps influence each other.

Moving forward, we deal successively with the distinctive character of scientific knowledge and then with faith and theological knowledge. Considering the implicit comparison, we can theorize how they might fruitfully engage each other.

The Distinctive Integrity of Science

The disciplines of philosophy of science, epistemology, and the study of methods in science are vast. To complicate matters, the differences among the sciences renders the word *science* analogous at best. These reflections, therefore, do not aim at comprehensiveness but at highlighting a distinctiveness in the scientific imagination and its authentic integrity when viewed from the perspective of theology. A similar discussion has gone on within the discipline of theology over the relationship of theology to the discipline of history since the nineteenth century and even earlier. The discussion between theology and science, by contrast, has been mostly but not exclusively pursued by theologians with some credentials in science rather than being a preoccupation across the whole discipline. This perspective originates in a theological imagination and, in a manner analogous to the dialogue with history, tries to show that science, while remaining a discipline distinct from that of theology, has a role within the discipline of theology. This can be shown on the basis of a first reflection on the object of each discipline, the way it controls its data or more generally its method, and how it verifies its conclusions.

Galileo and Darwin

To give an inherently abstract and analytical discussion a narrative concreteness, we recall the cases of Galileo and Darwin as referential examples of how scientific modes of perceiving and reasoning came to bear on a culture essentially shaped by religion. In our day these cases introduce a certain bias toward the scientific imagination, but they carry perennial meaning. The classic science that these cases represent may also be a thing of the past. But the drama in these stories highlights a saying of William James that extreme cases often illustrate vividly the essential logic of an issue.[3] In the case of Galileo, his Copernican scientific view of a heliocentric universe contradicted statements in scripture that said or implied that the sun rose and set in its revolution around the earth. Everyday language said the same thing: the sun rose; the sun set. The church's view echoed a general cultural assumption. In the case of Darwin, his view of evolution contradicted the historicity of the accounts of creation in Genesis and the general belief among fellow Christian scientists in the direct creation of new species. In this case, too, the positions representing Christian faith lay deeply embedded in a corporate cultural imagination, were spontaneously reflected in ordinary language, and were confirmed by ordinary perception. The views of both sides reflected the world as each found it from a certain limited perspective.

The Object of Science

The scientist does not strive to know transcendent reality. William Stoeger, a cosmologist interested in theology, more than once portrayed the way science proceeds, with care about how one generalizes across so many different sciences. He described natural sciences as "disciplines oriented toward the detailed qualitative and quantitative understanding and modeling of the regularities, processes, structures, and interrelationships ('the laws of nature') which characterize reality—relying on rigorous, repeatable analysis and experiment and/ or observation."[4]

This broad description of science presupposes that an object is able to be qualitatively and quantitatively defined, even if not exhaustively. By and large, the subject matter of science comprises worldly or finite reality. The object of the physical sciences may be further defined as material. Frequently, the sciences define themselves as being based on empirical evidence where this also refers to data that can be retrieved through apparatuses that detect the effects of experiments. From larger, more humanistic points of view, the materialism of science may be considered a limitation in its perspective, but such a deliberate limitation results in its precision and authority. We have to be careful with language here. That science deals with matter does not define it as materialistic. In fact, the physics of Newton and Einstein deals with mass rather than matter.

---

[3] William James, *The Varieties of Religious Experience* (United Kingdom: Collins, Fontana Library, 1971), 62.
[4] Stoeger, "Relating the Natural Sciences to Theology," 23.

The Control of Scientific Knowledge

Science concentrates on accuracy in its attention to limited and controlled sets of data. Science controls the material or object of its study by observation; that is, repeatedly examining its subject matter within defined conditions and recording the results. The pursuit of the empirical, the material, and the natural in specific detailed terms of what happens appears as virtue in this enterprise. On this point the stories of Copernicus, Galileo, and Darwin display the scientific imagination at work, observing the mechanisms of the natural world closely enough to make judgments about the certainty and dependability of conclusions or predictions about how things work in these conditions.

Mathematization, as a vehicle for describing and understanding the workings of nature, serves several functions in controlling the data from which science draws its conclusions. Mathematics helps to register and protect the exactness of the material evidence. Mathematical formulas encode functional descriptive language of how the various factors of a complex operation flow together. Equations provide an abstract shorthand description of how an operation works, how the various elements and forces interrelate, and in so doing explain the actual particular case. We do not usually think of mathematical equations as narratives, but the formula of the DNA molecule tells the story of life. The mathematization represents human construction, but it tells the stories of elements interacting in extremely complex patterns of amazing symmetry.

Mathematization also objectifies observed data and gives it a kind of abstract universal status. This marks an assumption in scientific work, namely, that patterns in behavior depend on an inner structure that accounts for the consistency.[5] The principle bears analogy to the correlation of actuality to potentiality in Aquinas: if something behaves this way, it must have inner ability to do so. The mathematical formula, then, releases the pattern from being a function of a witness's concrete experience and proposes it as a statement of fact that anyone can witness. The formula also implicitly proposes that it manifests a basic structure of the phenomenon. This process of universalization, too, increases science's authority. People consider a scientific proposal true until science positively disproves it. Copernicus made his case with mathematical observations. Darwin did not, but in *On the Origin of Species*, which some refer to as the last significant scientific book that can be read by a general audience, he made up for it by relentless appeal to example after example.

---

[5] Peter Atkins, *Galileo's Finger: The Ten Great Ideas of Science* (New York: Oxford University Press, 2003), 140–46.

The Verification of Scientific Knowledge

If repeated patterns of behavior reveal the structures of the beings that exhibit them, then scientific knowledge means something more than recording data. It generates larger conceptualizations about the process in question, and it alters or confirms the current view. The repeatability of the processes verifies larger conceptions of reality's structure. Scientific knowledge does not really prove its conclusions without the successful repetition of the process or experiment that originally established the outcome. Science continually revises formulas and laws that describe the basic makeup of reality by more sophisticated observation and more comprehensive construct. The capstone of the authority of science is that "it works," and the consistency of it working proves its objectivity. Galileo did not argue from texts; he invited his accusers to look through his telescope and think about what they saw. Humanists complain that this is instrumental reason at work, and so it is. And one has to marvel at what it has taught us.

The Objective Knowledge of Science

The knowledge generated by science can be called objective, not in the sense that all interpretations of the data are the same or equally satisfactory, but in the sense that the data have yielded principles that are empirical, public, and repeatable. The scope of its evidence and the logic of its method limit the knowledge that science generates. It does not speak of reality that transcends material and reductively empirical evidence; it does not use the language of spirit when spirit refers to immaterial reality. Scientists who assert that transcendent spirit does not exist express their faith rather than science, because science in principle can have no evidence of that which transcends the material world. The limits of science contribute to its authority; like any discipline, when it stays within the scope of its evidence, it proves itself correct until it fails. And its failure usually generates a reformed scientific view closer to the dynamism of reality. But the limitations of the object of science to the material aspects of the real also curtail the scope of its authority.

The cumulative truths of science have played the role of a lingua franca in our world and continue to do so. About twenty-three-hundred years ago Euclid composed a set of axioms in geometry that applied not only in Egypt but also in India and China.[6] All cultures could share the same geometry. The objective analytical language of science provides a stable reference point for communicating transculturally at any given time. When the Ebola epidemic broke out in Africa some years ago, it did not matter where the scientific means for fighting it came from if it worked. This makes science a powerful instrument for helping

---

[6] Atkins, *Galileo's Finger*, 276.

to unify the human race. Theology and religion might bear this in mind when they find cross-cultural communication difficult.

This deliberately simple portrayal of a scientific imagination renders it readily acceptable. It nests neatly in a human desire to know; it has self-imposed limits on what it can know; it consistently shows that the world is not as it seems; it has been driving culture in the West for centuries with analogues in other cultures; its impulse toward eclecticism and standardization provides possibilities for human unification, along with political dangers of being used for totalitarian purposes. But science remains limited to what its own evidence can show and subject to critique from other forms of knowledge when it exceeds its authority. The limits of science open a space for a comparison with another form of knowing that we have called faith and one of its particular instruments, Christian theology.

The Distinctive Integrity of Christian Faith Knowledge

Like *science,* the word *faith* also has a subjective and an objective referent. As an existential human response faith spontaneously codifies the object of faith into statements about it and about the world in the light of and in relation to it. As in the discussion of science, we begin with a focus on the subjective side of the faith that produces the more objective reasoning of theology. If faith generates a distinctive form of knowledge, what epistemology describes how that works? Can we establish a comparison with science by reflecting on the way faith's desire to know focuses on an object, and through theology controls the sources of its knowledge and produces a distinctive knowledge that has its own verification process? Because descriptive analysis of theological reasoning tends to ascend to an abstraction that disappears from sight like its transcendent object, the cases of Galileo and Darwin help to make the terms of the discussion available through example.

Galileo and Darwin

Earlier we noted that both of these scientists were men of faith in a period where faith nicely correlated with an objective vision of reality that was contradicted in one certain respect by their scientific findings. This explains the battle for correct knowledge: What is the correct vision of reality, and where does the evidence that clinches it lie? This public drama also went on within themselves. At some point Copernicus had to measure his growing scientific convictions against the public culture of faith in which he lived, and Galileo, who internal-ized heliocentrism, had to have done the same thing. How did Darwin quiet his doubts about his own convictions, which had gained shape well before the publication of *On the Origin of Species*? How did they understand the nature of faith knowledge that allowed them to live in contradiction of its public form?

The Object of Faith Knowledge

Human beings do not become aware of the object of faith knowledge by empirical perception. An object of faith makes itself known within and to human consciousness in response to a question about transcendence: Why does anything exist? By definition, the object of faith goes beyond anything that science can perceive and point to empirically. All sides should be attentive not to confuse an object of faith with an element or thing of this world or universe, which would automatically place it within the ken of science. The object of faith has to be something that cannot be perceived as sense data because it transcends them. If the object of faith knowledge did not lie beyond empirical and material data, it would not be an object of faith. This first important move sets up a qualitatively different sphere of experience from that of science and, by implication, a corresponding different aspect or dimension of reality.

All those who experience transcendence in their life will enjoy a unique experience. But it helps to delineate some parameters of the experience. Here are two. The experience of transcendence may take the "form" of excess. Primed by experiences of the boundless size of space, more careful reflection on the magnitude of the universe, or on the great beauty and joy felt when everything has come together, a person can have an experience of excess, a hint of some sphere or agency or source that accounts for what appears. The object of such an experience can be imagined as coming from beyond the horizon of the present situation, that expansive background that gives whatever appears a field for visual focus. In an experience of transcendence, the "beyond the horizon" of everything that exists makes the whole universe appear limited in relation to it.[7] The experience can be called dialectical, indicating a tension between what is and something other than it that sustains it and gives it value. Consequently, an experience of finitude, which so readily appears in the life-and-death cycle of nature, indirectly gives rise to the possibility of encounter with the ultimate excess of infinity. An experience of things as meaningful and valuable implies the question of a source and ground of that experience and that reality. Such is the horizon of infinite excess. An analogous experience, whether explicitly conscious or not, lies implicit, for example, in Thomas Aquinas's definition of

---

[7] The discussion of limits and what lies beyond them, when translated into terms that imply space and time, breeds confusion. Scientifically, there is no "beyond space" because it is a parameter of the universe. And God cannot be "beyond" or "above" finitude because it connotes occupying space. Transcendence encompasses all that is and, as infinity, exceeds finitude itself. All this shows how imagination works its way into all our efforts to transcend it.

God as "the pure act of being." The pure act of being refers to the unlimited and unimaginable dynamic power of being that exceeds the whole ensemble of beings within space-time and energizes them from within. In other words, the "form" of this experience "appears" as "excess" and "formlessness," the sphere transcending all form.

The other "form" of an experience of transcendence may pass through negativity. Evolution itself can generate this experience because the end result of the dramatic struggle within natural selection between creativity and corruption ends in death. Death spells extinction and annihilation: What is it for? Where is its meaning or coherent intelligibility relative to existence? For example, what are we to make of predation, the constant death-dealing evil of human beings against human beings that goes on not so secretly around us? In the kind of experience that elicits such questions, the finitude of everything presses in on consciousness as negation or negativity. Concrete experiences of negativity come as no surprise because it seems to be written into the structure of life itself. The many forms of physical, psychological, and socially inflicted suffering bear witness to it. Negativity, however, can only be recognized as such, that is, as negative, against a horizon of positivity, an impulse or desire for life and a drive toward wholeness. The thoroughgoing finitude of the world, which is not evil in itself, constantly appears as infected or endangered by the threat of negative forces. Every instance of being seems at risk; we are marked by the potential of negation before which we appear passive. Yet this same negation stimulates a search for transcendent leverage against it.

Theologians give various names to the object of this basic experience of transcendence, which is always shrouded in mystery. In this book, the object of an experience of transcendence is called *Presence.* The term has broad resonance. For example, if Buddhism were regarded less as a religion and more as a practice with an accompanying worldview, one could say that the aim of meditation is to discover Presence within the self that is no-self but exists within Presence.[8] Christians experience Presence as transcendent; Buddhists may think more in terms of ultimacy. The experience of Presence reflected in Christian theological language can be aligned with the idea of general revelation. All human beings potentially can experience Presence in different ways. More will be said about Presence in terms of Christian faith in the next chapter, but at this point, we can move forward with the idea that the object of faith knowledge may be regarded as transcendence experienced as an all-encompassing Presence. We have moved into a sphere of knowing that differs from scientific empiricism.

---

[8] *Presence,* of course, is not a Buddhist term, and neither is it a particularly Christian term. It is chosen for its openness and availability to common human experience prior to specific names.

The Control of Faith Knowledge

Revelation occurs within the experience of a human subject, and the idea of Presence provides a context for more specific description. As distinct from the general sense of mystery or the holy, a *particular* revelation points to a historical medium that qualifies the experience of transcendence.[9] A historical medium gives the experience of Presence its particular content. Without some historical medium, a community would have no specificity or common idea around which it could gather. In Christian theology, "revelation means primarily the encounter of God through a medium."[10] The medium, whether a sacred mountain, a book of recorded ordinances, or Jesus of Nazareth, is not itself the divine Presence but a finite thing that points to the transcendent and bears it within itself. This theory should not be regarded as mystical, except in the sense that all religious experience may be called mystical. It emerges from the conviction that immediate contact with transcendence or God from the human side does not seem possible. Such experience always runs together with our context and our self-consciousness and all the things that these involve. Nor can one rationalistically reason to God conclusively but only to a notion of God. We are restricted to faith in our knowing relationship with transcendence. Faith knowledge is *mediated encounter*, whose nearest analogy appears in the communication of one subject or self with another through external sign or gesture. We both know and do not really know other persons but must interpret their inner self-presence in the signals that are given.

Theological knowledge needs another control over anthropomorphism, the reduction of transcendent Presence to finite conceptualization. Anthropomorphism also extends beyond conceiving transcendence in human forms. It applies to any attenuation of transcendent reality to the limits of a finite or particular being. Negative theology *(via negativa)*, a medieval construct retrieved from a much earlier Near Eastern mystical tradition, still bears traction against this reductionism. Negative theology recognized that God as creator bestowed qualities on creatures analogous to "itself" as their cause. But it also appreciated the absolutely transcendent character of God, so that, though creatures may somehow be like God, God is not like creatures! Therefore, talk about Presence has this structure: We affirm something about Presence on the basis of a medium in this world that, like a sacrament, communicates Presence to our consciousness. But when human beings appreciate the transcendence of Presence, they must deny radically that any earthly meaning as such applies to Presence. We have to settle for a *realistic* projection of the actual character of Presence experienced within

---

[9] The idea of *particular* can be expressed as well by words like *specific* or *historical.*

[10] John E. Smith, "The Disclosure of God and Positive Religion," *Experience and God* (New York: Oxford University Press, 1968), 77.

ourselves, broadly guided by the mediating symbol, and applying it in a sense that we cannot comprehend.[11]

Therefore, the logic of the experience of faith governs the meaning of the terms used by theology about its transcendent object. The object of theology arises in the experience of faith and revelation. Theological language interprets and affirms what is experienced, and at the same time denies the adequacy of the conceptualization or language it uses. Out of that affirmation and denial, theology represents transcendent mystery. All true knowledge of Presence bears an apophatic character: the negation is not rescinded, but follows an imperative that disallows correlative one-to-one speech about transcendence equivalent to words about empirical objects. Much more will be said about the character of Presence in the light of Jesus of Nazareth, who is the medium of God for Christian faith. But we have enough here for a foundational comparison and contrast with scientific knowing.

The Verification of Faith Knowledge

The idea of verification with regard to faith knowledge retreats from the verification offered by science and takes refuge in a paradox connected with an epistemology of mystery. But we can construct a generous analogy around the sentence, "It works." Faith knowledge, like all knowledge, performs a function in life: it grounds the knowing subject and orients it toward the future. This sounds simple, but obstacles render the task difficult, and it sometimes breaks down in personal life, as in the case of Darwin. It remains too easy to say that a particular faith achieves a status of being self-justifying. A better idea posits that all live by some faith in some kind of ultimate or ultimacy. But at the same time, the language that points to the object of faith radically differs across religious traditions and the many forms of secular faith.

The verification of faith knowledge has to have an existential dimension because faith as a human response is existential. Just as there are a variety of religious experiences, ultimately as many as there are people, because we all live by some personal faith, so too will the actual grounding of one's existence, or orienting conviction, or fundamental moral disposition be completely embodied in the individual. Everything fits together personally. The convictions of faith also have a social dimension. Usually a community supports a given faith by sharing a common language, by gathering in ritual expression, by professing a common set of values and moral standards, and by offering mutual feedback.

---

[11] Thomas Aquinas, *Summa Theologiae*, I, q.13, a.2, and q.13, a.3, ad 2. Aquinas is saying that transcendent realities like God and Spirit are known by analogy with concepts and symbols like father and breeze. Analogy here means partly the same in a way we do not positively know, and radically different, because we only know what God is not and not what God is positively.

As long as these "work," one has a multifaceted communal verification. But it cannot be completely trusted. In Galileo's and Darwin's cases, social verification did not work and was so strong that it actually resisted observable scientific evidence. In other words, the social or communal criteria really do not add up to empirical verification but remain finite and culturally conditioned. They often lag behind new scientific, spiritual, and moral exigencies, and history only gradually alters corporate opinion. Faith's knowledge cannot be verified as decisively as scientific knowledge.

The "Objective" Knowledge of Theology

Faith knowledge also begins to become problematic when its existential character as subjective faith becomes occluded. Faith expresses itself in language and action that take on public meaning on the basis of its mediating symbols: doctrines, public ritual, community ethics, and other shared exercises. The personal character of faith takes on an objective dimension in the sharing of beliefs in propositional form, worship in commonly observed ritual, and a corporate morality structured by norms. These social forms tend to give personal faith the feel of objectivity. Of course, all objective knowledge consists of social subjectivity, but the verification of empirical knowledge operates in a considerably more straightforward way than in theological assertion. Theological knowledge does not share the absolute character of its object. The difference between interior faith clinging to transcendent Presence and the rote catechetical formulas that supposedly represent that faith is notorious. Theology has to reckon with that gap. The drama in the stories of Galileo and Darwin, in the actual and symbolic levels of their stories, resides in this tension. Objective faith knowledge does not amount to empirically based objective knowledge. It realistically participates in its transcendent "object" in ways that will be developed further in later chapters.[12] But in the contrast between beliefs expressing faith and overt knowledge that seems to contradict certain beliefs, theology must be "objective" enough to reflect critically on its own beliefs. When realistic faith knowledge loses its existential base and functions like acquired scientific knowledge, it has been corrupted, and it loses its character of mystery. When it contradicts empirical evidence with mysterious beliefs, critical reflection summons it back down to earth. Sometimes that process takes considerable time.[13]

---

[12] Faith refers to inner human commitment to a transcendent reality. Theology arises out of faith. But the existential basis of theology should not be confused with some form of subjectivism where the object or referent of theology really consists of the self and its experience. The next chapter supplies a rationale for why faith and theology can be realistic, that is, referring to reality beyond and other than the self.

[13] In this dialogue with science I have not attended to the question of true and false religion—not an incidental issue. But a positive ongoing relationship with science, not to

The Mutuality
of Science and Faith

We need a way of formulating a working relationship between these very different ways of thinking and interpreting reality. The world as science finds it gradually becomes a given. How does Christian faith positively construe the scientific view of the world as something to be cherished and included in faith itself? Or, how would a thoroughgoing scientist who is a Christian understand his or her faith? Can we construct a set of basic principles for interpreting Christian symbols in the light of a scientifically informed culture and at the same time, reciprocally, integrate the scientific story of the universe into the world of faith structured by Christian symbols?

In 1962, Thomas S. Kuhn published his widely known book *The Structure of Scientific Revolutions.*[14] The book describes the element of discontinuity in scientific learning characterized by the term *paradigm shift.* Originally a technical term, it was appropriated widely across disciplines and in everyday language to refer to radically new understandings of things. For example, the revolution in understanding our world and ourselves in it represented by the shift to heliocentrism has to be considered radical. Everything people experienced remained the same, but, with the shift, all of it was construed differently. I understand the term *paradigm* as an imaginative framework or template or worldview that includes assumptions, basic ideas or principles, and a working method that structures and guides interpretation. We are looking for a paradigm describing a positive, dynamic relationship between statements generated by science and faith or theology.

Let us go back to the keywords used by Ian Barbour to describe abstractly general outlooks on this relationship: *conflict, independence, intersection,* and *integration.* All these characterizations of the relationship bear some truth, but the first two overemphasize the specific differences in the ways of knowing, and the second two may not sufficiently respect those differences. The reflections that follow assume the perspective of the inquirer, one who has appropriated a scientific culture[15] and seeks to understand Christian faith from within that perspective. The discussion describes what a vital interchange between scientist

---

mention common sense and critical public values, does contribute to the authenticity of faith commitment.

[14] The fiftieth anniversary edition of this work is Thomas S. Kuhn, *The Structure of Scientific Revolutions* (Chicago: University of Chicago Press, 2012).

[15] I deliberately leave the idea of appropriating a scientific culture vague. The phrase refers less to the various cultures of scientists themselves, and more to the secular culture that uses the technology and gradually internalizes the worldview of the many scientific venues that influence us through education, communication, and industry. But the variations in this sampling of people remain large.

and theologian entails when they actually speak with each other in ways that are both critical from and of their respective disciplines and thus open to new insight.

Scientific Understanding as a Form of Faith

The sciences challenge philosophy and theology "to articulate more carefully and more critically their own perspectives on reality, on origins and destinies, on God's relation with the world. Obviously, this must be done within the cultural context, which is partially determined by science and technology themselves."[16] Theology, catechetics, and preaching all face the same problem: how to describe God's action in the world in a way that is coherent and intelligible relative to science and revelation.

Paul Tillich suggests a formula that can provide an initial framework to situate reflection on this relationship. The principle can be stated this way: Faith is the substance of culture, culture is the form of faith.[17] The principle operates out of an existential understanding of religion as rooted in elementary faith or ultimate concern. The second of the two maxims really binds faith and culture together: "Every religious act, not only in organized religion, but also in the most intimate movement of the soul, is culturally formed."[18] In all of its expressions every person's faith in transcendent Presence will take on the cultural patterns of language, ethos, and public interchange, and especially the basic form of its initial medium.

The history of Christian faith over two millennia bears witness to the dynamics of this formula. In each context of each period of this history faith soaked up a form of self-understanding and practice from the cultures it infiltrated. Our "Greek" doctrines, Catholicism's Aristotelian spirituality of action, Protestantism's evangelical preaching, and modernity's turn to experience have arisen out of and in dialogue with culture. These large terms should not bury the national sub-forms of faith or the ideologies of particular groups affected by schools of thought and special interests. Faith may remain the "same," but each form of faith can be analogous only when compared with others, that is, partly the same and partly different relative to the subject matter that it represents. The analogy subsists in the comparison of the proportional terms: faith expressed in first-century cultural terms relates to faith expressed in sixteenth-century Elizabethan terms, and faith expressed in twenty-first century scientific cultural terms, and so on. The relative proportions bear the analogy because no pure content of faith

---

[16] Willian R. Stoeger, "Faith Reflects on the Evolving Universe," in *Finding God in All Things*, ed. Michael J. Himes and Stephen J. Pope (New York: Crossroad, 1996), 162.

[17] This is an adaptation of Tillich's maxim "religion is the substance of culture, culture is the form of religion." Paul Tillich, *Theology of Culture* (New York: Oxford University Press, 1964), 42.

[18] Tillich, *Theology of Culture*, 42.

exists that can be used as a standard; faith's object always remains transcendent and has to be reckoned as such, and it never finds expression outside of some cultural form.[19]

With the principle of how culture and faith relate to each other as form and substance and its practical application in historical consciousness, we also have a framework for talking about how science and faith/theology interact as different forms of knowledge.[20] For this, we draw from Tillich's method of correlation, which he formulated as an ongoing hermeneutical process for negotiating theological interpretations related to a particular culture. With a slight shift of reference the dynamics of a mutually critical method of correlation also describe how culture and faith interact. Correlation means placing in conjunction the data of a faith tradition and the suppositions and questions of a present-day culture looking for spiritual meaning.[21] *Mutually critical* indicates the need for care not to compromise either faith or science in the resulting dialogue and exchange. Describing a new form for the expression of the substance of faith and opening up the imagination to deeper or more exalted interpretation of the dynamics of cosmos, life, and human freedom should be thought of as exciting and positive enterprises, but they require careful critical thinking that does not compromise a community's faith.[22]

Mutually Critical Dynamics of Appropriation

We are in a position now to introduce some rules for understanding the mutual relationships between a scientific imagination and faith knowledge expressed as theology. Some of these rules come from the epistemology of autonomous disciplines that have methodological canons and distinct limits on the range of evidence.[23] Others can be discerned in the comparison of these different ways of knowing.

---

[19] See Edward Schillebeeckx, *Church: The Human Story of God* (New York: Crossroad, 1990), 42.

[20] The phrase "forms of knowledge" is ambiguous; it refers to the dynamic process of two different kinds of knowledge reviewed in the first two parts of this chapter. The resulting convictions and propositions will be of different kinds.

[21] The paradoxical phrase "the data of a faith tradition" refers to the history of faith's expression.

[22] This may be too simply stated given historical, social, and political complexities. For example, Galileo and Darwin seemed to compromise the community's faith. But they had done the critical thinking. Communities of faith need time to appropriate new perspectives proposed by science, but this should not be an excuse for inactivity.

[23] The terms *science* and *theology* remain abstractions. For example, there are variations within scientific disciplines and subdisciplines. Science is not monolithic, and pluralism marks the discipline of theology.

No reductionism. Reductionism refers to the shrinkage of what can be known and, more radically, of reality to the criteria of what can be learned by the canons of a particular discipline. A strain of this exists in various writers of science, but is it intrinsic to any of the disciplines of science? Science may operate from materialist premises because its empiricism requires quantitative measurement that accounts for objectivity and precision. But to move from that methodological framework to an assertion that the spiritual or nonmaterial does not exist exceeds the limits of the discipline; there can be no material evidence for the nonexistence of the spiritual. The new atheism of some scientists does not draw evidence from their science but ironically expresses their faith.

But some criticisms of science go deeper. The practice of science raises some questions about the reductive materialist assumptions shared by many scientists.[24] A good example is found in statements such as these: "The basic stuff of reality is a quantum wave function, or a collection of particles and forces—whatever the fundamental stuff turns out to be. Everything else is an overlay, a vocabulary created by us for particular purposes."[25] "Consciousness emerges from the collective behavior of particles and forces, rather than being an intrinsic feature of the world. And there is no immaterial soul that could possibly survive the body. When we die, that's the end of us."[26] Thomas Nagel describes materialist reductionism as folding into a single explanation the understanding of all reality: "Everything that exists and everything that happens can in principle be explained by the laws that govern the physical universe."[27] Because of the material consistency of the evolutionary process, everything that exists today can be explained by looking back, step by step, to origins. This perspective gradually slides into explanatory theory: what exists later is no more than complexification of initial elements.[28]

---

[24] Behind this critique of science lies a theoretical question: Is science what scientists do? Or can scientists and philosophers of science establish some epistemological norms that define the logic of scientific disciplines? The tendency of this work is to look upon assumptions that are not scientifically established, or that cannot be, as analogous to faith commitments rather than principles of science itself. We will return to this issue.

[25] Carroll, *The Big Picture*, 142.

[26] Carroll, *The Big Picture*, 158.

[27] Thomas Nagel, *Mind and Cosmos: Why the Materialist Neo-Darwinian Conception of Nature Is Almost Certainly False* (New York: Oxford University Press, 2012), 18. This ideal was strengthened by Darwin, who provided a narrative by which everything may be understood to have emerged out of dynamic matter. See Nagel, *Mind and Cosmos*, 19. Nagel offers an extended analysis of the problem of scientific bias and a way of dealing with it (35–69).

[28] John Cobb also argues against scientific reductionism: This view simply ignores a whole range of subjective experience of the self—an intuitive, commonsensical self-experience or direct experience of the self. It is irrational to dismiss or ignore this sphere, because it is part of nature and shared at various levels by other species. See John Cobb, Jr., *Jesus' Abba: The God Who Has Not Failed* (Minneapolis: Fortress Press, 2015), 44; see esp. 79–108.

Three reflections counter the conclusions of reductive materialism and show, at least, that it represents no more than pure faith. We can begin with the evidence of the intuitive insight mirrored in Descartes's *Cogito* that human consciousness is a form of being. More will be said later about the realism of self-perception in a discussion of brain and mind. But it makes no sense to deny one's own existence as self-conscious subject. Second, the reality of life and consciousness can be affirmed on the principle of the continuity of evolutionary process by positing that some potential for or primitive form of these developments are part of reality itself. The principle of the consistency or integrity of nature suggests that some embryonic form or potentiality be found within the antecedents of mind that allows one to read nature holistically and recognize mind as a part of it. Third, science can also reflect on the positive character of evolutionary complexification to produce new "higher" levels of being. Evolution does not require that we exclusively look backward to understand reality in the present; we may and should also look forward from the past and recognize new forms of reality. John Haught expresses the point with forceful clarity. If evolution means that reality has a narrative character and still remains unfinished, then one cannot understand it adequately by only looking backward.[29] The universe as witnessed in our planet displays an evolution through emergence of greater complexity in new forms of being that are real. That shift of perspective, from looking backward to include looking forward, almost spontaneously reveals nature itself as a capacity to produce really new forms of being. A kind of "dominative" instrumental reason, as distinct from open contemplative wonder, seems to underlie the claims of reductionism.[30]

Reductionism in various forms can also be found in the discipline of theology. An example is a form of theology that, by inviting persons of faith to step into "another world" accessed by faith, also urges them metaphorically to step out of this world of material interchange. This results in a theology that bears little relation to the constant exchanges that make up life in this world. Here the theological imagination creates at least a strong separation or disconnection between the conscious life of faith and the logic of the material world. The person who has entered the spiritual realm of faith in many respects stands in opposition to natural processes. The critique, here, does not take aim at prophetic discourse that relates directly to this world but to esoteric religious experience that ignores critical reflection and cultural criticism in order to form isolated

---

[29] John F. Haught, "Cosmology and Creation," *Christianity and Science: Toward a Theology of Nature* (Maryknoll, NY: Orbis Books, 2007), 59–64, 130; idem, *God after Darwin: A Theology of Evolution* (Boulder, CO: Westview Press, 2000), 100–102; and idem, *Resting on the Future: Catholic Theology for an Unfinished Universe* (New York: Bloomsbury, 2015). This will become an important link to theological reflection on an absolute future.

[30] "But the subtle subordination of the desire to know to a reductionist will to control remains a significant element in the atmosphere of contemporary scientific and intellectual culture" (Haught, *Christianity and Science*, 187).

cult-like communities.[31] Large religious institutions can also assume defensive postures and retain in-group languages impervious to reasonable critique.

The antidote to both forms of reductionism in its various degrees lies in conversation. Conversation requires listening and hearing, taking into consideration the positions of dialogue partners, and an openness to new settlements. It entails remaining within the boundaries of one's own discipline and respecting the other. Theoreticians, of course, can more easily formulate the rules of conversation than put them in practice to the satisfaction of all. This prescription, therefore, does not ensure consensus, but it promotes insight and new learning. It formulates rules for an ongoing process rather than reaches a conclusion.

No anthropomorphism. Anthropomorphism refers to the natural tendency of the human imagination to envisage transcendent reality, specifically God, in terms of the human. Once God is recognized as personal, this almost inevitably carries with it the imaginative portrayal of God as a magnified human being, a "big person in the sky." In some theories of knowledge this cannot be escaped, because human knowledge always contains some residue of an imaginative representation of the object known. The situation requires explicit refusal to entertain familiar personal characteristics in transcendent reality as in the *via negativa* discussed earlier. Since by definition the object of faith transcends the entire physical world, affirmative language about transcendence intrinsically misleads. The strategy of negative theology addresses this. Other strong testimonies in the history of Christian theology, such as those of some mystics, explicitly resist this form of theological reductionism. This becomes a central issue when we consider Presence as the Creator God in the following chapter.

Science is a negative norm. The idea that science might provide norms for theology may be upsetting for some theologians with a proclivity toward theological reductionism. But, on certain issues, science represents "the world as it is," ambiguous as that idea may sound. For example, the evolution of life on our planet is not a scientific hypothesis, or a theory, but an accepted description of our history and state of being. Deliberately to ignore evolution or to refuse to think around it fundamentally undercuts the realism for which theology strives. Not every scientific discovery has a bearing on the human relationship with Presence, nor should the personal authenticity of faith be measured by the possession of knowledge. But the critical edge of theology cannot ignore basic cultural wisdom or a verifiable scientific description of the world.

The overt examples of heliocentrism and evolution open up the principle of how science can be normative for theology. Formulated as a "negative" norma-

---

[31] This abstract way of dealing with a dialectical imagination is not fully adequate but merely suggestive of an extreme. In many ways faith informs a prophetic imagination with transcendent leverage. The analysis here aims at structure and logic and not close description of complex motivations in particular cases.

tivity, this principle says that theology cannot deny what is commonly taken as established scientific conclusions about reality and retain its credibility. From one perspective the principle announces something commonsensical. What could be more obvious? But it is a hard-won conviction, because in different cultures faith has generated a language of the supernatural that seems to stand on autonomous ground in the face of common sense. Frequently, theology supplemented this enthusiasm by translating obvious metaphor into literal speech and backing it up with a metaphysics of the supernatural. From this perspective, then, negative normativity seems obvious to those who live comfortably in the sphere of scientific realism, but it challenges an imagination that prescinds from science and easily accepts a supplementary and sometimes rival supernatural world.

A searching imagination. From another perspective the principle of the negative normativity of science rests on a realism that generates positive outcomes for faith. It forces the faithful human mind to be attentive to the workings of nature. The negative normativity of science urges faith and theology to find transcendence not outside or above the workings of the natural world but within it. It gradually corrects the translation of *transcendence* from designating something in another place to a meaning that locates its referent inside this world but in a nonphysical or nonmaterialistic way.[32] This larger, nonreductive regard for nature can lead to what may be called an inspiration of the creative imagination. In nature one can read patterns that stimulate insight into transcendence at least in the form of questions. If, according to science, the behavior of the physical world opens up the imagination to inner structures that perform like the double helix, what is suggested as the inner reason for an "ascending" pattern of evolution toward beings of greater complexity? Does the arrow of time point in a direction? Is there a next step for human consciousness along the evolutionary ladder? In short, one cannot directly read the nature of transcendence from the dynamics of nature, but natural forces suggest metaphors for dealing theologically with nature's mystery in ways that are analogous to science. Science and theology share a pure desire to know and a searching imagination.

The Values Implied in Faith as Critical Moral Guides

Is there any point at which faith knowledge has leverage on science? The question of the openness of nature to transcendence frequently gives rise to a discussion of values. The world of values, both in theory and in fact, points to a sphere of experience that exerts an influence on scientific reason, and especially the use of technology. While this cannot be developed deeply here—but will be later—the following reflections at least call attention to this area.

---

[32] The idea of the spiritual in the sense of nonphysical and nonmaterial reality is planted here without further explanation in order to return to it in the following chapter.

To begin the discussion we turn to philosophy, cognitive theory, and science about the nature of the relationship between brain and mind or reflective consciousness. The relationship remains problematic, and I do not intend to resolve it. But strong reasons, not least of which is direct intuition, suggest that *human consciousness* refers to a real kind of being. It makes little sense for human consciousness to build an extraordinarily sophisticated body of knowledge that says, at the end of the day, that human consciousness itself may be reduced to an epiphenomenon that is less than fully real. If human consciousness directly signifies reality that is conscious of itself, we should be able to learn *from the phenomenon itself* something about the nature of reality.

The principle of direct evidence from experience can be extended further. There seems to be a universal tendency within human consciousness—in everyday life and in sophisticated philosophical and ethical reflection on it—to discover, argue over, and live by a set of values. A value is a quality of objects and actions that gives them an importance in themselves. Human consciousness recognizes and responds to values; it does not create them. Ontological, aesthetic, and moral values stand over against us and cannot be fully accounted for by interest alone. They refer to qualities of being or beings that are recognized in human consciousness as precisely that.[33] Nagel, too, defends a realist objective conception of values. In contrast to values defined subjectively as functions of human disposition and motivation, "the realist position is that our judgments attempt to identify the right answer and bring our attitudes into accord with it."[34]

Given the objectivity of values, one can begin to discern the way they relate to science. The explanation for knowledge itself generally correlates with a mode of behavior of an organism or species; knowledge fits the needs that the environment imposes. Science recognizes this objective form of functional

---

[33] This account of values is drawn from Dietrich von Hildebrand, *Christian Ethics* (New York: D. McKay Co., 1953). I am treating values as a given and not considering the evolutionary account of their origin. It is not clear to me whether explanation of their origin would change their status as a given. The human imagination, of course, *can* create values, as in forms of idolatry. But in principle a value declares itself and solicits a response. The objectivity of value is not undermined but affirmed by the fact that people fight over them. People dispute values *because* values are important and have a claim on human consciousness.

[34] Nagel, *Mind and Cosmos*, 99. The realist position, he adds, cannot be established empirically by any experiment; it is simply a better account of what is going on (104). The recognition of the realism of values also offers another way of exploring the phenomenon of faith. Charley D. Hardwick develops a valuational theism in response to thoroughgoing naturalism in *Events of Grace: Naturalism, Existentialism, and Theology* (Cambridge: Cambridge University Press, 1996). Values, he argues, are affirmed as objectively true and as being grounded in God (67). Faith operates in the sphere of valuation; faith in God creates a way of seeing reality and recognizing God as the source of human good (179). I return to value theory in Chapter 8.

teleology; the function of self-consciousness and knowing is to provide the basis for a certain way of behaving and dealing with the world. The critical mental abilities of human beings have the role of directing human behavior. If knowing were not oriented to human action, it is hard to imagine what else it would be for.

The conclusion of this brief reflection correlates fairly tightly with what most people take for granted: fundamental values direct human life; they give it moral seriousness by implying responsibility and even obligation.[35] And they spring from a matrix and a range of experiences that exhibit an autonomy analogous to that of faith. What one does with human science stands accountable to the sphere of value. This moral responsibility was experienced acutely by many of the scientists who led us into the age of atomic energy.

A Friendly Critical Exchange

In the framework of evolution and the dynamism of becoming over a vast period of time, the idea of an external designer of a process leading to a predetermined final product has been replaced by the process of evolution itself; that is, the character of intelligibility, goodness, beauty, and being are the products of development.[36] But the picture of the evolution of the universe as seen from our planet shows a certain direction of increasing complexity. Looking back from our perspective, intelligent beings appear as the result of evolution. At the same time, the future becomes an essential feature of both the dynamics of evolution and human experience that can also look forward into an open future. Human existence has a whence and a whither. The open place between past and future that appears in human consciousness becomes an essential indicator of the nature of reality that is available only to human beings, as far as we know. One cannot ignore this as a source of knowledge.

Meaning and value appear in human subjectivity within the larger context of an objective process of evolution. Human beings usually take meaning and value for granted in both personal consciousness and in the life stories or traditions of the community. Values and value judgments do not appear within the scope of the physical sciences. But the objective and subjective dimensions of experience should not be conceived as hostile to each other; consciousness is matter aware of itself; and human participation in being includes awareness

---

[35] H. Richard Niebuhr insightfully recognizes how the absolute value of truth operates in the world of science. One sees this most dramatically in the revulsion of the scientific community caused by deliberate falsification of evidence. See *Radical Monotheism and Western Culture* (New York: Harper and Brothers, 1943), 78–89.

[36] It may be helpful to parse this sentence in relation to the preceding discussion of values. It is the "character" or "form" of intelligibility, goodness, beauty, and being that develops, not their autonomous value.

of being enabled and restricted in movement by physicality. To an objective scientific imagination, direction manifests itself at best vaguely, slowly but surely, through complexification over vast stretches of time. For the scientific disciplines this falls far short of teleology in the sense of conscious purpose. But a personal desire for direction in life and a psychic need for purposeful activity that constantly show up in human experience form part of the cosmos. One can read something of the directionality of the cosmos in the human subject itself.

A sense of, or a desire for, direction has been augmented by human maturity and a sense of responsibility that has taken concrete form in cultural evolution. Teilhard de Chardin offered an allegory to illustrate how in the course of the Enlightenment and its aftermath in the nineteenth century human beings discovered a responsibility for human existence and for the planet. We are like a people in the hold of a ship, with little to do but fight or try to get along, who one day made their way to the bridge and saw that they were on a ship and that the ship was in motion. But where were they going? In a revolutionary corporate insight like that mediated by Copernicus and Galileo, they realized that "the time had come to pilot the ship."[37] Corporate humanity is directing our world forward into the future. I am going someplace or no place in it, with it, and as part of it. Both science and theology have to interpret this new experience of self and world.

The conversation between science and faith should lead to some form of an integrated understanding. This phrase seems too facile and feeble to carry the burden of meaning the project entails. But one reality can be understood in two or more distinct languages.[38] Describing the same reality puts the two languages in a dialectical relationship to each other. Without losing their autonomous status grounded in the canons of each discipline, both are bound to what is described and can influence each other. Possible *mutual influence* justifies the significance of the conjunction, the holding together, of critical scientific and theological perspectives and the languages they use to decipher reality. These two interpretations of one given reality produce a tensive understanding that remains active and dynamic rather than objectively "integrated." Each dimension remains distinct and autonomous, but they are held together so that each communicates something to the other even though they differ as ways of knowing.

---

[37] Pierre Teilhard de Chardin, *Activation of Energy* (New York: Harcourt Brace, 1971), 73–74.

[38] Edward Schillebeeckx, *The Church: The Human Story of God* (New York: Crossroad, 1990), 210–13. That light is best understood sometimes as particles and sometimes as waves bears an analogy to this maxim. The maxim plays a major role in the argument of Chapter 4. Mary Midgley accepts the broad maxim that science deals with facts and religion with interpretation and meaning. While they do not compete directly, they meet in the arena of a worldview that is needed for facts to be integrated among themselves and reality to have meaning, value and coherence (*Evolution as a Religion: Strange Hopes and Stranger Fears* [London: Routledge, 2002], 11–21).

A critical and a constructive appreciation of the conversation between science and faith includes several characteristics. Because these are autonomous ways of knowing, their conjunction cannot mean a fusion of distinct frameworks into a common consistent language. One cannot collapse theology into empirical data, as in "Jesus is risen into the consciousness of his disciples"[39]; or science into theology, as in "an autonomous ghost is working in the machine."[40] One has to wrestle with the two languages or interpretations that are different but mutually influencing each other.

Mutual influence does not mean a distinction that creates a split-level system of convictions and does not involve compartmentalization of human conscious-ness. Sometimes compartmentalization offers a therapeutic strategy for relieving the pressure of living one's faith in the face of continual critical questioning. But separate compartments do not offer a way of living an integrated or coherent life. The dialogue between science and theology does not imply life on a dual track. The ideas of split level and compartmentalization rightly insist that the disciplines of science and faith/theology cannot be collapsed into each other. But a form of integration can occur in the knower. Here, integration from the side of religious knowledge refers to holding distinct ways of knowing together to generate an active and open understanding of reality. It entails finding tran-scendence not in a sphere separate from this empirical world, but as a way of grasping a distinct dimension that lies within the empirical order. It does not appear overtly or empirically, but transcendence is mediated by and through external reality to a consciousness that is open to it. Empirical reality acts as a symbol or signifier of transcendence, or a value that stands autonomously before us and solicits an internal response.

A layered understanding of something organic provides a more accurate metaphor than split levels or compartments. One reality composed of layered interacting systems by definition offers a more encompassing and integrating understanding. When evolution is fast-forwarded through stages, it allows one to imagine the new stages of complexity emerging out of the dynamisms of earlier levels of being. Each new layer integrates the earlier systems into itself so that reality is "expanded." John Haught provides an example of this expansion on the level of self-consciousness and intentionality. Consider a hand holding a

---

[39] This view represents some existentialist theologians who cannot affirm a real resurrec-tion of Jesus.

[40] The phrase "the ghost in the machine" is Steven Pinker's. It refers to a separable spirit or self within the material human organism. He writes that "cognitive neuroscience is show-ing that the self, too, is just another network of brain systems." "Each of us *feels* that there is a single 'I' in control. But that is an illusion that the brain works hard to produce" (Steven Pinker, *The Blank Slate: The Modern Denial of Human Nature* [London: Penguin Books, 2002], 42–43). Without accepting Pinker's reductionism, he still challenges a facile soul-body distinction that serves theological interests.

pencil scribbling across a page and gradually beginning to form letters, words, and sentences. One sees in that extended visible act a manifestation of layers of vitality: physics describes the atomic structure of the matter/energy, chemistry describes the molecules that fit together and constitute life, and biology describes the hand of a living human being. These have gradually come together, without any intervention at all, and the writing inexplicably expands physical motion into meaning and linguistic communication.[41] Mind expands the brain with reflective intentionality and in so doing transforms all the enfolded dimensions into an organic whole and suffuses it and them with new value. From a scientific perspective the image of the hand reflects the integration of the world lauded in Psalm 104.

In conclusion, should the relationship of science and theology be understood as conflictive, independent, intersecting, or integrative? I do not see how science and theology as disciplines can be in conflict if each remains within the boundaries of its competence. Every conflict of which I am aware involves one or other practitioner exceeding the limits of the discipline. Independence more closely describes the methods of study defined by disciplinary canons. It also describes the practice of most scientists and theologians; they do not consult each other or exhibit cross-disciplinary interests. The few exceptions prove the rule, and it marks a tragic development. As disciplines, science and theology appear to be bodies of knowledge that coexist as different autonomous interpretations or aspects of a common object, the reality in which we live, and can be internalized as such. But the methods and the bodies of knowledge they produce also intersect inside human consciousness as it strives to learn. If there is to be integration, this is where it will happen, and this is how it should be understood.

The integration of science and theology has to be carefully proposed. Each discipline sheds light on a common subject matter from its particular perspective: various aspects of reality are open to query and inspection. A differentiated and integrated understanding of an aspect of reality occurs when someone appropriates each account of the subject matter in a way that leaves the autonomy of the disciplines intact. Integration cannot mean providing a pool of common knowledge generated by such different disciplines and used as material for building consistent meaning. Rather, integrating occurs in the knower who enjoys the capacity to see things from different points of view and entertain them together. From the perspective of theology the attempt at understanding transcendent revelation does not bypass the finite world; transcendence can

---

[41] John Haught, "Life and Spirit," *Christianity and Science: Toward a Theology of Nature* (Maryknoll, NY: Orbis Books, 2007), 147–48.

only appear to humans in it and through it. A scientific description of the world thus becomes a source for understanding the transcendence revealed through it. The meaning of transcendence always comes through its being mediated by the world of concrete knowledge and symbol, and that mediated form must be denied relative to its referent.

This outline of a dynamic relationship between science and theology as ways of knowing provides a background for a discussion of central Christian beliefs that structure in a formal public way the faith of the community. In each of the doctrines considered we raise principles or convictions from a discipline of science or from scientific culture that stimulate questions about the meaning of the doctrine. Addressing those issues will not produce a grand integration of science and faith. The intention focuses more narrowly on theological interpretation. How can science, particularly evolution, help enable a constructively positive and contextually more adequate and understandable interpretation of Christian doctrines?

3

Evolution, God, and Creation from Nothing

This chapter presents some crucial themes drawn from a Christian theology of creation. These ideas help formulate a basic context for situating our language about God. The chapter strives to communicate how language about God, which seems simple and straightforward, upon reflection appears filled with subtlety and nuance.

As noted in Chapter 1, not many years ago surveys indicated that approximately 40 percent of Americans did not accept evolution but thought that Homo sapiens was created the way we are today in a relatively recent "beginning." Newer polling indicates that these opinions are changing. But statistics still indicate a confusion between science and faith at this specific juncture.[1]

Creation marks one place where evolution and Christian faith cross paths. We have seen how faith and its theology on one side differs greatly from scientific method and knowledge. But it would be difficult to think deeply about the meaning of creation without considering what the vast majority of scientists regard as a roughly empirical and historical description of our universe, planet, and biosphere. This chapter examines how evolution requires adjustments in the Christian language and theology of creation. It aims minimally at showing that faith and science do not have to compete with each other on the issue of evolution but can learn from each other. It also suggests how evolution encourages revised conceptions of God and creation.

The topic is developed in four stages, beginning with some general conceptions about evolution and how it is related to the doctrine of creation. If we

---

[1] These statistics are ambiguous because one can pose the question of evolution in different ways, with naturalist or religious qualifications. Nevertheless, one has to be surprised at the lack of differentiation between religious and scientific sensibilities and how they become confused.

focus on the right questions, working through responses to them will greatly clarify the claims of theology in relation to the scientific consensus. In the end, questions revolve around formal conceptions of God and what the action of God creating is. To stimulate that discussion, we briefly review five different theological conceptions of God that are responsive to the demands of both faith and evolution. One cannot place in dialogue a critical scientific understanding of the world and a naive or uncritical conception of God. With these formal conceptions of God as a background, we reflect on some standard elements of the theology of creation as a way of showing how evolution and creation are distinct and different concepts that also intimately relate to and interact with each other. This marks the burden of the chapter, and it remains remarkably consistent with traditional creation theology, even as it responds to a new situation. The discussion concludes with a description of how, in the light of evolution, the idea of God, understood as creator, can resonate with the experience of people of faith and allow them to embrace evolution. Notice that none of what is proposed here has been drawn from or has anything to do with what has been called creationism.[2]

As an overture to the development of this chapter, consider this summary of what Hans Küng wrote over a decade ago: We have to get beyond anthropomorphisms, God as a big person, up there and out there. How are we to think of God "in the face of our new vision of the unimaginably broad, deep, and ultimately not fully comprehensible cosmos and the billions of years of the evolution of the world and human beings?"

"What is fundamental is that God is in this universe and this universe is in God. At the same time, God is greater than the world. We could follow Augustine in comparing the world with a sponge, supported and swimming in the eternal, infinite sea of the deity." God does not stand outside the world and intervene in it from outside: God is the dynamic ground of the being itself of the world. Not a part of the world, God is the infinite real dimension supporting all that is. The relationship between God and the world can only be thought of dialectically: "God is transcendence, but in immanence. God is an eternity, but in temporality; immeasurability, but in space." Thus the paradoxical expressions that ultimate reality is nirvana, void, absolute nothingness, shining darkness. These all pay reverence to God's absolute transcendence—not a person the way a human person is person; not an object from which we can distance ourselves. God then is not *a* person. As Küng asserts here, God cannot be reduced to the contradiction of personal and non-personal. One must rest with an incomprehensible God that is not less than what we know, but infinitely more, and thus able to sustain a

---

[2] A clear, patient, and persuasive dialogue with various forms intelligent design can be found in Howard J. Van Till, "The Creation: Intelligently Designed or Optimally Equipped?" *Theology Today* 55 (1998): 344–64.

coincidentia oppositorum.[3] This chapter is dedicated to sorting out the strands of this statement.

Evolution and Creation

The conviction that God created all reality collides with evolution at several points. One could say more strongly that evolution, as described by scientists, seems to call creation into question. We have to ask how aspects of an evolutionary worldview, the vision that now comprehensively pervades an appreciation of our whole finite reality, intersect with an understanding of God, especially as creator. To begin that discussion we raise to the surface preconceptions, opinions, and uncritical notions about evolution and creation that cause the friction between what scientists and theologians are talking about. Can we pinpoint a few questions whose answers will clarify conceptions of evolution on the one side and, more important, our theological conceptions on the other? Four questions, more pointed than those raised in the previous chapter, give our current subject matter focus.

One issue concerns the nature of the Big Bang and its theological shadow idea, creation. Intellectually, it is easy to imagine, but not picture, the Big Bang as a massive empirical event at the beginning of our universe. It would then follow for a person of faith that that event was creation. But such language misleads at several points. The so-called Big Bang represents less an event and more a scientific explanation of the origins of our universe by using knowledge drawn from physics, chemistry, and biology that sheds light on the question. The best explanations work within a framework positing that, from its beginning, the universe has continually expanded from an initial condition that was unimaginably dense and continually cooled from a condition that was unimaginably hot. Rather than an event, the Big Bang should be regarded as "a 'prediction' of the model which does not represent what really occurred" but in various ways reflects it.[4] Sean Carroll states it bluntly: "So the Big Bang doesn't actually mark the beginning of our universe; it marks the end of our theoretical understanding." We should not think of it as the beginning of time; "it's a label for the moment in time that we currently don't understand."[5] If the beginning of our universe

---

[3] Hans Küng, *The Beginning of All Things: Science and Religion* (Grand Rapids, MI: Eerdmans, 2007), 105–9.

[4] William R. Stoeger, "The Big Bang, Quantum Cosmology and *Creatio ex Nihilo*," in *Creation and the God of Abraham*, ed. David Burrell et al. (Cambridge, MA: Cambridge University Press, 2010), 158. An absolute beginning of things, even for our universe, and possibly very many others, remains somewhat murky. The evidence of science points to many universes and thus a prehistory to our universe.

[5] Sean Carroll, *The Big Picture: On the Origins of Life, Meaning, and the Universe Itself* (New York: Dutton, 2016), 51.

is not a particular event, and theologians consistently echo this by saying that neither should we think of creation as an event at the beginning of time, we can begin our discussion with the very basic question: What are we talking about? That question should spark critical attention. If creation was not an event, what do theologians think it is?

A second issue arises from the consistency or integrity of material emergence of the universe all the way to our species. Due to continuous material development the universe shares a constancy and uniformity from the beginning through time and space to our planet, emergent life within it, and the human species. The continuity of the evolution of the universe through various stages plotted by astrophysics shows a material consistency through the galaxies to our solar system, to our planet, to the emergent life within it, down to the human species and to each single person. This gives the reality of the universe a steady commonality and interrelatedness; everything comes from the same material elements, atoms, and subatomic particles. It is startling to imagine that, despite our tiny niche in the vastness of the cosmos, we can talk coherently about the whole of it. In a literal sense we are part of the universe, and we bear traces of the whole of it within ourselves.

This raises the question: Does God interact with finite or created reality? This question is frequently dismissed by science because there is no empirical evidence for it. We need a conception that acknowledges the consistent integrity and autonomy bequeathed to continuous material development. Our world of life evolved in continuity with the atoms and elements of the whole universe. Theologians who affirm God's action in the world need a conception of it that also acknowledges and works within the natural integrity of the universe. For example, by contrast, God not only was but is creator of the universe; surely the infinite power of creating also allows God to operate whenever and however God so wills throughout the universe. But neither God nor God's action comes under human scrutiny. And as we saw in Chapter 1, God as puppeteer takes on a heavy load of direct responsibility for the suffering of the world. The question is whether, where, and how God intervenes in the story of nature's emergence and evolution.

The issue does not revolve around imagining a closed as distinct from an open system of natural phenomena but is a larger metaphysical question.[6] Science explains things by the interactions of data and patterns of behavior without appeal to interventions from God. In so doing, science presents a challenge for theologians: If theology affirms God's action being involved in the same phenomena, it has to have some plausible conception of how this works. This issue pervades the dialogue between science and theology, where both sides

---

[6] I use the term *metaphysical* broadly to point to consciousness or thought about the underlying principles that govern reality, for example, in terms of causality or grounding. Creation falls into this sphere of thought.

tend to back away from God's intermittent intervention into the flow of nature and life.[7] This question of the integrity of the universe and systems within it carries profound significance for the theological imagination.[8] The question of how God acts in the world transcends an apology for the miracles of Jesus recorded in the New Testament. More fundamentally, what can the phrase *an intervention of God in history* mean today in a discussion of Christian faith in our scientifically constructed world? More particularly, what does this say about the suppositions of prayer to the creator God? If theology does not accommodate asking God to intervene in the processes of nature or the flow of human events, how should we understand what is going on in prayer of petition? Suddenly, we are confronted with a question about an overtly metaphysical theological issue that has direct pertinence to ordinary daily religious piety.

A third problem for the doctrine of creation accompanies the recognition that evolution is the blind process described in Chapter 1. That conclusion confronts head on a naive notion of God's providence that is a corollary of creation. It may be helpful to state the opposition between these ideas in order to set the question clearly. It can be entertained at different levels of consciousness.

On the one hand, creation, the direct action of God holding things in being, is a continual process, *creatio continua*, so that it can be seen to entail providence, God's "seeing" and guiding creation through time. This injects direction and purpose into the process. But Darwin explained in straightforward terms the mechanics of a blind process of natural selection that operated randomly over long periods of time. Given massive amounts of time, new species arise by a hit-and-miss series of possibility, opportunity, and event. If each moment of the series that generates change is blind, it is hard to assign sight to the whole process, at least empirically. Looking backward, one can read the successive events that led to the present in a coherent way, but the process from the past toward the future shows every present to be a random product. The underlying structure of an evolutionary universe and our world of living species, then, involves openness, indeterminacy, and lack of a specific purpose and endgame.[9]

What are evolution's implications for understanding God's providence and governance which are corollaries of God's creating? This question has a bearing on the two distinct levels implied in the second issue of divine intervention.

---

[7] There are sophisticated exceptions to this tendency. In fact, scientists and theologians use a variety of formulas or models to envision a response to this question. This book will not enter into this discussion or try to arbitrate it. I will rather find a resolution in creation theology itself.

[8] This works both ways. Much of the resistance to spirituality of a religious kind is based on an unreformed childlike imagination of God and God's work in the world.

[9] There is more to be said here, but this sets up the problem and helps to explain why evolution has been seen as deeply subversive of a religious imagination. As we move forward distinctions will help situate what can be established by science within the polarities of pattern and chance and what are the assertions of faith.

On the broad metaphysical level, Christian language exudes a sense that all reality participates in a teleological direction that spontaneously tends to draw evolution into itself. But here the deep underpinnings of conscious purpose are challenged. And the same is true on the personal level of an individual's life. Sudden wild attacks of randomness, like the death of a child, cut deeply into the basic orientation of people's lives. These considerations show that theology will not draw back the veil of mystery covering this subject matter. But it still has work to do.

Finally, we are led to the question of the very need for God raised in the previous chapter. Based on appearances, some conclude from evolution that the existence of God is not necessary: not for the being of the universe, because it can be simply presupposed as being there.[10] Not for the order of the universe, because evolution explains it: order is what evolution produced. And not for grounding ethics, because ethics can be based on reason in dialogue with the order in place. These are not scientific conclusions, but some scientists maintain these objects of faith. The question of the existence of God cannot be resolved on the basis of empirical evidence.[11]

This book does not argue for the existence of God; it addresses Christians who already believe in God. But evolution directs these essential questions to the theology of creation: What is God? What does God do? These questions must be given attention if we want to live in a culture influenced by the vast and differentiated world of science. The first question, What is God?,[12] is not intended to undermine the personality of God. Instead, it urges the use of an imagination that rises above the anthropomorphism of ordinary religious language and appropriates a language as critical as the one used by scientists to understand material exchanges of nature. The second question, What does God do?, finds its first and most direct response in the theology of creation. The rest of the book will say more.

These focusing questions place demands on both the scientist as such and the believing Christian. For a scientist with a consciousness attuned to appreciate empirical evidence, these questions remain as crucial as they are difficult. What are we talking about? Is God a "big person in the sky"? Theology will never be able to present direct empirical evidence for God. For the believing

---

[10] "There may be no ultimate answer to the 'Why?' question. The universe simply is, in this particular way, and that's a brute fact. Once we figure out how the universe behaves at its most comprehensive level, there will not be any deeper layers left to discover" (Carroll, *The Big Picture*, 203).

[11] For example, Robert Wright believes that science cannot dispel "deep mystery and all evidence of purpose" but neither does directionality demand the existence of God. Robert Wright, *Nonzero: The Logic of Human Destiny* (New York: Vintage Books, 2000), 331.

[12] John F. Haught, *What Is God? How to Think about the Divine* (New York: Paulist Press, 1986).

Christian, because these questions draw out conceptions oriented to a culture deeply influenced by science, they may also disturb naive faith. But Christians should at least be able to talk plausibly about how God's action relates to the workings of the physical world. And churches should be nurturing that possibility.

Theological Conceptions of God

Evolution raises some questions about God and creation. The impersonal question posed by John Haught, What is God?, is startling. It grabs one's attention. It calls for an explanation of the abstract definitions of God that follow.

We have seen that addressing the critical questions that are raised by science cannot rely exclusively on spontaneous commonsensical religious language. Its anthropomorphic character does not meet the critical imagination that scientific reasoning brings to the discussion. Of course, all language about transcendent reality relies on metaphor and symbol, because human knowing is tied by the imagination to the concrete world of sensible perception. But through "second reflection," which objectifies our own language and interrogates its meaning, we can set up an abstract language containing an intrinsic dynamic tension acknowledged by the person using it. For example, we believe that God is personal, but God is not a "big person in the sky." On the one hand, the words we use to refer to God are drawn from some kind of this-worldly experience; on the other hand, God as God cannot be reduced to anything finite. Such language, then, is dialectical: it both refers an imaginative predicate to God as God is encountered in faith, and simultaneously, it knows that God utterly and absolutely transcends the meaning assigned. Within faith, this is not doubletalk. Critical abstract language does not portray God as God is, and yet it opens an existential engagement that is both transcendently real and aware of its inadequacy.[13]

It should also be noted that the notions of God presented at this point prescind from explicit reference to Jesus of Nazareth, who is the central mediation of Christian faith in God. Christian faith in God is *christomorphic*; it takes a form derived from the ministry of Jesus. The conceptions of God that follow are substantially enhanced by a consideration of Jesus Christ.

God Is Pure Act of Being

In the thirteenth century Thomas Aquinas proposed a classic definition of God: "God is being itself, of itself subsistent," or, more simply, "God is subsisting

---

[13] There are a variety of ways to make this point; it is a relative commonplace in the discussion of faith knowledge as a basis for theology and it can be formulated in different ways. A constructive essay outlining the presuppositions of this discussion are found in Roger Haight, *Dynamics of Theology* (Maryknoll, NY: Orbis Books, 2001).

being itself."[14] This seemingly simple definition of God contains comprehensive meaning that borders on the mystical. Some of his allied formulas help explain it.

The term *being* opens the depth of Aquinas's formula. *Being* is the infinitive form of the verb *to be* or *is*. From one perspective the idea of the activity of being is abstract; one has to pierce the character of what is and focus on its existing. This is clarified by its opposite: nonbeing or nothingness. Meditation on the very being of things can yield a deep sense of wonder and awe and lead to the question of being: Why is there anything at all?

Aquinas deepens the Being that defines God by contrast with all finite beings in existence. All of them are particular; they have a finite nature, which enjoys the activity of being; they possess the action of being for a time and then cease to exist. All beings have a being that is limited by the kind of being it is and the individuality that instantiates it. By contrast, the essence or nature or kind of being that is God is itself the pure action of being and is not limited. God is subsistent being, being without any limitation and thus infinite.[15]

Another dimension of Aquinas's conception of God pushes beyond infinite being and penetrates more deeply into the character of God. Aristotle's foundational conception of things, which Aquinas appropriated, viewed them as a composite of an active meaning-giving form and a receptive stuff or potentiality that was shaped into an individual thing. In this language of act and potency, the term *act,* in a variety of different contexts and uses, communicated action, energy, power, dynamism, and generativity. In all finite beings this power is limited by the kind and individuality of the being it animates. In God, it is not limited. In fact, God's very nature and essence is actively "to be." This means that God is pure, absolutely undiluted, and unmitigated act of being. Such pure action of being is, of course, unimaginable, and this is what makes it a good definition of God. God "subsists" as pure infinite power of being of all that is. God is the pure act of being itself. The mystical dimension of this symbol appears in Meister Eckhart, who studied Aquinas.

God Is Ground of Being

This conception of God is associated with Paul Tillich, who used it with great effectiveness. It shares characteristics with Thomas Aquinas and more pointedly with Meister Eckhart's mystical appropriation of a Thomistic ontology of God. Tillich noticed how for Eckhart God was Being itself and divinity

---

[14] Thomas Aquinas, *Summa Theologiae* [*ST*], Part I, q.4, art.2.

[15] Aquinas, *ST,* Part I, q.3, arts.3–4. It will appear later that this pure act of being is singular with multiple effects; it is eternal, transcending time, and yet creative of temporal effects; its creativity is singular producing many beings.

was the ground of all being.[16] Tillich's existential theology, where subject and the known object infiltrate each other, aligns his language more closely with Eckhart than with Aquinas. The meaning of *ground of being* manifests itself as revelation. It refers not to a substance, or a cause, but to the absolute mystery of being that is simultaneously "abyss" and the source of meaning and dynamic principle of energy. "The religious word for what is called the ground of being is God."[17]

Another dimension of Tillich's conception of God as ground of being appears in his description of the structure of its manifestation and how it is encountered. This he calls "ecstatic reason." Human reason possesses an extraordinary ability to transcend the constraints of an ordinary situation, and "the mind is grasped by mystery, namely, by the ground of being and meaning."[18] At the same time, the pervasive character of "Being itself" and "ground of being" means that it may reveal itself in implicit or latent forms of consciousness. For example, in his meditation on elemental human courage Tillich finds the ground of being as the ontological source it takes to face life itself. "Every act of courage is a manifestation of the ground of being, however questionable the content of the act may be."[19] This opens up the range of experiencing the absolute mystery of God to everyone as a possibility in any phase of life.

Finally, it has to be emphasized that conceiving God as ground of being proposes a transcendence of God that simultaneously recognizes the immanence of God to all things; all things are rooted in God's power of being that sustains things from within. This is possible because God is not a substance or *a* being; God is the ground of *all* things or beings. But neither is God limited by things, for God is absolutely transcendent; Being itself is "above" all gods or conceptions of God.[20] We have to speak of God as if God were a definite being, but always with the awareness of the complete distortion that objectifying language imposes on God. "The God who is *a* being is transcended by the God who is Being itself, the ground and abyss of every being."[21]

---

[16] Paul Tillich, *A History of Christian Thought: From Its Judaic and Hellenistic Origins to Existentialism*, ed. Carl E. Braaten (New York: Simon and Schuster, 1967), 201–2.

[17] Paul Tillich, *Systematic Theology*, vol. 1, *Reason and Revelation, Being and God* (Chicago: University of Chicago Press, 1951), 156.

[18] Tillich, *Systematic Theology*, 1:112.

[19] Paul Tillich, *The Courage to Be* (New Haven, CT: Yale University Press, 1952), 181.

[20] See John J. Thatamanil, *The Immanent Divine: God, Creation, and the Human Predicament: An East-West Conversation* (Minneapolis: Fortress Press, 2006), 136–43. One can see at this point how closely these conceptions of God are aligned with the doctrine of creation. Much more will be said about the implications of these conceptual designations of God.

[21] Paul Tillich, *Biblical Religion and the Search for Ultimate Reality* (Chicago: University of Chicago Press, 1955), 82.

God Is Serendipitous Creativity

Gordon Kaufman, a twentieth- and twenty-first-century theologian at Harvard University, left us this conception of God that he constructed from a dialogue with evolution. The connection with creation is explicit. The idea agrees with the two previous conceptions that God is not *a* being but transcendent dynamic mystery.

Kaufman derives his notion of creativity from two sources of experience. The one is human creativity, something that we can experience within ourselves as an ability to "create"—to imagine new things and effect them. But the stronger and prime analogate for creativity connects with the experience of the world of development and evolution. Creativity is "the idea of the coming into being through time of the previously nonexistent, the new, the novel" that we have come to witness all around us.[22] "There is a serendipitous feature in all creativity: more happens than one would have expected, given previously prevailing circumstances, indeed, more than might have seemed possible."[23] In this definition the dynamism of evolution through chance variation and selective adaptation becomes inserted into the conception of God. Kaufman moves beyond thinking of God as a cause of reality to the dynamic energy of reality. "Creativity *happens*: this is an absolutely amazing mystery."[24] Kaufman is not moving from God to an idea of creator God; he is moving from an idea of creativity and trying it out as a metaphor for God. One cannot presume to know God and then move logically from there.

As in the two previous definitions of God, the abstract character of God as serendipitous creativity shifts the language of piety from a spontaneous,

---

[22] Gordon D. Kaufman, *In the Beginning . . . Creativity* (Minneapolis: Fortress Press, 2004), 55. Supporting Kaufman, Peacocke speaks of the structure beneath the story of evolution as one of creative energy that arises out of the interplay between law and chance, between stable patterns and randomness of event. One way of construing God is as source of energy and creativity of diversity (Arthur Peacocke, *Theology for a Scientific Age: Being and Becoming—Natural and Divine* [Oxford: Basil Blackwell, 1990], 65, 103). As a biologist, Holms Rolston finds the "grounds" of religious experience not in genes but in "fertility." Sheer genesis in natural history calls forth religious responses. "'Fertility' is precisely what evokes religious belief. The prolific Earthen 'fertility,' 'fecundity,' or generative capacity is what most needs to be explained in the spectacular display of life in which we find ourselves immersed" (Holmes Rolston, III, *Genes, Genesis, and God: Values and Their Origins in Natural and Human History [The Gifford Lectures, University of Edinburgh, 1997–1998]* (Cambridge, MA: Cambridge University Press, 1999), 296. Kaufman captures this with this image.

[23] Kaufman, *In the Beginning*, 56.

[24] Kaufman, *In the Beginning*, 56. "Precisely because of this close connection with the idea of mystery, 'creativity' is a good metaphor for thinking about God. If used properly, it preserves the notion of God as the ultimate mystery of things, a mystery that we have not been able to penetrate or dissolve—and likely never will succeed in penetrating or dissolving."

specific, and affective to a vaguer, reflective, and cerebral idiom. By removing the anthropomorphic and anthropocentric dimensions of a commonsensical perspective, the concept forces looser but more austere and abstract language fitted to the absolute and all-pervasive mystery of God. But one can speak of God's love for human beings and God's creative impulse toward human flourishing.[25]

In sum, this definition of what God is has the advantage of drawing into itself the awesome conceptions of reality that science has most recently provided our imaginations. These are actually statistical notions that blow open and leave our minds gaping. And behind all the groping for adequate images for the age, size, energy, and intricate dynamism of reality, we may be able to accept a mystery that goes by the name of serendipitous creativity.

God Is Incomprehensible Mystery

For Karl Rahner, the word *God* points to incomprehensible mystery. Sometimes he says "Holy Mystery." John Haught believes that "the idea of mystery [is] the most appropriate designation for the divine."[26] With it, we begin to sense that these "definitions" express different aspects of the same transcendent God. But three qualities help draw out distinctive notes in Rahner's usage: his approach to mystery, the ontology of the approach, and mystery's pervasive character.

Rahner embraced a partly Thomistic, partly Kantian, and partly existentialist analytical approach to God that deftly combined the human knower and what that knower can know. He looked on human knowledge as being-that-is-present-to-itself. To know ourselves is to know something about being itself. The clarity of self-consciousness, the ability to know the self even as the self entertains contact with the world outside the self, represents the distinctiveness of human knowledge. He also holds that human knowledge can be in conscious contact with infinite reality, obliquely, through the sense that the whole of the reality we know is finite and limited. The idea of mystery is connected with this glimpse of infinite transcendence through the sense of finitude. In this negative or "dialectical" way, human beings are able to perceive reality against the horizon of an infinity that is as real as it is mysterious. This objectivity can be experienced, at least indirectly, so that "incomprehensible mystery" also implies a being engaged by Holy Mystery. The very word *God* cannot be neutral: it points to something that draws people in and makes a claim on them, which each one has either to accept or reject.

This existential description of an encounter with incomprehensible mystery can be characterized in objective terms. However mysterious these terms remain, they carry an experiential residue. The classical language of "participation" gets

---

[25] Kaufman, *In the Beginning*, 66–68.
[26] Haught, *What Is God?*, 116.

at this side of the experience of absolute mystery. Rahner expresses this again in dialectical terms: radical closeness to God bestows genuine autonomy. "The radical dependence and genuine reality of the existent coming from God vary in direct and not in inverse proportion."[27] Because God creates autonomous beings, and sustains them, dependence on God guarantees their being and their value: "Genuine reality and radical dependence are simply just two sides of one and the same reality."[28]

Finally, incomprehensible mystery carries a pervasive and comprehensive character that can accompany human existence in life across time. The metaphor of a horizon helps to describe this. God's relation to the world is not as a being relating to other beings, but as the grounding power of being: "The infinite expanse which can and does encompass everything cannot itself be encompassed."[29] This presence of God to the world as ground describes a permanent horizon of existence and not merely a subjective experience. And the consciousness of it can run very deep.

God Is Transcendent Presence

This definition of God as transcendent Presence is from contemporary theologian Thomas O'Meara's metaphysics of revelation.[30] In many ways this definition absorbs the others into itself. It does not compete with the other conceptions but provides a distinctive focusing image that reflects human experience. The fuller range of its effectiveness will become manifest throughout the development of this book. What follows are comments on the meaning of *Presence* and some of the merits of its usage.

God as Presence reflects a modern idea of faith knowledge where the meaning of the term resonates with experience and, on the basis of analysis, also refers to objectivity. It holds together an experience of transcendent Presence to consciousness and the realist conviction that it refers to something other than the self. A real transcendent Presence makes itself known within human experience. It appeals to a common experience of believers in God that some mysterious power works within and is irreducible to anything that is caused either by themselves or their environment. Many people have experiences of transcendence; such experience seems common enough to consider it a universal possibility.[31] But

---

[27] Karl Rahner, *Foundations of Christian Faith: An Introduction to the Idea of Christianity* (New York: Crossroad, 1994), 79.

[28] Rahner, *Foundations of Christian Faith*, 79.

[29] Rahner, *Foundations of Christian Faith*, 63.

[30] Thomas Franklin O'Meara, "Towards a Subjective Theology of Revelation," *Theological Studies* 36 (1975): 401–27.

[31] The experience and acceptance of transcendent Presence is usually understood in personalist terms of faith. But Edward Schillebeeckx construes such faith arising out of a social

it takes myriad different forms because of its contextual mediation. Recognition of a required mediation of transcendent Presence explains religious pluralism. In itself, the nature of the transcendent reality that is present remains open in this formula. But unlike the others, it connotes or suggests a personal presence. *Presence* more explicitly implies that the "ground of being" is also the ground of personhood. Following Tillich, then, the "ultimate concern of a person cannot be less than a person."[32] Presence implies "personal Presence." But this should not lapse into the anthropomorphism that God is *a* person.

This definition of God has several qualities that recommend it. It is a deliberately vague and diffuse concept that says something but in a way that can be construed differently. The metaphor of God's Presence offers a way of talking about the many aspects and dimensions of the fundamental interaction between God and human existence in a single inclusive metaphor and symbol. It expresses a foundational contact between God and human beings that holds together and releases many different experiences and conceptions of how God is active within history according to context and mediation.

In an evolutionary framework, where reality moves through continuous time, God's transcendent Presence within the process smooths out long-term antitheses into compatible polarities of coexisting aspects of reality. These antitheses are either overcome or can be held together: God/world; God/human beings without competition; grace/nature; grace/free will; theology/science; church/world; Christian life/worldly life. In every case Presence, though experienced, remains transcendent; it does not operate as a part of the finite world to which it is present.

Another quality that recommends this definition of God is that it can be appreciated by those who are theologically critical and those in the context of popular religion. The appeal of the metaphor is direct: God as transcendent Presence satisfies the critical dimension of faith that it be a concern about the ultimate as well as the immediate and spontaneous character of ordinary experience and language about God. It makes a direct appeal to a common experience of believers in God of some mysterious Presence that is irreducible to anything that arises out of themselves or from interactions with external influences.

---

political experience of life that requires some form of utopia. He roots the experience of transcendent Presence in hope's demand for a coherent seriousness of reality in the face of suffering and injustice that affects all. See Edward Schillebeeckx, *Christ: The Experience of Jesus as Lord* (New York: Seabury Press, 1980), 740–41. I'll return to this in Chapter 8.

[32] Tillich, *Systematic Theology,* 1:156. Wesley Wildman warns against this reasoning because it entails anthropomorphism. Speech referring to God has to be dialectical. Wildman also recognizes the open character of "ultimate reality." See Wesley J. Wildman, *Science and Religious Anthropology: A Spiritually Evocative Naturalist Interpretation of Human Life* (Surrey, UK: Ashgate, 2009), 25, 205–6.

These five conceptions of God do not give us all we need in order to appropriate in a positive constructive way all that evolution is telling us about God and ourselves. But they give us a start. One does not have to remember the nuances of these conceptions to appreciate what follows. But it is essential to recognize that science teaches us that we cannot think about God in baby language when addressing the world that has been described with the mature and measured language of science. Much more can be said about God by examining the teaching of Jesus of Nazareth, which is concrete in contrast to these abstract conceptions. But a reflective theological conception of God is absolutely necessary for an intelligent dialogue between theology and evolution. Many of the so-called problems that arise for faith in the face of science stem from some kind of anthropomorphism, either on the side of faith or on the side of, not science, but scientists who know less about faith and theology than I do about science. Let us now consider some basic reflections from the theology of creation that integrate these conceptions of God with reflections on the language of creation that engages evolution and the problems it creates.

Reflections on Creation

Since Darwin published his *On the Origin of Species* in 1859 right up into our own day, evolution has threatened Christian faith. The age and size of the universe seem to dwarf the human and dethrone anthropocentrism; the tight integrity of nature seems to edge out God's intervention in the world and our lives; the randomness of evolution seems to subvert confidence in divine purpose; scientists do not speak of God and do not need the divine. As in an article in Aquinas's *Summa Theologiae*, these problems raise questions that require answers.

The first part of an answer lies in more considered conceptions of God, and the five concepts previously examined raise the level of the dialogue with evolution to a critical pitch. Now we turn to classical theological conceptions of creation that remain surprisingly relevant in a conversation with twenty-first century science. Because space does not permit a comprehensive theology of creation, we limit the discussion to distinctions that seem relevant to the issues at hand. Three salient theological understandings of creation mark the terrain. The first says that the essence of creation consists of an ontological relationship that is not empirically perceptible but that can be experienced in a rudimentary way. The second maintains that the transcendence and immanence of God relative to the world express perspectives on God's single Presence; they include each other. The third proposes that God's "action" in the world does not compete with natural forces, especially not human freedom, but subsists within them as an entirely constructive impulse toward a positive future. Together, these three convictions provide a space that allows evolution to open up a new understanding of God.

The Immanence and Transcendence of God

A second salient feature of the doctrine of creation is that God creates out of nothing: *creatio ex nihilo*. This, too, cannot be imagined, because empirical data only bear witness to existing reality generating reality in new forms. This raises the question of how this doctrine arose. Not from the Bible in any clear or undisputed form. Even when the original text is well translated by the English *creation,* it remains uncertain that it intends the idea of "from nothing" in the ordinary sense of "nothing at all."[33] Because it is unimaginable, the concept of nothing involves a sophisticated logic. We need to ask about the source of "out of nothing" and why it is important.

Whether or not it can be found in the scriptures, the idea of creation out of nothing became important in the second century. Christianity was in full dialogue with Greek culture at this point, and the issue of the universal sway of the Jewish God was in play. Creation out of nothing reinforced monotheism in a polytheist context. "Only by recognizing the creation to have been *ex nihilo* is the supremacy of the Divine will to be given full expression, and thus can justice be done to the testimony of the Scriptures."[34] Creation out of nothing gave the Christian God absolute sovereignty over all things and along the way made matter, the primal stuff, good, because it too was created by God. This early insistence on the goodness of matter has relevance today, when theology tends to emphasize the value of spirit and science the solid validity of materiality. If the main polarity of creation finds focus in being and nonbeing, and the intrinsic unity of creator and created resolves it, the hostility between spirit and matter may be laid to rest.[35] The decisive issue, then, resides in the relation between God and creatures.

The phrase *creation out of nothing* implies the possibility of saying there is nothing between God and creation. This way of speaking highlights the entailment that God is directly present to what God creates. No preexistent material

---

[33] For example, the text of 2 Maccabees 7:28 seems explicitly to paraphrase "out of nothing" in this way: I beseech you to "recognize that God did not make [heaven and earth] out of things that existed." But ambiguity arises in two places: first, the terms *chaos, formlessness, the void,* or *the deep* in Genesis 1:1–2 in one sense point to "something" and in another sense refer to "nothing," because what they indicate is unformed or not specified. Second, it is difficult to know the meaning intended, and this can only be sorted out intra-textually or culturally and with ambiguity. See Ernan McMullin, "Creation *ex Nihilo*: Early History," in Burrell et al., *Creation and the God of Abraham,* 13–16.

[34] McMullin, "Creation *ex Nihilo*: Early History," 20. One could argue that the nuanced form of the doctrine is implicitly contained in scripture, and that it took explicit form within the new context and its problems. But why would that be necessary?

[35] The dynamic unity of spirit and matter "has rich potential for a meeting with modern science, where it is increasingly evident that matter, as congested energy, is just as much a mystery as anything we might call spirit or soul" (Janet M. Soskice, "*Creatio ex Nihilo:* Its Jewish and Christian Foundations," in Burrell et al., *Creation and the God of Abraham,* 39).

or medium channels God's creating finite existence. The context for conceiving this stipulates that God continually creates and that creation does not involve an act in or of the past but is ever actual. This, in turn, includes God's constant Presence within the depths of all reality. This conception has always been taught with the "omnis" that follow from creation: God is omnipotent, omnipresent, and omniscient. But these qualities of God frequently succumb to an objective anthropomorphic imagination of God as a supreme being over against finite beings.

By contrast, the five conceptions of God characterized above, namely, God as act, ground, creativity, mystery, and presence, more easily allow God's immediate and direct presence to finite reality as a whole and to every entity within it. They alter the framework in which the classical qualities of God are understood. All things are intrinsically constituted by and exist within the creating power that is God. The frequently used theological term to describe this is *panentheism,* which etymologically signals that all things exist within the power of God so that God is the "within" of all that exists. We need to say more about how God relates to the world in order to resolve the paradox this sets up and that Langdon Gilkey described as "the world is totally and essentially dependent on God *(non ex materia),* and yet the world is not identical with God *(non de Deo)."*[36] How can we talk about absolute dependence and ability to be over-against at the same time?

A purely theological consideration of the transcendence and immanence of God offers an entry point into a first understanding of the relation between God and the world. Theology sometimes represents God's transcendence with language depicting God as "totally other than" or "absolutely different from" created reality. But frequently this language rests on a tacit supposition that God is *a* being, with a determinate nature, so that taking the language at face value creates an unbridgeable gap or difference between God and creatures. It is true that such language often works rhetorically. But on a deeper level it sets up a dualism or disconnection between God and creatures that attenuates or cancels God's immanence.

The five conceptions of God offered here revive the simultaneity of the transcendence and immanence of God by recognizing that God is not *a* being that is infinite, but, like a verb, God is act or energy or dynamism. Once we construe God as not *a* being and not related externally to finite beings as object to objects, transcendence and immanence can begin to coalesce into a unified or nondual reciprocity.[37] There are many ways in which God can be said to be "over-against" relative to the world, especially regarding some human dispositions, actions,

---

[36] Langdon Gilkey, "Creation, Being, and Nonbeing," in *God and Creation: An Ecumenical Symposium,* ed. David B. Burrell and Bernard McGinn (Notre Dame, IN: University of Notre Dame Press, 1990), 229.

[37] Thatamanil states this clearly in the case of Paul Tillich (*The Immanent Divine,* 137). But, *mutatis mutandis,* the principle also reflects the thought of Thomas Aquinas, Meister

and their effects. But on the metaphysical level of creation, it makes little sense to conceive as totally other the very act and ground of finite being. We need a finer-grained language than transcendence and immanence.

Before going there, however, it might be helpful simply to note how this conversation engages the imagination as, for example, in the case of the gender of God. On the one hand, the formal but dynamic "definitions" of God offered earlier transcend considerations of gender. On the other hand, all words, concepts, and more generally language carry an implicit imaginative referent, so that gender may be operative at some level of appreciation. God both transcends gender and invites descriptive language appropriate to a context. The use of gendered language, like all the predicates we apply to God, becomes subject to what Thomas Aquinas called the simultaneous affirmation and negation of whatever we say of God.[38]

Creation as Absolute Dependence on God

A reflection on *creation* might well begin with an elementary consideration of the meaning of the word. *Creation* refers to what God does. Since God and no other creates, the primary meaning of the term is subjective in that it refers to God acting. In a secondary sense *creation* refers to the effect of God creating. God's creation means our whole universe and perhaps others including everything in them. The whole finite world is the creation of God. Usually the distinct usage is clear from the context, but in some instances both aspects of creation may be in play at the same time as in the proposition that creation is a mystery.

It may be important to note that we know more about objective creation than subjective creation. We live in and are part of the objective creation of God, and we learn something more about this mystery every day. However, the creating act of God is unimaginable and impenetrable mystery. God's action shares in the definition of God as incomprehensible mystery. We talk about God creating, but we literally know nothing about it in any positive sense.[39]

In fact, our speaking about God creating often deceives. For example, we say that "in the beginning God created heaven and earth," which leaves the impression that God's act of creation transpired at the beginning of time. Was

---

Eckhart, Nicolas of Cusa, Karl Rahner, Edward Schillebeeckx, Gordon Kaufman, and Robert Neville, who are resources for this reflection.

[38] "Such names as these, as Dionysius shows, are denied of God for the reason that what the name signifies does not belong to Him in the ordinary sense of its signification, but in a more eminent way" (Aquinas, *ST,* Part I, q.13, art.3, ad.2). Thomas thus used sexist language to deny its applicability.

[39] Thomas Aquinas was clear on this: we can know *that* God exists; we cannot know *what* God is; at best, we can also know what God is not (*ST,* Part I, q.3, intro; Part I, q.12, arts.12–13).

it not the beginning of time? But this places God's action of creating within and subject to time, a point in time, whereas God's creating constitutes the ongoing condition of the possibility of existence.[40] Creation is not about temporal origin but an ontological statement, that is, about being or reality and its ultimate dependence on a metaphysical creator. "It is not about a creation event, but about a *relationship* which everything that exists has with the creator."[41] The classical idea of an ongoing creation by God *(creatio continua),* referring to creation from the perspective of time, implies that this relationship to God is a permanent structural condition of all that is. Finite existence is because of a constant participation in the power or ground of being.

Yet one can find a place in nature that bears witness to creation, that is, within human self-consciousness. Drawing on principles that are relevant to this reflection, we can stipulate that human existence exists as part of nature and not in a neutral place above it looking out on it. Also, because human consciousness is nature conscious of itself, deep structures within human consciousness can reveal something about nature. On those assumptions, the phenomenology of the human subject by Friedrich Schleiermacher seems archetypal; that is, the depth of human existence consists of an open space of freedom and agency in the world, yet relative to its own existence the human mind or spirit knows only passivity and dependence. We have no power over our being or not being but depend absolutely on a power of being that we do not control.[42] This provides no more proof of creation than does Aquinas's argument for the existence of God from efficient causality. But it connects creation to human experience.

To conclude this fundamental consideration of the meaning of the term *creation,* we cannot move forward without underlining the sphere of understanding to which this language appeals and how empirical reference does not define it. Evolution convinces us that our universe and ourselves occur in time; evolution conveys a story. We can, therefore, look backward toward origins and forward toward where it is heading. But that temporal story does not and cannot reveal the whole of being's character as being created; creation is not an empirical structure. For example, one can meditate on and marvel at the anthropic principle, but to think it is an argument for creation misinterprets what creation is: an intrinsic and invisible relationship with the ground of being that is intimated in the question of why there is being at all.

---

[40] Thus, by contrast to God's act being a temporal act, Robert Neville speaks of God's single act of creation as encompassing all of time in the singleness of God's not-temporality. See Robert C. Neville, *Philosophical Theology,* vol. 1, *Ultimates* (Albany: State University of New York Press, 2013), 230.

[41] Stoeger, in Burrell et al., *Creation and the God of Abraham,* 172.

[42] Friedrich Schleiermacher, *The Christian Faith* (London: Bloomsbury, 2016), 12–18. This phenomenology slides seamlessly into Schleiermacher's theology of creation, 149–56.

The Relationship between God and the World

This third cluster of ideas from creation theology digs more deeply into the entailment of creation out of nothing and places a crucial distinction between what Thomas Aquinas called first or primary causality and secondary causality. The distinction helps define a framework that enables a language for addressing God's relation to the world as understood by science.[43]

The key terms, here, are drawn from a distinction between God's action of creating that Aquinas calls "primary causality" and the "secondary causality" witnessed within the finite or created world.[44] Primary causality refers to how God acts, to what God does, as creator. By contrast, what happens in the finite world, all the processes of the universe, including what we do, are called secondary causality. The distinction clarifies that the two forms of action are different, with a difference that requires that they coexist. God creates and, as immanent Presence, supports reality against nonexistence. By contrast, the world that God sustains by creating consists of a dynamic network of causes interacting with one another.[45]

The distinction seems clear, except for the fact that God creating remains absolute mystery. But first causality, understood formally as what God does, plainly differs from and is defined by contrast with what creatures do. God is not and cannot be a secondary cause because God is not a creature. Nor can any created object be a primary cause because that is what God does. Wherever anything exists, God is present as creator but not as secondary cause, not as agent of this world, not as the performer of any finite action, but as the sustainer

---

[43] Christian theology asks how one might conceive God's special action in history as distinct from God's universal presence and action; that is, can God intervene and act as a cause within the framework of history? William Stoeger sets the question in "Conceiving Divine Action in a Dynamic Universe," *Scientific Perspectives on Divine Action: Twenty Years of Challenge and Progress*, ed. Robert John Russell, Nancey Murphy, and William R. Stoeger (Berkeley, CA: The Center for Theology and the Natural Sciences; Vatican City: Vatican Observatory Publications, 2008), 225–27. Steven Pope offers a brief overview of the concepts of primary and secondary causality from Thomas Aquinas in *Human Evolution and Christian Ethics* (New York: Cambridge University Press, 2007), 103–7.

[44] Elizabeth Johnson notes that "the best way to understand God's action in the indeterminacy of the natural world is by analogy with how divine initiative relates to human freedom" (Elizabeth A. Johnson, "Does God Play Dice? Divine Providence and Chance," *Theological Studies* 57 [March, 1996]: 16). There is wisdom in recognizing conscious experience as a part of nature. And one can think in both directions. There are examples of Aquinas's analysis of causality in nature that also describe the coincidence of freedom and grace.

[45] Stoeger notes how the idea of creation out of nothing clearly underlines the nature of God as transcendent Pure Act, and not *a* being, as a way of resolving how God acts in history. That means "*creatio ex nihilo* and the ideas closely connected with it . . . provide a fundamental basis for properly understanding God's action in the world—both God's universal, creative action, and God's special action" (Stoeger, "Conceiving Divine Action in a Dynamic Universe," 226).

of the finite agent.[46] The creative sustaining power of God suffuses reality and is present in every worldly activity, including what goes on in black holes, in the buzzing motion of subatomic particles within the relatively huge space of an atom, and even in evil actions. But not as a secondary cause.[47]

This distinction between first (creative) and second (finite) causes sets up a theological framework for understanding how God acts in the world and in history.[48] Several facets distinguish this large conception of things. Most important, God acting as primary cause means that God does not intervene in the world, in the process of evolution, or in historical events.[49] One should not think of, let alone expect, an intervention of God in this world. The reason for this does not derive from the world as a closed system, but from God's presence to finite reality: God has no other "place" from which to intervene. Nor does God disrupt the laws of nature that God sustains or interrupt history that unfolds through a web of natural processes. God creating means an always already active Presence in everything that transpires as its primary cause. God cannot be God and a secondary cause at the same time any more than God can be creator

---

[46] Aquinas writes that "because no creature has an absolutely infinite power, any more than it has an infinite being . . . it follows that no creature can create" (*ST,* Part I, q.45, art.5, ad. 3). But the reverse is also true: because all things operate according to their nature, God as infinite creator cannot act as a finite being but operates precisely as creator sustaining finite beings in existence.

[47] Thomas Aquinas, *Summa Contra Gentiles,* bk. III, chap. 70. Here Aquinas says that both agents produce the same effect "immediately, though in different ways." This crucial point responds to objections based on the imagination that God acts as a secondary cause. For example: "The active powers of human agents inescapably limit God's freedom. If some of the causal work is done by natural agents, it cannot *all* be done by God. There cannot be two sufficient causes for one event" (Ian G. Barbour, *When Science Meets Religion* [San Francisco: HarperSanFrancisco, 2000], 161). There can be, because different kinds of agency are noncompetitively entailed in every worldly action. In the end the self-limitation of God is a bogus concept. The pure act of being cannot be self-limiting.

[48] For a discussion of other conceptions of how God acts in the world, see Pope, *Human Evolution and Christian Ethics,* 107–10. A good example of another conception is Keith Ward, "Divine Action in an Emergent Cosmos," in Russell, Murphy, and Stoeger, *Scientific Perspectives on Divine Action,* 285–98. Ward proposes God acting in the world on the model of the human spirit acting in the brain; it thus understands God's action as a secondary cause like a ghost in the world machine.

[49] *Intervention* can have several senses; it may suggest "from the outside," or "suppressing natural laws," or acting as a secondary cause (Denis Edwards, *How God Acts: Creation, Redemption, and Special Divine Action* [Minneapolis: Fortress Press, 2010], 45–47). Alvin Plantinga shows the complexity of even establishing a meaning for "divine intervention" that is distinct from continuous creating causality in a world of quantum mechanics. He finds "nothing in current or classical science inconsistent with special divine action in the world" (Alvin Plantinga, *Where the Conflict Really Lies: Religion, Science, and Naturalism* [Oxford: Oxford University Press, 2011], 125). In this discussion, however, Plantinga does not distinguish God's primary causality from secondary causality.

and creature at the same time. It makes little sense to read this as a shocking denial of ordinary Christian faith and behavior; it makes great sense to stress the Presence of God in every event or occasion of religious experience.[50]

Another subtler reason against God's intervening into the course of world events and trying to discern God's plan in the events of the world lies in its implicit anthropomorphism. Reflection on God's eternity, something implied in all of the proffered names of God, provides insight here. God's eternity, which can only be signaled negatively as the denial of time, means that God's creating transpires as one eternal act. "The act of creation is a single one, in which what is past, present or future from the perspective of the creature issues as a single whole from the Creator."[51] The denial of time in God reinforces the absolute difference of God from our temporal imaginations emphasized earlier. God's purpose for the world and its execution do not consist of temporal unfolding. God remains creating Presence to all that is, and all that becomes, all that was and will be, already is present to God. This framework of absolute mystery and Presence renders the very idea of a divine intervention in the world mistaken, an anthropomorphic confusion. It imagines that God accomplishes things one after the other.[52]

God's special action in history is often conceived in terms of God acting as a secondary cause. But it seems more coherent to conceive it as an influence that works in and through secondary causes that make it a particular mode of God's universal creative action. God's creative Presence and this-worldly causality need to be understood in relation to each other as distinct but working within each other.[53] This requires an insight into how a single effect emerges out of two distinct causes. How do infinite and finite causes relate to each other? From the perspective of God's creating first causality, God, as the ground and energy of being itself, provides the power of being by which the finite agent operates. From

---

[50] Stoeger, "Conceiving Divine Action in a Dynamic Universe," 240. See also Niels Henrik Gregersen, "Special Divine Action and the Quilt of Laws: Why the Distinction between Special and General Divine Action Cannot Be Maintained," in Russell, Murphy, and Stoeger, *Scientific Perspectives on Divine Action*, 179–99.

[51] Ernan McMullin, "Evolutionary Contingency and Cosmic Purpose," in *Finding God in All Things: Essays in Honor of Michael J. Buckley, SJ*, ed. Michael Himes and Stephen J. Pope (New York: Crossroad, 1996), 155.

[52] Pope develops this idea in terms of God's knowledge using McMullin's language in *Human Evolution and Christian Ethics*, 102–3.

[53] God's primary causality operates within, not upon, finite reality. The mind grasps this through what may be called an intuition of levels of reality that correspond to different questions being asked. Once this is in place, it guarantees the integrity of the sphere of secondary causes. Because "primary cause is the source of existence, it effects its own work in the actual structured patterns of relationships through which is realized the ordering of the world" (James Pambrun, "*Creatio ex Nihilo* and Dual Causality," in Burrell et al., *Creation and the God of Abraham*, 219).

the perspective of finite agency, it is altogether natural that a finite cause produce effects according to its finite nature. These two causalities operate together but on different planes. As Aquinas writes: "It is also apparent that the same effect is not attributed to a natural cause and to divine power in such a way that it is partly done by God, and partly by the natural agent; rather, it is wholly done by both, according to a different way, just as the same effect is wholly attributed to the instrument and also wholly to the principal agent."[54] This "wholly"-"wholly" language means that these agencies are not over against each other; they do not exist in a competitive relationship.[55] We have here a nondual unity of being in which secondary causality enjoys real being, power, and agency by the power of a primary creative Presence of Being itself.[56]

The concomitant natural and divine action sheds light on evolution. Science from its many different perspectives analyzes the processes by which evolution moves through time. On the basis of many motives for faith, theology recognizes a divine agency in the whole process as well as in its minutest detail. And as in twentieth-century physics, the factor of time has become a major element in this vision. Creation consists of a narrative; creation entails duration or moving "through" time; creation is unfinished. This brings eschatology back into the picture. The future becomes a necessary consideration for understanding anything in motion. This leads to a conception of the human as incomplete, moving forward, toward something spread out in front of human consciousness, into a future in which human beings may consciously and responsibly participate.[57] Human action ordinarily involves orientation toward an outcome. Evolution thus invites a reorientation of Christian self-understanding toward cooperative action, supported by God's creating Presence, and oriented toward a goal. Consequently, evolutionary creativity infiltrates every facet of Christian self-understanding and theology.[58]

---

[54] Aquinas, *Summa Contra Gentiles,* bk. III, chap. 70.

[55] Küng, *The Beginning of All Things*, 157–59. As Johnson puts it: "In this system of thought it is incoherent to think of God as working in the world apart from secondary causes, or beside them, or in addition to them, or even in competition with them" ("Does God Play Dice?" 12). John Webster recognizes the fallacy of a competitive view that encourages a choice between the glory of God and the initiative of human existence. See John Webster, "'Love Is Also a Lover of Life': *Creatio ex Nihilo* and Creaturely Goodness," *Modern Theology* 29 (April 2013): 167–68. I cite Webster to show that these distinctions engage philosophical and evangelical theologians alike.

[56] "It is also evident that, though a natural thing produces its proper effect, it is not superfluous for God to produce it, since the natural thing does not produce it except by divine power" (Aquinas, *Summa Contra Gentiles,* bk. III, chap. 70).

[57] John F. Haught, "Cosmology and Creation," *Christianity and Science: Toward a Theology of Nature* (Maryknoll, NY: Orbis Books, 2007), 128–30.

[58] Responding to the question "What does God do?" Rolston thinks in terms of an ultimate and constant source for fecundity and novelty across the billions of years and the quantum transitions of increased levels of life. In the creation narratives the point is empowerment

In conclusion, we've come a long way from a simple conception of creation meaning that God put everything into existence a long time ago and thus is responsible for all that is. The mysterious idea of creation remains subtle and filled with dimensions that invite new scientific discovery. Transcendence and immanence seem like antagonistic ideas, yet they name qualities of the same Creator; each is understood to entail the other when God is not *a* being but pure Act. The relationship between God's first causality and Presence within all finite causality enjoins a nondual unity of two distinct dimensions of movement and being. Reality cannot be fully measured on the surface or reduced to sensible data. The idea of God's special action in history fades away; the particularity of God's action in any event does not require it, because God's action as first cause always operates particularly within individual beings and events.[59] Recognition that the primary action and causality of God is entirely different from the activity observed within a finite world and yet inseparably entailed within it is utterly basic. It introduces a new deep perspective that simultaneously revises simplistic constructs of the dynamics of reality and transform faith and science as different ways of interpreting the same phenomena. Evolution describes in empirical terms the constant dynamism of creation. It provides a magnificent witness to the power of God's creativity. It suggests visible clues to how God's creating in this universe unfolds, even though that remains utterly mysterious on an empirical level. And, finally, this creating still goes on, and we participate in it.

The Resonance of Creation Theology

Repeating something said earlier in this chapter, the idea and word *God* carries an imperative to respond. *God* engages and solicits a response because God purports to make a difference in life. By extension, the theology of creation sets

---

and not design, an empowering that places productive autonomy in the creation" (Rolston, *Genes, Genesis, and God*, 370). Karl Rahner translates this into metaphysical terms: "The agent's rising beyond and above itself in action and becoming takes place because the absolute Being is the cause and ground of this self-movement, in such a way that the latter has this fundamental ground immanent within it as a factor intrinsically related to the movement" (Karl Rahner, *Hominization: The Evolutionary Origin of Man as a Theological Problem* [New York: Herder and Herder, 1965], 88). See Denis Edwards, *Jesus the Wisdom of God: An Ecological Theology* (Maryknoll, NY: Orbis Books, 1995), 105.

[59] Stoeger explains how so-called special divine action can be understood as a subset or aspect of primary causality, because primary creative causality always occurs within concrete particular events. "Again, the divine creative relationship is highly differentiated with respect to each entity and system within the universe—and God's action flows from the character of that relationship." In short, one should understand "special divine actions as richly differentiated modes or expressions of God's universal creative action" (Stoeger, "Conceiving Divine Action in a Dynamic Universe," 246–47, 240).

out a vision of reality whose affirmation should carry a set of human reactions, attitudes, convictions, and affective responses that correlate with the set of affairs that are described. "The issue of creation is not just a question about things but a question about ourselves as well."[60] Or as David Kelsey points out, affirming something involves the self. "To affirm the doctrine of creation from nothing is to take on oneself a range of attitudes toward, and intentions to behave in certain ways in, the world."[61] This concluding section underlines several fundamental moral attitudes that intrinsically accompany an appropriation of a theology of creation along the lines that have been laid out here.

Acceptance of the doctrine of creation implies the acceptance of God who is personal. This simple assertion hides the deepest of mysteries, because God cannot accurately be imagined as *a* person, and sometimes God appears in context to be impersonal.[62] Focusing on God as loving creator radically transforms an impersonal world. Without altering a single fact, a recognition of a personal creator God gives everything a new, deeper, personal, intentional, meaningful character, even though these qualities remain mystery. Value plays a major part of the transformed character of reality in the framework of creation. *Value* here means "the quality of having importance in itself." Creation dialectically bestows in-itself importance on what is created. This dialectic arises out of the very logic of creation: God creating something other than God and giving it an "in itself," which, as absolutely dependent on God, has importance in itself. The person who believes in creation also acknowledges the intrinsic reason why human life especially cannot be cheap. Frequently, we say it has absolute value. But why? The immanence of God to all that is bestows a seriousness to the world, to life, and to human decision that they could not have without it. On the scale of values known to us now, human life ranks the highest.[63]

The transcendence of God also summons forth fundamental moral commitments. One of them sets out a negative norm: If God is God, then no finite reality can assume that position. The intuition of God's transcendence includes within itself recognition of the fundamental inversion of idolatry, which, when it is deliberate, is an active moral failure. The world is not God, and nothing in it or of it is God. A relation to God immediately exposes idolatrous claims even

---

[60] Robert Sokolowski, "Creation and Christian Understanding," in Burrell and McGinn, *God and Creation: An Ecumenical Symposium*, 183.

[61] David Kelsey, "The Doctrine of Creation from Nothing," in *Evolution and Creation*, ed. Ernan McMullin (Notre Dame, IN: University of Notre Dame Press, 1985), 178.

[62] The taut character of this tension must be honored; the mystery of God includes, for some, an experience of God's personal love in creation and, for others, God's cruel absence from it.

[63] Needless to say, this raises some ecological issues. But they do not have to be discussed here.

in the act of their seducing or oppressing freedom.[64] At the same time, the same intuitive feel for the transcendence of God supplies the hope (Schillebeeckx) and courage (Tillich) to work through obstacles that confront human freedom. For Schillebeeckx, impasse, blockage, and negativity consistently bring out from our deepest inner resources hope that existence is positive and the motive force to meet the challenge. Resistance to human suffering, especially in praxis, reveals a fundamental human hope that gives humans a glimpse of an objective hope, or a possible object of hope. "All our negative experiences cannot brush aside the 'nonetheless' of the trust which is revealed in man's critical resistance and which prevents us from simply surrendering man, human society and the world entirely to total meaninglessness. This trust in the ultimate meaning of human life seems to me to be the basic presupposition of man's action in history."[65] We noted earlier how Tillich finds within "the courage to be" the power of the ground of Being that implicitly enables it.

Another fundamental moral disposition that follows an understanding of creation is gratitude. The Christian spontaneously thinks of God creating freely and believes that love drives the enterprise. When this understanding of all reality has its scope narrowed to the single person's existence, the natural response is gratitude. When one achieves a certain amount of self-possession, sheer appreciation of and gratefulness for one's being seem to be an appropriate part of one's identity. Gratitude should help define the freedom or moral disposition of the Christian.

But we have not yet factored in the many people who may be so dehumanized that they are unable to appreciate the sheer value of their own existence—that has to enter into the discussion. The experiences of impasse, sometimes unto death, of persistent massive dehumanization, and of evil cast a shadow over the positive glory of God manifest in creation. Whereas the distinction between God's "causality" or Presence clearly distinguishes God from the mechanisms of material world, it also seems to undermine the practice of the prayer of petition engrained in Abrahamic faiths. First on a metaphysical level and then practically, what is going on when we pray to God out of our need?

Further reflection on the nonintervention of God actually shows how deeply it supports the Christian practice of prayer of petition. One can notice three aspects of prayer out of need that shed light on its logic. The first consists in the radical dependence that is presupposed in turning to God in need. As Rahner states:

---

[64] Creation out of nothing means "that the world genuinely is other than God but also implies one has the attitude of respect rather than reverence toward all that is not God. Reverence is an attitude appropriate to what is divine. Creation is other than God. There is no aspect or component of creatures that is unqualifiedly 'divine'" (Kelsey, "The Doctrine of Creation from Nothing," 180).

[65] Edward Schillebeeckx, *The Understanding of Faith: Interpretation and Criticism* (New York: Seabury Press, 1974), 96–97.

"Such prayer is the cry of elementary self-preservation, a naked expression of our instinctive clinging to life, arising from the very depths of human life and human anguish."[66] The prayer implies a recognition that one's personal life/identity radically (in its being) depends on God. Therefore, second, while this may or may not be recognized, God's response to such prayer can be found in the prayer itself. Christians should stress the already present and personal power of God within the person who prays. As was earlier noted, it makes no sense at all to emphasize the nonintervention of God into the world when God is already fully and personally present to the world and to each person in it. Third, what may be lacking and really being prayed for is an active recognition of God's Presence and its translation into courage, action, and hope for a resolution of the impasse. God does not do in the world what human beings are called to do. But God is Presence, who accompanies and empowers.

How does this translate to the psychologically conscious level of everyday spirituality? What would God be like if God responded to my wishes and not those of others? What would God be like if I were grateful to God for saving my life in a plane crash but not the lives of others? The issue lies in the character of God's response to human need. All human fears and limitations should be laid before God in prayers of petition. As Juan Luis Segundo states bluntly: "If our love is faced with the illness of a loved one, it is only logical that it find expression in a petition for that person's health. To ask for this is not to ask for miracles. We are simply voicing the limit confronted by our love, and the victory of our hope over that limit."[67] Rahner makes the point that petition should be childlike in submission to the will of God. Fair enough. But Segundo, by contrast, thinks of the prayer of petition as a consciously adult act of responsibility. We need to be empowered to do what we have to do. The child asks his or her father for many things; adult Christians ask the Father for the gift of the Holy Spirit to help them do what they have to do (cf. Luke 11:13).

Finally, in parallel with and perhaps drawing on the *Spiritual Exercises of Ignatius Loyola*, Teilhard de Chardin speaks of a spirituality that is sustained by the two hands of God. Ignatius proposes these two dimensions underlying a spirituality based on creation theology. First, God sustains in being each individual person because God's primary creative agency holds each being in existence, thus working within every gene riding on every DNA molecule. Second, by indirection, God works for the individual through every external agent that accompanies a human person through every stage of growth.[68] Teilhard calls these two simultaneous empowerments the two hands of God, the one directly

---

[66] Karl Rahner, "Prayer in Our Needs," *On Prayer* (Collegeville, MN: Liturgical Press, 1993), 76.

[67] Juan Luis Segundo, *Our Idea of God* (Maryknoll, NY: Orbis Books, 1974), 46.

[68] Ignatius of Loyola, *The Spiritual Exercises of Saint Ignatius*, trans. and commentary George E. Ganss (Chicago: Loyola Press, 1992), paras. 235–36.

internal to one's being, the other from outside the person.[69] Teilhard's conception of the ontological structure of every person provides a framework for gratitude as a basic moral response to reality. Ignatius's contemplative exercise leads a person to an intimate appreciation of a response of love. Both reflect the spiritual power contained in the ontology of creation.

---

[69] Pierre Teilhard de Chardin, *The Divine Milieu: An Essay on the Interior Life* (New York: Harper and Bothers, 1960), 47–51. Teilhard also calls these two vectors constituting every person the "double thread of my life" (50–51). The two hands of God correlate with God's primary causality relative to a person and God operating in the secondary causes that shape an individual's life.

4

Creation as Grace

Theology has developed distinct vocabularies for God's creative causality, the action of the divine Spirit, and grace. But they seem to refer to the same thing, God acting in the world. Comparative analysis of these languages yields more comprehensive insight into God's Presence in the world and simplifies our speech about it. The discussion intends to reinforce a sense of an all-encompassing God, who does not act in the way humans imagine but is always near as sustaining Presence.

Building on the previous chapter, this chapter examines more carefully Christian theological language about how God acts in an evolutionary world. Since the time of Augustine, Western theology has worked on the supposition of a "fallen human condition" preventing human beings from opening themselves up to God without the "divine help" of grace that was freely and overtly offered by God to some but not to all. This understanding implied a two-tiered human history involving an order of creation and an order of redemption: a fallen human subjectivity and the phylum of people restored to union with God through the operation of the grace mediated by Jesus Christ. The question of the relation between God and human existence was thus compounded by a second separation from God: not only were creatures not God, they were also alienated from God. A "double gratuity" constituted the proper relationship with God: the free act of God creating human beings and the free act of God's prevenient and saving grace. In the medieval period the term *supernatural* hardened the premise that Christians lived in two distinct relationships to God. In the Western Christian vision these two distinct spheres structured the whole of human history.

To be more precise, the language of *supernaturalism* and *second gratuity* resulted in a framework in which an appropriation of God's Presence was sharply distinguished from the natural order. God's revealing action came from a source apart from the mechanisms of the world and of evolution. Revelation, mediated through a particular history, became a separable add-on, distinct from the rest of public history. In the modern period God's action in revelation began to be understood as occurring in human subjectivity, and the language of the exchange between God and human beings became existential and drifted away from public history. But that left religious language unconnected with the harder scientific conceptions of reality and almost immune from critical appraisal. It is one thing to say that faith has its own reasons, but the content of faith has to be consistent with everyday life. As a counterpoint to various kinds of unfettered supernaturalism, this chapter once again appeals to creation theology to find the full power of grace operating within the natural sphere of matter. The discussion thus follows from and fits organically into the findings of the previous discussion of creation.

One finds three distinct spheres of Christian language about how God acts in our world. The first is the language of creation. I offer a reprise of the certain relevant aspects of creation theology as a distinct language for thinking about God's action in the world. The second sphere draws from the Christian scriptures, the Old and New Testaments of the Bible, and specifically the language of the divine Spirit, which is the most directly applicable of many ways of talking about God working in history. The third sphere of distinctions dealing with God acting in the world comes from the history of the theology of grace. This reflective language expands biblical ideas about the Holy Spirit as Christian communities faced particular problem areas in the Christian life. The hypothesis governing this analysis holds that the distinct vocabularies and discussions of creative causality, the action of the divine Spirit, and grace all refer to the same thing, so that comparison will show a common conviction beneath the different issues that are addressed and the different terms that are used. The discussion intends to reinforce a sense of an all-encompassing God who does not act as a secondary cause in the world but works as the primary agent present to and sustaining the created world.

The Language of Creative Presence

The phrase *creative Presence* stems from the idea of primary causality, the category Thomas Aquinas used to refer to God's ongoing creating act. Recall that *creatio ex nihilo* became clear in the defense of monotheism and the universal scope of God's creating. "Creating out of nothing" skips off the tongue when it is read in the catechism. But the concept is intrinsically complex, and it leads into paradox and mystery. Since the primary meaning of creative Presence entails God acting, it absolutely transcends the power of the human imagination; it refers to incomprehensible mystery corresponding to no sensible data. It also refers directly to God as activity or actualization, and not at all to a substantive actor. In various ways this dynamism correlates with the heuristic images of

God offered in the previous chapter: God as pure act of being, ground of being, serendipitous creativity, incomprehensible mystery, and presence. In what follows we highlight four aspects of God's creative Presence that provide points of comparison with other Christian languages referring to God's action in history.

God's Creative Presence

It is like nothing else; it can be compared with no other action; it is completely mysterious and incomprehensible. We noted earlier that Gordon Kaufman perceived analogies, weakly in human creativity and more strongly in the process of evolution. But the essential point in God's action is "out of nothing." Kathryn Tanner approaches God's transcendence linguistically by noting how predication about God utterly fails to communicate the meaning of God in comprehensible terms. God is not a being among others, not of the same kind of being as others: "In sum, God transcends the application of all ordinarily contrastive terms."[1] Even the statement that God is beyond identity and difference does not communicate positive sense because, as Aquinas says, although we can affirm that God is, we have no idea of what God is. To say that God is incomprehensible mystery, then, admits that the term *God* does not designate positive sense or meaning. "God is identified, in other words, by this very failure to mean."[2]

From a Christian perspective, Tanner continues, God is both transcendent relative to the world and intimately immanent or involved with the world. To affirm both these things at once, God's transcendence must be understood so as to acknowledge that God radically differs from the world, "that the difference between God and the world is not like any of the differences among things within the world."[3] God is totally other than finite reality. And yet, inversely, God's presence to the world has to be a total engagement with the world and every aspect of it. God's involvement with the world "should have an unlimited scope and be utterly direct in manner. That . . . is the point of creation *ex nihilo*."[4] It renders God's Presence totally accessible but totally imperceptible in any direct manner.

Realist Extrapolation

The tension between utter difference and direct Presence generates existential meaning for the phrase *creative Presence*.

---

[1] Kathryn Tanner, "Creation *ex Nihilo* as Mixed Metaphor," *Modern Theology* 29 (April 2013): 139.

[2] Tanner, "Creation *ex Nihilo* as Mixed Metaphor," 139.

[3] Tanner, "Creation *ex Nihilo* as Mixed Metaphor," 147.

[4] Tanner, "Creation *ex Nihilo* as Mixed Metaphor," 148.

Because creative Presence creates human existence, reflective human consciousness participates in the creating event from "inside," so to speak. This does not give human beings any positive perception of God's creativity. But, by indirection, the recognition of our own being as radically dependent in being "reflects" passively the action of creation. Rather than a direct positive meaning, human beings assign a vague and obliquely derived content to the notion of God by a process of experience and extrapolation. Because God creates human beings, God is immanent to human existence. Humans' extrapolations are not merely projected psychological feelings but are rooted in and point to the very ground of human—and all created—existence. In other words, because *realism* means "consciously being in touch with an object other than the self," human beings experience the transcendent God, other than the self, in their dependent identity. Human beings participate in the creating Presence of God and consciously resonate with it. A person affirms God's creative Presence both realistically and incomprehensibly.

God Not Less than Creation

Commonsensical reasoning produces the axiom that God cannot be less than what God creates. It has to be used with care and may be qualified by the phrase "by human reckoning." It implies that God cannot be less than personal. By human calculation, God must not be less than conscious, deliberate, and free.

These qualities of creative Presence are questioned not only by empirical-minded scientists and philosophers, but also by theologians who see a side-door anthropomorphism reentering the theological imagination.[5] While it is difficult to rule out this spontaneous tendency in language about God, there is no reason to suspend the general rule of predicating qualities to God: one must radically deny that any quality drawn from worldly experience applies *as such* to God. In other words, these qualities must be denied before being affirmed. The character of God is not affirmed in ordinary analogical terms but dialectically, so that God cannot be construed in anthropomorphic terms.[6]

Creation's Complexity

Another aspect of God's creative Presence is important for understanding how genuine chance and human freedom both relate to God's action. To the extent

---

[5] For example, Wesley Wildman reflects on how deeply anthropomorphism affects all theological discourse in "Ground-of-Being Theologies," in *The Oxford Handbook of Religion and Science,* ed. Philip Clayton (Oxford: Oxford University Press, 2006), 612–32.

[6] From another point of view analogy can be retrieved structurally. If the difference between creating Presence and creature is affirmed as simply total, all contact with God would be denied, including the construct itself of creation, and all God-talk would be suppressed. This highlights the tensive character of dialectical affirmation.

that languages characterizing God's action in the world are anthropomorphic, they lack the nuance that evolution presses upon us. God's creating Presence operates in two distinct, interacting, and noncompetitive ways. On the one hand, God's creative Presence sustains every being and action of every creature that exists: God supports both their being and their acting. Moreover, finite being is real, other than God, with an autonomous existence guaranteed by the creator. On the other hand, relative to any single creature, God's creating Presence also operates in the finite beings and agents that surround and influence it. God's creative Presence operates simultaneously in two ways: directly within each creature, and indirectly through the many forces and agents, also sustained by God, that affect a given being. Thomas Tracy explains this dual agency: "First, the Creator acts directly in and with every action of the creature as its sustaining ontological ground. . . . Second, we can also say that God acts by means of the action of created causes, and we can attribute the effects of these causes to God as divine acts."[7] Creaturely autonomy opens up space for genuine human freedom within the tight integrity of evolution. And the interaction of forces integrates chance into God's creative Presence through this web of this-worldly causes, from things whose provenance remains unknown in the chaotic maelstrom of causes to things that are ontologically indeterminate as evolution moves forward. Randomness, therefore, is a mechanism created by God and a structure of God's creative Presence.[8]

In summary, the understanding of how God acts in the world expressed by creation theology offers a highly reflective and disciplined conception of this active relationship. This makes it appropriate for a conversation about how evolution should influence how we speak about God's action. I now want to represent in a comparative mode the more instinctive language about God acting in the world drawn from scripture. This language resembles the everyday language used by Christians. Behind this implicit comparison of the operation of the Spirit of God and God creating lurks the question whether any essential differences separate these two languages other than the difference between the uncritical character of spontaneous faith language and a more considered theology.

---

[7] Thomas F. Tracy, "God and Creatures Acting: The Idea of Double Agency," *Creation and the God of Abraham*, ed. David Burrell et al. (Cambridge, MA: Cambridge University Press, 2010), 225. We saw this structure in Teilhard's metaphor of "the two hands of God," but it requires criticism. It communicates a comprehensive presence of God. But due to the distinction of the human and divine dimensions of action, which will be considered further on, God's intentions cannot be read into the evil actions of human beings. God sustains human action that does not cohere with what we learn of God's intentions from Jesus of Nazareth. Not everything that happens to us reflects God's will.

[8] "As a technique of indirect divine action, ontological chance provides flexibility and a capacity for novelty that a purely deterministic system would lack, but it also entails that God's intentions take a more complex, conditioned form" (Tracy, "God and Creatures Acting," 228).

The Language of the Spirit of God

The reflective language of creation theology seems to be left behind when we try to understand the various meanings of the phrase *the Spirit of God* used in the scriptures and thereafter. The context is pre-evolutionary. The language presupposes a stable world, like that of a stage, on which events are being played out. There is no evolutionary sense that the world itself, the "stage," is a narrative. The point of this discussion lies in an effort to understand Spirit language as it has been used in the tradition of the Christian community and, after that, to appropriate it in a way that coheres with other ways of speaking about God at work within the world.

It seems like an easy task to lay out the meanings of *the Spirit of God* according to its usage in the past. The metaphor of spirit or wind abounds in power and versatility for expressing the invisible work of God that only appears in its awesome effects. The commonsensical usage causes no problems: God as Spirit refers in various ways to what the creator God actually does in the world. But reflective theology always looks for more clarity: What does the Spirit of God refer to? The simple question yields several different answers.

The strategy, here, consists of laying out some of the important usages and meanings of *the Spirit of God* from the scriptural tradition, so that, in the end, the specific understanding of the term in this project will be recognized as coherent, plausible, and faithful to the historical stream of Christian self-understanding. This approach passes through the Jewish scriptures, to the explosion of functions accomplished by the Spirit in the New Testament, leading to the theological tradition of speaking about how God works in the world.

God's Spirit in the Old Testament

The quest for the meaning of the Spirit of God must begin with the metaphor itself. The word for spirit in Hebrew is *ruah*, and it was rendered as *pneuma* in Greek.[9] The same word referred to the wind and to the breath of a living being. In this latter sense *ruah* suggests life, and it is not surprising that the Spirit of God is associated with the power animating living beings. The notion of wind imaginatively suggests a power or energy that is invisible in itself yet manifestly present in its effects. In the passage from life to death, the life-giving spirit, once there, quits or leaves. Since Yahweh the creator God dwells in inaccessible

---

[9] For a brief history of the biblical use of the symbol "Spirit of God" and how it has been employed in the history of theology to refer to God's presence, power, and action within human beings and the world at large, see Dennis Edwards, *Breath of Life: A Theology of the Creator Spirit* (Maryknoll, NY: Orbis Books, 2004), 33–49. The Hebrew idea of *Shekinah* has a more particular provenance and sense and requires a distinct analysis, found below.

transcendence, the symbol of invisible presence with visible effect becomes a way of finding or recognizing God at work in the world. This does not quite answer the question, What is this Spirit of God? Thus far, we have only talked about how the term was used. We must begin there before risking definitions, which the scriptures themselves do not provide, and look at several different but analogous usages and interpretations.

The Spirit of God sometimes refers to the source of a power exhibited in nature, especially in a person, that exceeds native ability: a serendipitous capability that seems extraordinary suddenly appears and can just as easily disappear. For example, in the Book of Judges, when the people of Israel were occupied and dominated by the king of Mesopotamia but repented and asked God for help, "the Lord raised up a deliverer": "The spirit of the Lord came upon him, and he judged Israel; he went out to war, and the Lord gave King Cushan-rishathaim of Aram into his hand" (Judg 3:9–10). Sometimes "the Spirit of the Lord took possession" of someone (Judg 7:34). The idea is that Spirit represents divine power acting within a person. Persons may be filled by the Spirit with an ability exceeding their strength. "I have filled him with divine spirit, with ability, intelligence, and knowledge in every kind of craft" (Ex 31:3). When they wrote of the Spirit of God, then, the biblical writers were not describing God but noting an ability to act in a way that manifested God as the source of the agency. "In the Old Testament the spirit [that is communicated by God] is not a personal being. It is a principle of action, not a subject. It belongs properly to Yahweh alone; it is communicated to living beings but it never becomes a part of the structure of the living being in such a way that the living being possess the spirit as its own."[10] One should not read these texts as a direct witness of God acting within a subject as secondary cause, but rather as God's power of being enabling a person to act in concert with divine intention.[11]

The Spirit of God indicates the source behind the power of public figures who shape the history of the people of Israel as people of Yahweh. God's power accompanies and works on their behalf. The narrative of the Book of Judges is carried along by the phrase, "Then the Spirit of the Lord came upon" a certain figure, as if the Spirit controlled the story. It both does and does not make God the main actor of the narrative; God is mixed up in the unfolding of the events, but as an empowering force working in agents rather than being an empirical

---

[10] John L. McKenzie, "Aspects of Old Testament Thought," *The New Jerome Biblical Commentary* (Englewood Cliffs, NJ: Prentice Hall, 1990), 1290.

[11] I cannot parse the legitimacy of this distinction between Yahweh, Yahweh's power, and the power interiorly manifested in creatures but which is not their own in the context of today's understanding of God's transcendence and immanence. The distinction clearly protects God's transcendence, but the status of the divine power that is not divinity itself remains fuzzy. I do not assume that all usages are the same or how far McKenzie's generalization is true.

actor. The Spirit of God communicates power to the charismatic actor who, like an instrumental agent, channels God's intention forward. Dismissing this today because of its anthropomorphic terms does not do justice to a profound sense of both realism and wonder it communicates. On the one hand, certain actors do what they do; on the other hand, what they do fills one with awe and curiosity at how it could have been done at all. A strong faith in God, along with some critical adjustments, has to bolster the plausibility of this language.

After the transition of the government of Israel from the charismatic leader to the monarchy, the operation of the Spirit of God tended to be attached to the institution and the person of the king. The Spirit of God resided in the king, who acted in the name of Yahweh. The occasional intervening character of the Spirit of God became less prominent. "The emergence of the monarchy as an institution was a break with the old dynamic conception of the spirit of God. Now the spirit was a permanent gift to the anointed (i.e., king) of Yahweh; this gift points in a special way to the intimacy between the king or the 'Christ' [anointed] and God, and to his special gifts (and that is true above all for the messianic king)."[12] It began with Samuel anointing David as king: "Then Samuel took the horn of oil, and anointed him in the presence of his brothers, and the spirit of the Lord came mightily upon David from that day forward" (1 Sam 16:13). The explosive character of the Spirit evanesces; someone becomes filled with Spirit; its transmission is connected with rites and anointings, laying on of hands, and succession in office; the Spirit becomes connected with the institution and the role of leader.

The later prophets exhibit other ways in which the Spirit of God makes itself felt in Israel's life. In Isaiah, the Servant of God possesses the Spirit. The Servant Songs represent a fusion between older charismatic views of a communicated Spirit and an office or dedicated function. The Spirit of God will enter into a messianic king:

> The Spirit of the Lord shall rest on him,
>> the spirit of wisdom and understanding,
>> the spirit of counsel and might,
>> the spirit of knowledge and the fear of the Lord. (Isa 11:2–3)

The Spirit of God also empowers the Servant of Yahweh in Isaiah:

> "Here is my servant, whom I uphold,
>> my chosen, in whom my soul delights;
> I have put my Spirit upon him,

---

[12] Edward Schillebeeckx, *Christ: The Experience of Jesus as Lord* (New York: Seabury Press, 1980), 537.

> he will bring forth justice to the nations. . . .
>> He will faithfully bring forth justice.
> He will not grow faint or be crushed
>> until he has established justice in the earth;
>> and the coastlands wait for his teaching." (Isa 42:1–4)

In Isaiah 61, the Spirit of God is fully at work in the prophet who announces God's triumphal establishment of justice in Israel and the world.

> The Spirit of the Lord God is upon me,
>> because the Lord has anointed me
> he has sent me to bring good news to the oppressed,
>> to bind up the brokenhearted,
> to proclaim liberty to the captives
>> and release to the prisoners. (Isa 61:1)

The postexilic period looked forward to still more expansive manifestations of the Spirit of God. Ezekiel announces in God's name that the Spirit of God will be poured out on the whole people of God and not just individuals, prophets, or kings. Speaking to all God's people, he says: "A new heart I will give you, and a new spirit I will put within you; and I will remove from your body the heart of stone and give you a heart of flesh. And I will put my spirit within you, and make you follow my statutes and be careful to observe my ordinances. Then I shall live in the land which I gave to your ancestors; and you shall be my people, and I will be your God" (Ezek 36:26–28). This oracle makes plain a personal intimacy that was less evident earlier even if it were implied. The bond between God and people appears more interpersonal and even affectionate. Isaiah also announces that the Spirit of God will be poured out upon all the people of God and, when it is, justice, righteousness, and peace will reign (cf. Isa 32:15–17; 44:3–5). These witnesses suggest a new context and language for thinking about the Spirit of God. The texts point to a utopian interpersonal relationship between God and God's people.

We may conclude these sweeping illustrations of various functions of the Spirit of God by recalling the text inserted at the head of the Hebrew Bible that associated creation itself with the immanent power of God described in majestic Spirit language: "In the beginning when God created the heavens and the earth, the earth was a formless void and darkness covered the face of the deep, while a wind from God swept over the face of the waters" (Gen 1:1–2). Wind sweeping over a vast body of a formless sea symbolizes God's power. When spoken through the command of God's words, Spirit is able to organize light and darkness, give form to land and boundaries to sea, and shape an interconnected whole teeming with life (cf. Ps 104). The Spirit of God reflects intelligent power and seems to be referring to God acting directly in the world.[13]

The Spirit of God in the New Testament

The metaphor of wind, breath, or spirit for the manifestation of God's presence and power at work in the world explodes in the New Testament. Its associations are so extensive that one is forced to choose a few wide categories to illustrate how flexibly Spirit language was used. It took different forms to show the many ways in which God worked in Jesus and in the community that formed around him. Four uses or places highlight where the power of the Spirit of God works in the New Testament: in Jesus's person and ministry; in the group and movement he left behind; in the salvation the Spirit communicates or actualizes; and in the role of Advocate.

To begin, the divine Spirit works behind and within the person of Jesus. Luke's Gospel demonstrates this dramatically; the Spirit of God punctuates the span of Jesus's existence as the Spirit of God came upon the charismatic leaders in Judges. The Holy Spirit was active in Jesus's conception: "The Holy Spirit will come upon you, and the power of the Most High will overshadow you; therefore the child to be born will be holy; he will be called Son of God" (Luke 1:35). In the accounts of Jesus's baptism the Holy Spirit "descends" upon him and implicitly anoints him as God's beloved Son and agent (cf. Luke 3:22; Mark 1:9–11; Matt 3:13–17; John 1:29–34). After his baptism Luke portrays Jesus as "full of the Holy Spirit" and "led by the Spirit in the wilderness" (Luke 4:1–2). Jesus, then "filled with the power of the Spirit, returned to Galilee" (Luke 4:14) to begin his ministry there in a formal way. In a dramatic scene in his home village of Nazareth, Luke has Jesus stand in the synagogue to read the words of Isaiah:

> The Spirit of the Lord is upon me,
>   because he has anointed me
>   to bring good news to the poor. (Luke 4:18)

By the power of God Jesus was able to "cast out the demons" (Luke 11:20). Holy Spirit language accompanies Paul's understanding of Jesus's resurrection (cf. Rom 1:4; 1 Tim 3:16). Before he ascends to the Father, as depicted by Luke,

---

[13] This synthetic hermeneutical opinion tries to cut through the variety of inflections of Spirit-talk across different periods of Jewish history in search of a present-day appropriation. It is deliberately broad and tentative. Edwards concludes: "The Spirit can be understood as the immanent divine power that enables evolutionary emergence, continually giving to creation itself the capacity to transcend itself and become more than it is. The Breath of God breathes life into the whole process of an emergent universe. The Holy Spirit is the immanent divine principle drawing creation toward an open future" (Edwards, *Breath of Life*, 48).

Jesus promises his followers that the Holy Spirit will come upon them (cf. Acts 1:8), and so it does at Pentecost, when "all of them were all filled with the Holy Spirit and began to speak in other languages, as the Spirit gave them ability" (Acts 2:4). Analogous to Judges, Luke and the New Testament generally do not propose that the Holy Spirit operates as an empirical actor in the history of Jesus and its overflow into a Jesus movement through the first century. But Luke definitely reads the Holy Spirit as divine power at work within these events. The term *Christ* means that God anointed Jesus of Nazareth with the Holy Spirit and with power" (Acts 10:38).[14]

After Jesus's resurrection, the Acts of the Apostles presents a wide canvas of historical developments influenced by the power of the Spirit of God mediated by the risen Jesus and working within the whole community. The writer, Luke, lays out the reasoning behind the narrative in terms of an outpouring of the Spirit of God. The Book of Joel contains a prophecy of expectation:

> Then afterward
> I will pour out my spirit on all flesh;
> your sons and your daughters shall prophesy,
>   your old men shall dream dreams,
>   and your young men shall see visions.
> Even on the male and female servants,
>   in those days, I will pour out my spirit. (Joel 2:28–29)

In Luke's theology the event at Pentecost fulfills this prophesy: "Divided tongues, as of fire, appeared among them, and a tongue rested on each of them. All of them were filled with the Holy Spirit" (Acts 2:3–4).

Luke then puts Joel's vision from the past into the mouth of Peter to explain to the people who gathered to find out what was going on with the enthusiastic followers of Jesus of Nazareth (cf. Acts 2:14–41). These are more theological reflections than historical records, but they catch the deep conviction that alone kept the Jesus movement alive. In his speech Peter describes this "coming to pass" as transpiring "in the last days" when history itself is coming to fulfillment. Something new is going on here. Historically, all of this can be readily explained by the profound impression that Jesus of Nazareth had on those who encountered him. Theologically, however, the impact included a conviction that Jesus was anointed by the Spirit of God, who had introduced a new age. The tiny communities of followers of Jesus moved forward in the conviction that the risen Jesus was present to them as divine Spirit and power.

The idea that the Spirit of God supplied a dynamic divine impetus to the development of the Jesus movement expanded with the events narrated in Acts.

---

[14] Schillebeeckx, *Christ*, 534.

Although the sources are not sufficient for a close tracking of this growth, markers show a development of the Jesus movement from a Jewish to a Jewish-Gentile one, and then to a movement with a universal scope. Acts tells a story of a Roman Centurion who sought baptism, and a series of events that led to Peter declaring: "'Can anyone withhold the water for baptizing these people who have received the Holy Spirit just as we have?' So he ordered them to be baptized in the name of Jesus Christ" (Acts 10:47–48). In the year 48 or 49, leaders came to a formal decision that a Gentile did not have to become a Jew to become a Christian, thus opening wider the doors of the movement.[15] Paul captures this well through a reference to the Holy Spirit. Writing to the Corinthians, Paul says: "For just as the body is one and has many members, and all the members of the body, though many, are one body, so it is with Christ. For in the one Spirit we were all baptized into one body—Jews or Greeks, slaves or free—and we were all made to drink of one Spirit" (1 Cor 12:12–13). By the 80s, the self-understanding of Christians had still larger horizons: "Make disciples of all nations, baptizing them in the name of the Father and of the Son and of the Holy Spirit" (Matt 28:19).[16]

We turn now to the theological question of what the Holy Spirit does relative to salvation. Edward Schillebeeckx, in his magisterial christological study of salvation and grace in the New Testament, responds to the issue: "No difficulty is found in also ascribing to the Holy Spirit all the gifts of salvation which are ascribed to Christ—salvation, deliverance, redemption, justification, sanctification, access to the Father, etc."[17] Thus, for example, Paul says that "you were sanctified, you were justified in the name of the Lord Jesus Christ and in the Spirit of our God" (1 Cor 6:11; 1 Pet 1:2). The gift or bestowal of the Holy Spirit is a guarantee of final salvation (cf. Eph 1:13–14, 4:30). The Spirit dwelling within a person communicates life over death, freedom from bondage, and a sensibility of life and peace (Rom 8:2–11). A reciprocity between faith and the Spirit within suggests that they entail each other: they dwell together in a person (cf. Acts 11:24; 2 Cor 4:13). The Spirit, too, creates a bond in a community and becomes a basis for the union of the members with each other (cf. Phil 2:1; 2 Cor 13:14). The Spirit actualizes the unity and peace of the community (cf. Eph 4:1–6). The texts can be multiplied, but these make the point that what was accomplished by Jesus Christ for human salvation flowed from both Jesus and

---

[15] "Becoming a Jew" refers principally to circumcision, among other things that were no longer required (see Acts 15:22–29).

[16] In summary, scientist Ian Barbour writes that, as for biblical symbols, beginning with the creation account and then all through both Testaments, "I submit that it is in the biblical idea of *the Spirit* that we find the closest parallel to the process understanding of God's presence in the world" (*When Science Meets Religion* [San Francisco: HarperSanFrancisco, 2000], 176–77).

[17] Schillebeeckx, *Christ*, 534.

the Spirit. The Spirit generated and empowered Jesus as the Christ, and Jesus mediated the Spirit to his followers.

Schillebeeckx concludes that Christ and Spirit are intimately related: "According to the New Testament, Christ and the Spirit evidently perform the same function."[18] To further explain this relationship, he first has to stipulate that the language of the New Testament should not be read as analytical ontology; the scriptures are not setting out definitions. Closer attention would show that this language and way of thinking describe the way things happen. This language of faith affirms God's action on the basis of what people of faith encounter in the events flowing from the appearance of Jesus. God is a God of life because God bestows life, and a God of love who loves, and bestows light because people see in a new way. Jesus is the anointed Christ because he does these things. So too, the Spirit does these things as God's agency or mediating power. In some respects we have come some distance from Old Testament usage. But in other respects the continuity is clear. One knew that Jesus was anointed by the Spirit of God because of the things he said and did. The Spirit of God "overshadowed" Jesus with a power of divine provenance so that he was able to do them.

Finally, the Gospel of John and the First Letter of John introduce another term for the Holy Spirit: *Advocate*. In the discourse at the last supper in John's Gospel, Jesus says: "I will ask the Father, and he will give you another Advocate, to be with you forever" (John 14:16). A couple of features stand out here: first, it is clear that the Advocate is the Holy Spirit (cf. John 14:26). And the emphasis of Jesus's saying falls on this new gift of the Holy Spirit as being a successor to Jesus, doing for them what he did while with them, but now permanently to compensate for his absence. The Advocate, Jesus says, "will teach you everything, and remind you of all that I have said to you" (John 14:26). The Spirit Advocate will dwell within the disciples, but calling the Holy Spirit Advocate amounts to a personification, comparing the indwelling Spirit to a person performing a human-now-divine function. The content that the Advocate offers is drawn from Jesus's teaching. John's Jesus says it very clearly: "When the Advocate comes, whom I will send to you from the Father, the Spirit of truth who comes from the Father, he will testify on my behalf" (John 15:26). In so doing the Advocate will pass judgment on the world for failing to recognize the teaching of Jesus (cf. John 16:8–11). But the Spirit of truth will also "declare to you the things that are to come," not on his own authority, but on the basis of the teachings of Jesus and, in him, of the Father (John 16:13–15). As if to demonstrate the nonsystematic use of this language, John designates the risen Jesus as the Advocate with the Father for the world (cf. 1 John 2:1–2). The roles of the risen Jesus and the Spirit were sometimes confused.

---

[18] Schillebeeckx, *Christ*, 535.

The Spirit as Shekinah

The Spirit of God, especially as seen in the Book of Judges, shows God acting. The quality of the term *the Spirit of God* most useful for our understanding today lies in God's action occurring inside human subjects.[19] The transcendent God does not act empirically as a finite actor; God acts inside of created agents. At the same time, practically speaking, the biblical language of God working within appears interventionist. The power given a person comes from outside the creature's autonomous ability and agency, and it appears to be "in addition to" creative causality. The idea of *Shekinah,* in many respects a synonym for *the Spirit of God,* has a different connotation. It conceives of God not as occasionally interventionist but as residential. It stresses the permanent immanent presence of God in the world. "It was an interpretive effort to bridge the gap between heaven as the place of God's eternal residence and the earth as the place of His real activity, esp. His involvement in Israel's history."[20]

Shekinah is a term used in commentary and explanation of the Hebrew Bible after the canon was completed, rather than being a biblical symbol.[21] Drawn from the root of the word meaning "to dwell," it refers to "the radiance, glory, or presence of God, 'dwelling' in the midst of his people."[22] The metaphor allows one to recognize a theme that runs throughout both testaments accenting the idea of Presence and "God dwelling in his sanctuary," or among or within his people. In Exodus, God says, "I will dwell among the Israelites, and I will be their God" (Ex 29:45). "My presence will go with you, and I will give you rest" (Ex 33:14).

When Moses built a tabernacle for God in the desert, it became the place of God's presence. "Then the cloud covered the tent of meeting, and the glory of the Lord filled the tabernacle" (Ex 40:34). After settlement in Canaan, during the confederacy of tribes before the kingship, Israel had a central place for worship in Shiloh. Later, under David, it became the Temple in Jerusalem. This was the place of God's "habitation," and people made pilgrimages to it (cf. Deut 12:5ff.). God dwelt in the Temple, and at certain times no one could enter "the house of the Lord, because the glory of the Lord filled the Lord's house" (2 Chr 7:2).

---

[19] Notice how use of the word *inside* implicitly calls up its opposite, *outside.* But God works within creation because God is there. God is other than creature but not outside the human subject: no *outside* opposes *inside.*

[20] "Shekinah," *Encyclopedia of the Bible,* https://www.biblegateway.com. For a brief history and definition of *Shekinah,* see Gloria L. Schaab, "A Procreative Paradigm of the Creative Suffering of the Triune God: Implications of Arthur Peacocke's Evolutionary Theology," *Theological Studies* 67 (2006): 552–53.

[21] See Elizabeth A. Johnson, *She Who Is: The Mystery of God in Feminist Theological Discourse* (New York: Crossroad, 1993), 82–86.

[22] R. A. Stewart, "Shekinah," in *The New Bible Dictionary*, ed. J. D. Douglas (Grand Rapids, MI: Eerdmans, 1962), 1174.

Sometimes *Shekinah* operated as a synonym for *God,* protecting God's transcendence from anthropomorphism. It allowed one to speak more directly about God's dwelling within the world and God's being present to and within the world.[23] Although close to the term *the Spirit of God,* it conveys a sense that is more permanent and even local. God's presence really fills the world. Isaiah refers to God's glory found within creation and shining forth from it. Implicitly, God's glory already resides throughout creation, but Isaiah predicts that one day it will become manifest for all the world to see: "I am coming to gather all nations and tongues; and they shall come and shall see my glory" (Isa 66:18).

In sum, in many ways a synonym of *the Spirit of God, Shekinah* is less occasional and less interventionist. It draws attention more closely to the idea of God as Presence in the world as in the primary causality of creation. It expands the idea of God's Presence in the world prior to and distinct from a functional and intervening God acting within but coming from some place "outside" creation. The history of the theology of grace in Catholic thought takes a turn analogous to this in the twentieth century.

Grace as Functional Theology of "God as Spirit"

During the course of the second and third centuries the tradition bears witness to reflection on the role of God as Spirit in ways analogous to the language of the scripture. But after the Nicene declaration that the Word or Son of God was of the same nature as the Creator and Father God, theologians entertained the question of whether the Holy Spirit also shared the single divine nature, and this reflection led to the doctrine of trinity. Once the doctrine of trinity was established in the late fourth century a good deal of theological attention to the Holy Spirit was drawn up into the relation and role of God as Spirit to God as Father and to God as Son, in short, trinitarian theology. However, in the West—and this analysis is focused on Western theology, especially beginning with Augustine— a functional theology of the Spirit continued under the category of grace. In later Augustine grace was called "*auxilium Dei,*" and this divine help, in terms of content, referred to the Holy Spirit. In opposition to Pelagianism, grace, or God's help, or the Holy Spirit interacted with human freedom for salvation. After Augustine a good part of the theologies and controversies over the meaning and function of grace refers to God's work as Spirit within the human person. As a result, one finds a functional theology of the Spirit of God at work in the world, somewhat obscured under the category of grace, that develops the role of the Spirit of God found in the scriptures.

---

[23] See Kohler Kaufman and Ludwig Blau, "Shekinah," *Jewish Encyclopedia,* http://www.jewishencyclopedia.com/articles/13537-shekinah.

What follows is a commentary on a series of theologians to bring out particular aspects of their theology of the activity of God as Spirit in the world. The commentary in large part presupposes historical reconstruction of various theologies of grace.[24] But the interpretations are straightforward in highlighting aspects of these theologies that show how God as Spirit interacts with human life. They demonstrate the correlation between God acting in the theology of grace with God acting as Spirit and as creative Presence.

Augustine and Bernard of Clairvaux: God as Spirit within Freedom

Augustine reacted spontaneously and almost viscerally to what he took to be Pelagius's suggestion that free will, informed by God's commandments, had enough equipment to attain salvation. This undermined the necessity of Christ for salvation and underestimated the damage of the Fall to our wills. Augustine's ample experience and self-reflection taught him the degree to which the freedom of the human spirit is so curved in upon itself that, without help, it cannot escape its self-absorption. In response to the internal wounds of sin, Augustine determined two important roles of God as Spirit under the name of grace. First, the Spirit of God, working within human freedom and prior to any input on its part, released a selfish will from its inversion. This was done from inside the human will, where the Spirit of God has free reign. Second, the Holy Spirit continued to work within a person, sustaining and cooperating with the human will, to carry forward its self-transcending action. Augustine called this "cooperative grace": "God operates, therefore, without us, in order that we may will; but when we will, and so will that we may act, God co-operates with us."[25]

The idea of cooperative grace could easily promote speculation on how the powers of God as Spirit and human freedom commingled. Centuries later, in response to this issue, Bernard of Clairvaux clearly showed he understood that God and human freedom operated differently and not in competition:

What was begun by grace alone, is completed by grace and free choice together, in such a way that they contribute to each new achievement not singly but jointly; not by turns, but simultaneously. It is not as if grace did one half the work and free choice the other; but each does the whole work, according to its own peculiar contribution. Grace does the whole

---

[24] I have analyzed the theologies of grace of Augustine, Aquinas, Luther, and Rahner in *The Experience and Language of Grace* (Mahwah, NJ: Paulist Press, 1979), and of Calvin and Schleiermacher in *Christian Community in History,* vol. 2, *Comparative Ecclesiology* (London: Bloomsbury, 2014).

[25] Augustine, "On Grace and Free Will," *Basic Writings of Saint Augustine,* vol. 1, ed. Whitney J. Oates (New York: Random House, 1948), ch. 33, 761.

work, and so does free choice—with this one qualification: that whereas the whole is done *in* free choice, so the whole is done *of* grace.[26]

It is hard to miss the parallel structures of the Spirit of God working in human willing in Bernard's construct and the working of God's primary causality working within finite operations that Aquinas described over a hundred years later that was cited in the previous chapter.[27] The language of Aquinas on creation is structurally identical with the confluence of God as Spirit and human freedom each doing the whole good work. This noncompetitive relationship of each within the other captures something essential of the God-human relationship.

Aquinas: God as Spirit Empowering Human Being

Thomas Aquinas dramatically altered Augustine's language of grace by adapting it to the categories of being he appropriated from Aristotle. But he left the dynamics of the operation of God as Spirit that Augustine proposed largely in place. The major shift envisaged grace as a created result within the human person that was caused by the effectiveness of God's love. Behind Aquinas's treatise on grace, then, lies Augustine's God as Spirit understood as God's love.[28]

The distinctive character of Aquinas's theology of grace arises from the teleology inherent in his Aristotelianism. The operation of human nature flows through the powers of mind and will that generate behavior oriented toward the goal of existence. That will be translated in future catechisms to become "human beings were created to love and serve God and thus reach salvation." In this scheme grace, behind which is God's loving Spirit, fills human abilities with God's empowerment thus enabling a Spirit-filled person to act out a life that is oriented to the supreme goal of union with God. In other words, the Spirit of God imbues this-worldly human activity with an expansive power of love that enables sanctification on earth and blessing in the end. It enables a spirituality of action in everyday life.

Luther and Calvin: God as Sanctifying Presence

Despite their differences, we place Luther and Calvin together on this point. Together they represent how the Spirit of God refers to God's immediate personal

---

[26] Bernard of Clairvaux, *On Grace and Free Choice*, in *Treatises*, vol. 3: *On Grace and Free Choice* (Kalamazoo, MI: Cistercian, 1977), para. 47, 106.

[27] Aquinas wrote that a single action and effect happening in the world is simultaneously wholly produced by the finite agent and wholly produced by God's primary causality (Thomas Aquinas, *Summa Contra Gentiles*, bk. III, chap. 70).

[28] Thomas Aquinas, *Summa Theologiae [ST]*, Parts I–II, q.110, art.1.

and sanctifying power. First, relative to Luther, the language of grace gravitates around Christ and atonement more closely than the Holy Spirit. But the Spirit of God leads us to Christ. What Luther adds to our understanding is thoroughgoing personalist language that serves as an antidote to Aquinas's objective ontological language. He depicts union with God in interpersonal biblical terms: a union of subjectivities through a clinging to Christ by a faith moved by the Spirit.

Calvin has a more developed understanding of the role of the Spirit of God in human life. God as Spirit "is the bond that unites us to Christ."[29] The inducement of "faith is the principal work of the Holy Spirit" (3.1.4). The Holy Spirit is God as Spirit operating within the human subject that reveals to our minds and seals in our hearts the truth of God's promise offered publicly in the ministry of Jesus (3.1.7). This illumination and power of appropriating, in turn, drives what Calvin calls the process of sanctification, which is a life in the Christian community that is faithful to the guidance of God's law. In rudimentary form this structure drives a Christian life not unlike what is found beneath the Aristotelian superstructure in Aquinas. It describes an ideal form of life in the Christian village, town, or city in which each member of the church plays his or her providential role, and together they aim to become a holy community.

Schleiermacher: God as Spirit Animating the Community

Friedrich Schleiermacher's conception of God as Spirit combines simplicity, depth, and comprehensiveness that these schematic observations cannot convey. The Spirit of God refers to God. The Spirit is "a specific divine efficacious working in believers."[30] The efficaciousness of the Spirit of God is not unrelated to the experience of absolute dependence discussed in the previous chapter. The realism of that experience rests on the real presence of God at work in creation. "The Holy Spirit is the union of the Divine Essence with human nature in the form of the common Spirit animating the life in common of believers."[31] For Schleiermacher, God as Spirit refers to the creating power of God that places God within all created reality but with specific reference to human beings. And still more specifically, in the church the Spirit is christomorphic, the Spirit of Christ.

The personal spiritual power of this conception appears in the seamless consistency of Schleiermacher's conceptions of salvation and the church. Jesus saves by communicating his God-consciousness to others, that is, his particular efficacious resonance with God as Spirit through his ministry. This efficacious

---

[29] John Calvin, *Calvin: Institutes of the Christian Religion*, ed. John T. McNeill (Philadelphia: Westminster Press, 1960), bk. 3, ch. 1, para. 1. References in the text are to book, chapter, and paragraph of the *Institutes*.

[30] Friedrich Schleiermacher, *The Christian Faith* (London: Bloomsbury T and T Clark, 2016), no. 123, p. 572.

[31] Schleiermacher, *The Christian Faith*, no. 123, p. 569.

Spirit thus defines the divine lifeblood of the church, which Schleiermacher refers to as the inner invisible sustaining power of the church. "Thus the *invisible* church is the totality of the effects of the Spirit as a connected whole."[32] God's creating and personal Spirit holds the whole visible church, across all its denominations and divisions, together as one body of Christ.

Rahner: Spirit as God's Self-communication to Creation

Rahner's functional theology of God as Spirit within his theology of grace, although it is largely taken for granted today, contains a lesson of brilliance in simplicity. In his first move he went back to the Catholic Scholastic theology of grace and argued that the primary referent of the term *grace* was God's loving presence to humanity. He then argued that God willed the salvation of all humankind, that God's will could not be ineffective, and that these points must make a difference in creation itself.[33] Finally, he postulated and identified in the working of human knowing and willing an inner orientation to the "supernatural" gift of God's Spirit to every human being. This inner orientation itself results from God's presence as Spirit.[34] For Rahner, all people all the time are responding to God's gracious presence.

The comprehensive character of Rahner's reappropriation of the theology of grace as the dynamics of the presence of God as Spirit can be seen in some of the elements of traditional language that it preserves. Rahner's theology of the Spirit corresponds neatly with Augustine's conception of God working within human subjects. By rearranging Thomistic language so that grace refers primarily to God's loving presence as Spirit to human existence, as distinct from its effect in persons ("created grace"), he short circuits the objectivist Aristotelian language that does not adequately portray an interpersonal relationship. In so doing, Rahner spontaneously appropriated the language of sin and forgiveness so prominent in the Reformers. He also highlighted in Catholic language what Schleiermacher had anticipated: the retrieval of the functional theology of the Holy Spirit so obscured by trinitarian preoccupation. Like Schleiermacher, he associated the graceful operation of God as Spirit with creation theology, while

---

[32] Schleiermacher, *The Christian Faith*, no. 148, p. 677.

[33] Two articles represent this early work of Rahner: "Some Implications of the Scholastic Concept of Uncreated Grace," *Theological Investigations* (Baltimore: Helicon Press, 1961), 1:319–46; and "Nature and Grace," *Theological Investigations* (Baltimore: Helicon Press, 1966), 4:165–88.

[34] To my knowledge Rahner never withdrew the idea that this offer of God's personal self-communication as Spirit was supernatural. Indeed, he called it a "supernatural existential." *Supernatural* in Rahner does not mean "added on to creation of our world" or to human nature but calls attention to the gratuity of God's personal relation to the world. I do not see the necessity for the term *supernatural* or *double gratuity,* especially in the light of its negative legacy, because the whole vision, including creation, is conceived as gratuitous, as grace.

at the same time preserving the christomorphic character of a Christian theology of the Spirit. And finally, he saw grace operating in all people because God creates out of love. Grace, in Rahner's view, does not appear as an add-on but as a further drawing out of the dynamics of creation and the work of God as Spirit with an accent on God's love.[35]

Spirit as God's Personal Presence

This cursory examination and interpretation of the meaning and function of Holy Spirit from the perspective of the history of the theology of grace in the West yields an understanding that is quite consistent with scriptural usage. The most significant development occurs in the explicit affirmation that the referent of "the Holy Spirit" is God. The affirmation in the history of doctrine that, like the Word or Son, the Spirit too is consubstantial with the Father and the Son renders explicit what some argue is implicit in scriptural usage. But Augustine's theology of grace did not take advantage of the substantial divinity of God as Spirit making it coterminous or co-present with God's creating Presence. Because of his obsession with sin, his treatment of grace became overly functional; he did not capitalize on the divinity of the Spirit and its indwelling. In the modern period, especially in Schleiermacher and Rahner, the theology of grace was transformed in a manner analogous to the difference between *the Spirit of God* and *Shekinah*. Grace and the Spirit of God should be understood within the framework of God's creating and loving Presence within the whole of reality, especially relative to humans who can respond.

God's Dynamic Presence within Finite Reality

Having described these three "languages" used to characterize the power of God working in the world, we now examine what happens when we realize that they all refer to the same reality. This does not mean that they are all saying exactly the same thing, because each language has a different provenance. Each rests on a somewhat different set of suppositions and has a distinctive purpose that allows it to bring out particular facets of the common "what." That fact gives each language a reason to be maintained. But at the same time, and this is the

---

[35] "God's bestowal of grace began with time itself. It is interwoven in our history. Through the work of the Holy Spirit, all creation has been pressured from within to evolve" (Judy Cannato, *Field of Compassion: How the New Cosmology Is Transforming Spiritual Life* [Notre Dame, IN: Sorin Books, 2010], 148). In Denis Edwards's view, the universal offer of God's grace "is Rahner's way of describing the core of the good news of the kingdom preached by Jesus, the idea of a gracious, liberating God at the heart of reality" (Denis Edwards, *Jesus the Wisdom of God: An Ecological Theology* [Maryknoll, NY: Orbis Books, 1995], 68).

relevant point, the common referent provides a wider perspective that modifies each single language when it is used by itself. The larger horizon for each language prevents it from reducing the entire picture into a narrow point of view. This abstract introduction takes on more concrete meaning in what follows.

We return to the term for God described in Chapter 3: *Presence.* This shorthand form draws into itself the other phrases used to "define" God: pure act of being, ground of being, creative serendipity, and absolute and incomprehensible holy mystery. It also subsumes the phrases used earlier in this chapter: "primary causality" and "creative Presence." All of these terms refer to God, not as *a* being, but as dynamic act or power of Being. Presence also includes God as "Spirit" as it appears in the scriptures and explicitly as "Holy Spirit" in the theological languages of grace we have considered. It should be evident that the mere words are not creating this assimilation. Rather, they simply refer an experience of the same reality of God.

Before launching into a brief phenomenology, we must define its point of view. This theological description cannot be called neutral or objective. And yet the naturalist seeker and the materialist scientist are included in its audience. The language falls far short of evidence or proof, but it strives for some measure of experiential credibility. The language may resonate with the longtime faith and belief of some; for others, it will amount to speculative hypothesis at best. But in both cases it aims at a certain level of coherent plausibility that cannot be simply ignored. What is being described is Presence, not as it is in itself, but as it has for so many appeared in consciousness.

Presence as Personal Power of Being

Since the Enlightenment in the West, projection has explained for many the dynamic source of the experience of Presence. The term *projection* can be explained in different ways, but the broad intent maintains that the experience of Presence derives from some form of corporate or personal self-consciousness projected outward onto a nonexistent referent. Or, as in the case of Ludwig Feuerbach, the referent is really an ideal form of corporate humanity. When Christians affirm with their scriptures that human existence is the image of God, we are really projecting God in the image of ourselves. And the result provides comfort, stability against unsettling history and chance, and a whence and whither of existence itself.

One cannot maintain that the existence of Presence as the distinct power of being can be proven when so many remain unconvinced. But many who live within this power and to whom God is such a Presence affirm that they do not need proof, that the experience appears self-authenticating, and that the processes of reasoning implicitly appeal to the experience. But can that experience be characterized in general terms? Does the conviction that the ultimate power of my being transcends the million vectors of influence that converge on myself, and that consciousness of it comes to me rather than being generated by me, possess some objective rationale? On the one hand, I do not see how such a conviction can be established from outside the experience itself. On the other hand, the experience has some qualities that definitely point in that direction. For example, dependence entails otherness, and my dependence in being transcends me. Since I am a part of the universe that is conscious of itself, is it not the dependence of the universe's finitude itself that I experience? Or, to rephrase the same idea positively, because I am part of the physical world that is conscious of itself, my experience of dependence is the world being conscious of itself. One can read reality in the self. And if I really experience an inner acceptance, affirmation, and accompaniment, no amount of insistence that this is pure self-affirmation will sound convincing. Faith in a real Presence of transcendent otherness appears more solid and surely more generative and promising than faith in reason or in humanity on its own.[36]

Presence cannot be less than personal. To describe Presence as personal in this slippery and somewhat dialectical way warns against anthropomorphism. This occurs when *personal* refers to the quality of persons, and this makes God a person and thereby sets up a context of meaning that inescapably causes confusion. The more one reflects on God, the more one is forced to an intrinsically subtle language, reminiscent of Pseudo-Dionysius the Areopagite who so influenced medieval theology: whatever we say of God, we also resolutely deny that our language and experience can adequately represent God's transcendent reality. God always and in every respect exceeds our ability to imagine and conceptualize. The phrase *not less than* tries to keep the tension of God being personal without being a person; it represents the limit and finitude of the human imagination before God.

The phrase *not less than* opens up two important qualities of the language about God employed here: what it does not tell us, and what it proposes. It should be clear that talk about God cannot be like everyday language, in which evidence frequently fills the words with one-to-one correspondence of content to object. This relationship includes wide variations because ordinary speech is filled with metaphor and allusion. Yet we understand what others are talking about because we have analogous experiences. But we have seen how the referent of *God* leaps out of the sphere of ordinary speech. Therefore, what does speech about God communicate that is not truly false, or at least severely limited because our experience is so particular and limited?

---

[36] For example, the object of faith of Sigmund Freud, pure human reason, once historical consciousness has undermined the universality of its premises and the coherence of its logic, seems weak by comparison. See Sigmund Freud, *The Future of an Illusion* (New York: W. W. Norton, 1961), 54.

Without a lengthy treatise but in a blunt statement, language about God points to a possible consciousness whose object cannot be represented but which can be experienced dialectically as that which transcends the words. Language about transcendence does not merely limit and confine; it also points out a direction, invites an opening of experience, psyche, and mind to appreciate transcendence as it immanently affects the knower. Almost all resistance to religious language reads it representationally without taking into account its dialectical character. Such language invites an opening up of the mind to transcendence, but without an apophatic dimension, so-called religious language is either corrupted or not religious at all.

Presence as Communicating and Revealing

God as Presence relates in countless ways an experience of dependence in our existence upon a transcendent source. Passively, God emerges in consciousness as Presence; in response, we infer God actively revealing God's self. But the language of God's self-communication requires two qualifications that protect against anthropomorphism. The first reminds us that the revelation of God does not communicate empirical information, some kind of discursive data about ourselves and the world. The metaphor of Presence helps to protect against thinking of ordinary or verifiable types of communication. The second qualification insists on a critical awareness that the idea of self-communication includes the spontaneous reflex that converts God into an infinitely large person.

While an extended theology of revelation would be out of place here, we need some idea of the kind of communication with God that Christian theology calls revelation beyond the lines drawn in Chapter 2. The twentieth century turn to existential description of how two human subjects communicate with each other in deeper ways than verbal transaction has transformed the framework for thinking about revelation. Thinkers such as Maurice Blondel and Karl Rahner attended to the dynamics of a human subject searching for ultimate reality; personalist theologians like Emil Brunner exploited the dynamics of subjective "encounter" to describe God communicating *through* "gesture" and "word" at a deeper existential level. This elemental symbolic or sacramental structure of communication formed the basis of Edward Schillebeeckx's classic neo-Scholastic theology of divine communication.[37] Recognizing that the core of revelation consists of "encountering Presence" frees the language of revelation from literal interpretation and thereby gives it a noncompetitive place in a dialogue with other forms of knowing.

---

[37] Edward Schillebeeckx, *Christ the Sacrament of the Encounter with God* (New York: Sheed and Ward, 1963).

Having adopted a large framework for understanding revelation as subjective encounter with Presence, how can we protect God language from anthropomorphism, from projecting God as a person interacting with human subjects? Honoring the dialectical or negative structure of speech about God and the particularity of all revelation accomplishes this. Positive affirmations about God are negated into positive mystery. God's Presence is experienced as creative energy, sustainer, acceptance, empowering Spirit, divine help, a ground for courage, and loving ground of being. God's Presence appears as benevolence and blessing. Other considerations build on and compound the mystery. We said earlier that all revelation is general because God is universal Presence. We must also say that all revelation is special because, as revelation, it always occurs in concrete specific places and mediating events to particular persons. Because all revelation is received by specific human subjects in particular circumstances, it will always bear the distinctiveness of those who receive it in faith. But this means that, because of its particularity, no single revelation can completely rule out others; all revelation comes as historical, particular, partial, and unable to exhaust what is revealed. Revelation of ultimate reality as personal God has to be placed in dialogue with revelatory experiences that seem to be opposed. One could hardly expect anything else of the absolute and incomprehensible mystery of Presence.

Presence Experienced as Love

Focusing now on the Christian tradition of Presence in the lives of people carried in the history of the theology of grace, we draw out the typical ways in which Presence is experienced. Generally, God has been experienced as loving Presence. But the meaning of the term *love* varies so greatly within cultures and so frequently has been rendered simplistic, superficial, and sentimental, that the word may run counter to experience. *Love* often means desire for another, which, although frequently represented artfully in Christian tradition, too often suggests dominating or possessive intent. Or does *love* refer to a longing to be united with the other in a mutually enhancing relationship? This seems better to describe love of God from the human side and may also aptly represent God's will. Christians most often depict God's love as altruistic: God wills the flourishing of creatures for their own sake. This fits a logic that Christians find in the act of God creating, even though it seems to be challenged by the many threats to existence that fill God's creation. This last point needs discussion and will be addressed in the following chapter. For now, we consider the Christian perception of the components of God's loving Presence with four key words: *acceptance, forgiveness, healing,* and *energizing.* These do not represent a "supernatural" order; they flow from the

Presence of God to the created order. They do not flow deductively from a direct knowledge of God but have been experienced by Christians schooled by the teaching of Jesus.

The meaning of creation arises out of an experience of absolute dependence upon and being in relation to a Presence that accounts for the world's and one's own being. *Acceptance,* on the basis of being created, understates such an elemental self-awareness. Many Christians think of God's providence reaching themselves as individually intended beings. In the context of evolution and the consistency of nature, the idea of the universe going forward from the Big Bang to produce each human person, and thus myself, is stunning. One cannot imagine this going forward from the beginning, but to one who has encountered creating Presence, looking back, it describes the events that account for one's being there. God and evolution, each have each fully produced each one of us. God as creator Presence adds unspeakable depth to the status of being in general and cosmic acceptance of each one's individuality.

God as loving Presence is *forgiving* presence. Christianity has a serious tradition of attention to sin and has continually engaged the problem of evil, and we take up these issues in the next chapter. But while many can accommodate the way nature deals out random tragedy, others cannot fathom God creating predatory human beings. The experience of forgiveness offered by Presence addresses this, but it can only appear plausible to those who recognize their own rather than others' need for it. Forgiveness operates within the conjunction and distinction of one's being and acting. While it is true that we are what we do, this cannot reduce an inner identity to a set of behaviors without remainder. Creating Presence accepts the sinner while condemning direct action or participation in anything that injures God's creatures. Forgiveness is acceptance by creative Presence of the very things that God created. Although it comes with creation, it is not cheap.[38]

Creative Presence, in the face of debilitating guilt, *heals* people. The recreating power of divine forgiveness really constitutes regeneration and new being. Many people experience a lingering sense of guilt that forgiveness by the injured parties cannot relieve: one cannot forgive oneself; nothing can wipe away the fact of what one did. Such guilt can weigh down and cripple freedom. Divine loving Presence has the transcendent power to heal such wounds and release freedom from such a trap. Infinite loving Presence can restore the integrity of being; it can recreate wholeness and restore inner freedom.

---

[38] It is embarrassing to treat Christian forgiveness so quickly in the light of the extraordinary depth of the tradition and its intricate dynamics. See James K. Voiss, *Rethinking Christian Forgiveness: Theological, Philosophical, and Psychological Explorations* (Collegeville, MN: Liturgical Press, 2015).

Finally, we cannot forget that divine and loving Presence is creative. Presence does not just stimulate psychic *energy* but, metaphysically creative, it reasserts the power of being. Augustine called this dynamic energy cooperative grace when he thought in terms of freedom arising out of sin and turning toward value. Divine Presence, on the level of primary causality, operates personally within human beings a freedom that is striving to serve the world rather than itself. Divine Presence empowers both metaphysical and moral self-transcendence in the universe.

Recapitulation

How does what we know about reality and ourselves from a scientific perspective correlate with our basic doctrines? This book is exploring how evolution influences the way we think about and formulate Christian belief. How does evolution influence a theological understanding of the classic questions of how God relates to and acts in the world? This chapter deals particularly with three seemingly distinct areas of theology: creation theology, particularly *creatio continua*; the biblical language of the operation of the Spirit of God; and the language of the theology of grace. In all three theological domains one finds spontaneous everyday spiritual language referring to God's providence, the charismatic actor charged by the Spirit, the inspiration of the community and its scriptures, the illumination of the seeker, the call of the prophet, the conversion of the saint, the courage of the life of witnesses, the various forms of grace that one has received in the course of life, and the permanent grace that supports a faithful life.

How do all these experiences of giftedness by and commerce with God relate to one another? The task of theology includes sorting out and providing some coherence to various sets of terms that have developed out of distinct circumstances and specific problems. Frequently, particular issues engaged by a specific theologian or at a distinctive time have generated diverse traditions that have traveled forward as autonomous spheres of thought and even subdisciplines. Theological loci or places of focused attention divide the Christian theological vision into "parts." The all-encompassing framework of the evolution of the material world and our lives in it throws new light on the whole Christian vision and a refreshing new perspective on the patterns of speech we inherit. It also supplies a new perspective from which many topical divisions appear archaic and irrelevant.[39]

---

[39] Roberto Ungar traces the breakup of a unitary conception of being and history into distinct spheres of being to the merging of Christianity with Greek metaphysics and ontology. He thus sees science and naturalism effecting a healing of holistic thinking. See his notion

A comparison of the theological languages of creation, of the Holy Spirit, and of grace shows that these three distinct sets of terms, discussions, and analyses refer to the same subject matter of God dealing with the world and especially human beings. In other words, the reality being referred to by God's ongoing creation, by the working of the Holy Spirit, and by the operation of God's grace in people's lives is the same. This appears most clearly when one asks what God does in this world generally but also and especially relative to human subjects. The responses of the theological languages of creation, the Spirit, and grace are remarkably the same. And the reflective definitions of God offered in the previous chapter reinforce that insight.

The comparison and then conflation of these three theological languages address problems that are existentially serious. Theology continuously suffers the criticism that it is detached from real-life problems of everyday people. A wide gap separates the discipline of theology and daily life experience, and the debates in which theologians engage often have little to do with the spontaneous religious language that people use when they reflect on their lives before God.[40] One reason for this may be found in a hidden premise of the discipline of theology itself that accounts for how theology has drifted away from everyday experience. The false premise can be described this way: when one enters the world of the Bible and its revelation one encounters a self-authenticating authority of faith that brooks no criticism from experience of the world outside the text. The world of Christian faith is self-contained. This can result in a separation of spheres: profane and sacred, nature and grace, the language of the world and of the church, of matter and spirit. These tacit separations become hostilities that prevent a discovery of the spiritual within matter and the constitutive relevance of our materiality to our spirituality.[41]

God is not a "big person in the sky," but a mysterious overwhelming and loving Presence within all material reality. Human subjectivity not only makes the cosmos conscious of itself, but it can also distinguish the vast unimaginable extension and complexity of the universe from an agency that creatively holds the whole of it in being. Human consciousness experiences itself as dependent on evolved matter and on the physical universe. But the human subject can also discern a Presence in the world that transcends the world. The relation of world

---

of "only one regime" in Roberto Mangabeira Unger, *The Religion of the Future* (Cambridge, MA: Harvard University Press, 2014), 143–62.

[40] This may be expected in a technical discipline; not many ordinary people pick up technical books on the formation of our planet or the nature of light. But then neither do believers in science assemble each week and recite a creed.

[41] I hesitate to use the term *dualism* here because it does not communicate anything until it is explained with reference to the case in point. There are many realities that involve tensions between various forces; some are vital hybridities that gain energy from the opposition of forces. The terms *dualism* and *duality* have fairly consistently taken on negative connotations.

to God runs deeper and is far more mysterious than the relation of brain and mind, which implies some kind of dynamic hybridity of dimensions. God absolutely transcends the world of matter, and the meaning of the term *spirit* is simply "negation of matter," so that matter can be completely immersed in a transcendent power that is both other and immanent to it. There can be no empirical trace of the reality of God in matter because all matter is already within the embrace of the material nothingness that "spiritually" and creatively energizes finite being. The world can be called the sphere of God because God is the within of all that is. The experiences of God, grace, Holy Spirit, divine help, transcendent acceptance, continual creation, accompaniment, forgiveness, empowerment, consolation, and hope are not experiences of the self-writ-large; they are rooted in a real creating Presence of the act and ground of being, the incomprehensible mystery of the dynamism of creation that supports both the universe and the individual in it. This conflation of theological symbols and languages helps theology return to the sources of its meaning and intelligibility. When this is translated into practical or even popular religion, it becomes the source of conscious gratitude that supplies the ground of all prayer.

5

Ambiguity
in the Heart of the Human

This chapter examines a Christian theological appreciation of darkness and light at the core of human existence. It revisits the doctrine of original sin in the light of evolution. The doctrine of an original sin and fall represents profound issues for understanding human beings. But in the end, evolution exposes the dysfunctionality of the doctrine and preserves the positive character of human existence established in the doctrine of creation while acknowledging the ravages of sin.

Christianity, at different times, has accented one or the other of two sides to humanity: its luminosity and its darkness. Human beings possess spiritual and even godly qualities: they enjoy reflective self-knowledge, freedom, and creativity. Human beings also exhibit a denser and sometimes demonic dimension: they are shortsighted, self-absorbed, and destructive. Throughout our history, various "dualisms" have marked our appreciation of ourselves in relation to the world: light vs. darkness, good vs. evil, spirit vs. matter, soul vs. body, grace vs. sin, eternity vs. time, life vs. death. These dualities are less obvious in Judaism and, to some extent, were derived from Greek culture, but they have survived in the West.[1] We need to take stock of these oppositional binaries.

If one enters the discussion of the human through the doorway of evolution, many of these contrasts and oppositions fall away or are softened. Because human existence arises simultaneously out of creation and evolution, the analytical account of conflicting tendencies takes on a new aspect. Many antitheses become dynamic polar tensions that, like law and chance, interact to generate creativity. As we discuss in this chapter, just as evolution has revolutionized our understanding of the human, it must also transform the Christian understanding of the doctrine of sin.

---

[1] Jonathan Sachs, *The Great Partnership: God, Science, and the Search for Meaning* (London: Hodder and Stoughton, 2011), 63.

The discussion follows a simple logic. Because the credibility of the biblical story of a first sin has collapsed as history, we have to find a new framework for understanding the tensions of human existence. This requires clarity about the classic doctrine of original sin and why it no longer seems relevant. With that in place, we can formulate some deeper issues that attend the doctrine and underline the pivotal role it has played in Christian self-interpretation and language. The loss of the historical sin of Adam and Eve should not jeopardize theological convictions associated with this doctrine, for example, salvation. Finally, while insisting that the term *original sin* is inappropriate today, we consider an evolutionary interpretation of sin that responds to the issues addressed by the classic doctrine and fits with the doctrine of creation that insists that what God creates is good.

Before launching this discussion, however, let us focus its subject matter in contrast to several related questions. It aims at showing that evolution does not allow a doctrine of an original sin and fall. But the doctrine persists, and its language continues to infect Christian self-understanding, public worship, and prayer. While many theologians agree at this point, others create a new doctrine, use the same name, and thus continue to promote its harmful influence. It unduly affects the understanding of Jesus Christ in the West in restrictive and negative ways. This chapter, therefore, aims at showing why this doctrine should be allowed to disappear. The discussion does not propose a comprehensive theology of sin. We accept the reflections on social sin that emerged in the nineteenth century and were so brilliantly applied to American industrial life by Walter Rauschenbusch. We agree with liberation theologies that rightly describe the social nature of human existence and the social forces, both positive and negative, that shape the individual. But social sin does not justify continued use of the language of original sin. At the same time, however, the doctrine of original sin did have an explanatory function; whether or not this was legitimate, it accounted for sin in and of the world. The phenomenology of social sin does not take up that function of the doctrine but remains a description of actual human life. Here, evolution helps to explain the roots of sin. It allows the doctrine of original sin to be retired and encourages personal and social analyses of sin to dig deeper into the ambiguity of human nature.

The Doctrine of Original Sin and the Fall

Like the doctrine of creation, the Christian teaching on sin seems straightforward until one begins to think about it. The theological opinion that it stands alone as a doctrine backed by empirical evidence is an oversimplification. The teaching on original sin and the Fall have a long and intricate history in Western theology, which has continuously reinterpreted the teaching with subtle distinctions that sculpt it to contemporaneous understandings of the world. Each denomination of Christians has a version of the doctrine that fits its larger culture. For example, some Christians baptize infants, while others see no need. Space prohibits a history of how the doctrine developed in ways too varied to be generalized and too deep to be captured as an outline. The doctrine of original sin has also left a legacy too influential to be minimized as it is today, and too misleading to be left in its objective symbolic form. We have to begin, then, with a description of the doctrine in broad terms that most Western Christians will recognize.

The Pillars of the Traditional Doctrine

Before stating a working summary of the doctrine of the source of sin, we might consider four pillars of experience and language that support the teaching and loosely function as landmarks of its development. The first is the story of the sin of Adam and Eve (Gen 3). The story overflows with symbolic meaning. It describes the first sin, whose character lies in a fundamental disobedience of God's command, and it results in expulsion from paradise and subjection to pain and labor in order to survive in the world we know. Adam and Eve, the original archetypal humans, introduce sin into the world at the bidding of the evil serpent. The story teaches that human beings, not God the creator, are responsible for the existence of sin in the world. It also represents a testimony of repentance on the part of its authors.[2]

Saint Paul constructs a second pillar for the doctrine of original sin from his own experience and offers a view of sin as an objectified power or force in the world. This can be seen, first of all, on a personal level when Paul writes about his own inner experience. The context indicates that the law is good because it states God's will. Then Paul asks: "Did that which is good, then, bring death to me? By no means! It was sin, working death in me through what is good" (Rom 7:13). "For I do not do the good I want, but the evil I do not want is what I do. Now if I do what I do not want, it is no longer I that do it, but sin that dwells within me" (Rom 7:19–20). Paul puts words to the dynamics experienced by many that desires and impulses wage a war within the person who strives to act rightly.

Paul speaks of the other bigger idea of sin as a power and force in public history. It correlates with his appreciation of Jesus Christ as a second or new Adam, a new head of the race and source of a new phylum of human beings. The newness revolves around obedience; as Adam was disobedient, Jesus Christ was obedient even to death. But in developing that positive theology Paul also noted a relationship between Adam's sin and sin as a force in the world. He

---

[2] Sin does not come from God, because God's creation is complete before sin, and creation is good. Sin thus emerges from within human freedom, not without the evil forces that tempt it from without (Paul Ricoeur, *The Symbolism of Evil* [Boston: Beacon Press, 1969], 232–60).

wrote: "Therefore, just as sin came into the world through one man, and death came through sin, and so death spread to all because all have sinned" (Rom 5:12). In contrast to Christ's obedience being salvific for all, Paul writes of Adam: "For just as by the one man's disobedience the many were made sinners" (Rom 5:19). Paul may have meant that Adam was a source, a first in a wave of human actions. But when these words were fused with an experience of sin as an objective power and a conception of a world filled with demons and the evil influence of Satan, they became ripe for thinking of sin as a condition or a state or the nature of being human to which the salvation of Jesus Christ responded.

A third pillar of the concept of original sin and a fall was contributed by Augustine. The experiential context of Augustine consisted in his profound sense of gratitude for God's grace in his life, celebrated in the *Confessions*. After writing that marvelous testimony, when Pelagius caught his attention as espousing a spirituality of free will in obedience to the law of God leading to salvation, Augustine reacted: Could anyone bypass the grace of Christ and attain salvation? In response to Pelagius, Augustine interpreted the language of Paul just cited as referring to the sin of Adam that implicated all humankind. All human beings, in a sense human nature itself, were involved in Adam's catastrophic action. This fall of the species from an initial pristine state of existence so tainted humanity that a condition of sin and guilt was spread through generation itself to all of humanity. In effect, original sin refers to a scenario in which all human beings are born into a state of inherited guilt. "Augustine is responsible for the classic elaboration of the concept of original sin and for its introduction into the dogmatic deposit of the church."[3]

One further pillar supports this doctrine: a vast body of theological speculation. This is a hard doctrine, and we will discuss its weaknesses later. But it prevailed in the West along with a legacy of reflections, distinctions, and correlative implications.[4] In modern theology, for example, the doctrine of sin might be distinguished from the idea of a fall in an effort to move out of mythological language and make the idea of a human condition of sin more realistic existentially. This seems like a positive move, but it does not overcome the negatives attached to the doctrine of original sin.

What is the doctrine of original sin and the Fall? In one sense original sin is the sin committed by Adam and Eve in the creation story.[5] More commonly, the

---

[3] Paul Ricoeur, "'Original Sin': A Study of Meaning," in *The Conflict of Interpretations: Essays in Hermeneutics* ed. Don Ihde (Evanston, IL: Northwestern University Press, 1974), 278.

[4] For a compact history of the development of the doctrine and some present-day theological interpretations of it, see Tatha Wiley, *Original Sin: Origins, Developments, Contemporary Meanings* (Mahwah, NJ: Paulist Press, 2002).

[5] Pius XII taught that original sin "proceeds from a sin actually committed by an individual Adam and which, through generation, is passed on to all and is in everyone as his own" (*Humani Generis,* August 1950, no. 37).

term *original sin* refers to the effects of that fateful event, to the condition of human nature into which all human beings are born.[6] In the Augustinian tradition, besides being deprived of God's grace, original sin results in diminished human powers: intelligence is dulled, human will is weakened, and its scope is restricted, or, as Luther phrased it, held in bondage. Humanity, in the sense of each individual person, comes into existence lacking the liberty to open itself to God. Human beings cannot achieve that for which they are created without further help, grace, from God.[7]

Problems That Undermine the Doctrine

We have outlined the doctrine of original sin with little commentary on the different cultural contexts that influenced the development of its main elements. Each aspect of the doctrine emerged within a specific culture and set of issues, and the doctrine has migrated through centuries of theological schools and denominational foci. Since the Enlightenment various objections to the doctrine have risen to the surface. Current North American intellectual culture is not sympathetic to the doctrine of original sin in its classical form, and many adjustments have been made for those who hold it in this environment. For some, this means the demise of the doctrine of original sin; in fact, it commands little attention in some systematic theologies. Others retain the doctrine but interpret it in new ways. These difficulties raise the question of whether a doctrine can still be professed when the suppositions and the reasons for its affirmation have fallen away.

In what follows we highlight some of the problems surrounding the concept of original sin. It should be clear that these objections address that doctrine and do not minimize the phenomenon of sin itself. Dividing the objections into three overlapping spheres helps to show that the plausibility of the doctrine appears fragile from many points of view.

Initial problems with the doctrine of original sin and a fall come from the discipline of history and other empirically based modes of thinking. Most Christians have adjusted to the fact that the story in Genesis is not historical, even though for centuries it was understood that way. But once the story of a sin and a fall becomes a symbolic representation of something much deeper and more

---

[6] In Catholic teaching original sin refers to a deprivation of original grace and a right relationship with God that is proper to each person as a result of the first human being's sin (*Catechism of the Catholic Church,* nos. 417, 419).

[7] Another meaning of *original sin* can be found in a secular or scientific vocabulary. It refers to a broad, impressionistic appreciation of human nature as selfish and unruly, and it bears social and political undertones. Do we share a positive open understanding of the human or a pessimistic view of human nature that favors more rather than less social control? See D. T. Campbell, "On the Conflict between Biological and Social Evolution and the Concept of Original Sin," *Zygon* 10 (1975): 234–49.

complex, the doctrine begins to appear vague and mystifying; less tangible, accessible, and real in everyday or naive terms; and finally, less relevant.

Science, too, particularly evolution, has compounded the problem of original sin and a fall. An evolutionary understanding of the emergence of life allows no space for a catastrophic event that so radically altered human nature. On the contrary, evolution confirms what critical history had already established: the doctrine did not refer to a historical event. Like the misinterpretation of creation as an event, instead of an interpretation of our relationship with God, so too the symbols of original sin and a fall explain nothing. They simply declare or confess that human beings are sinful.[8]

Evolution, as an imaginative framework that now accompanies a scientific view of reality, also flatly contradicts the idea of a pristine ideal existence in the past. In a narrative conception of reality with an evolutionary bent toward more complexity, ideals represent where we are going, what we can hope for, rather than what we have lost. Historical consciousness and the evolutionary journey of an unfinished world have inverted the worldview that forms the supposition of the doctrine. In sum, original sin was not a historical event; it was evolutionarily impossible. The doctrine is a symbolic mythological expression, not meant to be taken as a realistic historical event, not an explanation of anything, but a confession of something that is recognizable by all: human existence is sinful. This last affirmation implies that much more is going on than that human beings do not achieve their moral potential. Some inner mechanism has to be acknowledged here, and the doctrine of original sin does not account for it.

Anthropologically, the idea of a first sin that results in a change in the state or condition of human nature, its deprivation of an original wholeness into which one is born, teeters on the edge of contradiction. One cannot conceive of a state of lacking a holiness that one should possess even before the exercise of human freedom because responsibility refers to knowing activity that responds to moral imperative and value. A hereditary transmission of sin is impossible; what is communicated by heredity cannot be called sin until it is ratified by freedom. The broadest analogy cannot accommodate sin in an individual prior to the exercise of freedom.

The concept of an original sin and the effects of a fall also run into theological problems. The etiological myth, in trying to account for sin in the world by assigning its source to human provenance in a single act rather than God creating, develops a concept of human nature without grace that directly opposes creation theology. The evil tendencies it leaves in human hearts are unaccompanied by God's Presence and grace, and this deprivation implicitly undercuts the goodness of God's creation. Some theological explanations of the doctrine confuse

---

[8] A "literal" understanding of the scriptures tends to underestimate the ability of the composers and editors of the scriptures to know when the language they are using is figurative.

temptation with sin, or instinctual and impulsive desires with intentional and thus responsible action, and the confusion communicates distance from God. The end result leaves the doctrine skewing the relationship between the creator God and human existence in a negative way by introducing a state of alienation, or opposition, or enmity, or even an adversarial relationship at a point prior to the exercise of human freedom. This is nonsense in the light of scripture's creation faith and theology that depict God pronouncing creation good and the motive of creation as God's love.

In the end, the doctrine of original sin in its classic form contains serious problems. This leaves the theologian with two options: keep the doctrine and change its meaning, or allow it to disappear. The first retains the language of original sin and its effects in some kind of fall and reinterprets it by addressing the problems as they arise. This option has resulted in various interpretations of the doctrine that explain it in new ways; theologians give it a new logic and rationale while preserving the name. This makes it a living doctrine always subject to new interpretation.[9] The other option consists of formally dropping the language of original sin from current Christian self-expression, something that is actually happening among many reflective people and theologians. The rationale for this move lies first with the problems themselves and, second, with the misinformation that the ordinary religious language of original sin communicates. An inescapably strong cultural bond connects the phrase *original sin* and the story of Adam and Eve, one that cannot be overcome easily on a public level. The spontaneous connection inevitably carries with it mistaken conceptions.

A decision to discard the idea of an original sin should not be made casually; such a decision usually happens collectively and gradually. In what follows we consider what is at stake in this doctrine and three major reinterpretations of what is formally called original sin. We then discuss sin in an evolutionary context. Only then will it appear that the notion of original sin is redundant or unnecessary and that the origins of sin can be fruitfully understood in an evolutionary framework that is consistent with creation.

Deeper Issues at the Heart of Human Existence

Before turning to constructive theology, we must reflect on what is at stake in the doctrine of sin and how it occupies an important place in a Christian sensitivity to

---

[9] Scholars frequently describe the doctrine in its scriptural form as an etiological myth, as the word *original* implies. For centuries it carried explanatory power that it lost with its historicity. It was also a transcendent mystery because it transpired "in the beginning" and had some appeal to faith. Interpretations of the doctrine today tend to be no more than existential-psychological or social-phenomenological descriptions of human existence and thus do not require faith. And they do not attend to the explanatory role as satisfactorily as does evolution.

the character of human existence, to Christian anthropology. Educated Christians today are faced with a strong temptation to dismiss the doctrine of original sin and the Fall as a vestige of premodern thinking. A sense of the development of intellectual traditions would support this view; no doctrinal formula can remain stable in history. But too much Christian language has been tied to this doctrine to treat it less than carefully and seriously. This does not mean that the language of original sin has to be preserved as essential to the Christian message. The language of the doctrine has so infected other positive Christian conceptions that one has to describe its mechanisms with care. The following discussion does not adequately engage this large, prominent, and far-reaching topic, but something must be said. We begin by highlighting some considerations that show the importance of the doctrine of sin.

What Is at Stake?

The doctrine of original sin carries symbolic weight. As already noted, its imaginative connection with the biblical story of Adam and Eve helps explain this. This symbolic narrative, coupled with the doctrine of an inherited sinful condition of being deprived of grace, even though sinful by analogy, generates elementary convictions that operate without being noticed. For example, what does the sacrament of baptism, which enjoys almost universal usage among Christians, say about the status of human beings before God as they come into existence? Is the language of a wounded human nature really appropriate? The practice of infant baptism suggests that pristine human existence comes into being already tainted by sin, someone else's. Although many churches committed to adult baptism may avoid this logic, the association of baptism with inherent sin runs deep. The doctrine of inherent sinfulness does not cohere with the doctrine that what God creates is good.

The doctrine of sin, with deep roots in original sin, underlies basic christological commitments. What is it about the human that calls for the salvation from God that Jesus proffers? What is the universal condition of humankind that Jesus of Nazareth as the Christ addresses so that people can relate to him as savior and to God with a sense of acceptance and righteousness? In the large doctrinal narrative of creation, fall, and redemption, original sin, understood as a universal human condition, constitutes, or at least profoundly influences, the fundamental supposition of the Christian story. The basic logic of the Christian vision seems to depend on universal guilt or, if not guilt, a condition contrary to what God intends. The steady erosion of the intelligibility of original sin has thus also subverted the core language that expresses Christian beliefs and the language of public prayer. The intimate connection of original sin with Christian beliefs in God and the mediation of Jesus Christ gives the conception of an original sin considerably more relevance than it can or should bear. Consequently, when original sin becomes unsteady, the whole doctrine of salvation in terms of redemption begins to wobble.

The doctrine of sin has also had a significant bearing on the conception of the church and its mission. If the world, that is, all human history, unfolds as a history of sin, and Jesus Christ is its universal savior, then the mission of the church must strive to draw all people into itself as the sphere of salvation. Such has been the interpretation of the mandate of the risen Jesus preserved in Matthew's Gospel: "Go, therefore, and make disciples of all nations, baptizing them in the name of the Father, and of the Son, and of the Holy Spirit" (Matt 28:19). The deployment of the mission of the church has come under close scrutiny and criticism in these times, and the doctrine of original sin has played a role. It infiltrated a more positive motivation and practice of church mission. It often depicted a sinful world that, without the church's mediation of salvation, amounted to no more than meaningless process leading to destruction. As that view grows less plausible, as people grow more respectful of other religions and cultures, the universal role of the church in history appears to be undermined.

The doctrine of original sin has had a history; it rose to prominence in Western theology through the influence of Augustine. In the modern period it has been losing its plausibility. By being interpreted in new ways, its old form has almost been interpreted away. But what are some of these reinterpretations, and have they saved the notion of original sin?

Attempts to Save the Doctrine of Original Sin

The pressure on the doctrine of original sin understood in naive terms has been exerted since the dawn of the modern period of Western culture. And theology has consistently responded. A number of major lines of thought have sought to preserve an impulse toward sin that exerts its influence on all individuals prior to the exercise of freedom without being identical with personal sin. One might call this a kind of "pre-formal" sin, or tendency to sin, or temptation, resulting in an inescapable situation of sin.

One of these consists of an existentialist interpretation of what the tradition has called original sin. It works within a developmental view of the human person. The freedom of each person gradually develops into a more autonomous responsibility for choices and actions. As a person develops biologically and psychologically, freedom emerges from what Paul Tillich calls a "dreaming innocence" of moral responsibility into a sphere of self and others, of self and society, of right and wrong, of good and bad.[10] With their first choices, persons fall into an existence morally estranged from their essential being. This entails a sense of one's desires and one's will in contrast to the desires and norms larger than the self that exert pressure to conform. If in Christian faith the rightness and goodness of one's human action consist in their conformity to the will of God, this development appears by contrast as an inclination to autonomy and egoism and temptation to sin. An inclination toward self-indulgence taints every action, so that sin lies embedded in the developmental dynamics of freedom to assume control of the self and to put one's own desires ahead of anything external or imposed.

A second way of interpreting a condition of sin, and thus an interpretation of original sin, focuses its attention on our social makeup; it sees the influence of sin on the person moving from society to the individual. The premise of this interpretation can be found in a social anthropology and the sociology of knowledge. Developmentally, persons are socialized into cultures of meanings, values, and behavior patterns that gradually communicate to each one the consistency and nature of things. Within this framework one can conceive of original sin as a corporate "sin of the world." This refers to various social patterns of thought and behavior that incorporate sinful attitudes, biases, hatreds, and aggressive tendencies, which, in turn, shape the emergence of people's freedom.[11] This happens in passive and active ways; that is, social forces operate both from outside the self, acting on each person, and become internalized to shape attitudes and channel responses actively. From the viewpoint of an existentialist interpretation, the sin of the world appears to be communicated to a person from the outside. But from a holistic social understanding of human development, internalized social patterns of understanding, desiring, and acting constitute an

---

[10] I have psychologized a deeper ontology of Tillich whereby "dreaming innocence" refers to the pure potentiality of a being to reach its essential being. But it does not, for it awakens into actual existence, which is finite, particular, flawed, and beset with the forces of destiny that shape its actuality and leave it estranged from essential being. The tension between authentic freedom and the limitations of destiny is never overcome in this life; rather, authentic freedom and the limitations of destiny define it (Paul Tillich, *Systematic Theology,* vol. 2, *Existence and the Christ* [Chicago: University of Chicago Press, 1957], 32–39). Tillich was inspired here by Søren Kierkegaard, who also existentialized original sin: the first sin of Adam is the sin of every person. As human freedom latent in the human spirit emerges out of innocent ignorance, it is accompanied by dread because it faces a range of good and evil choices whose quality can only be learned by the exercise of freedom itself. Sin, therefore, arises out of an innocent but ignorant freedom pushed by concupiscence into choices before their value can be assessed (Søren Kierkegaard, *The Concept of Dread,* trans. Walter Lowrie [Princeton, NJ: Princeton University Press, 1944]) 23–46).

[11] Piet Schoonenberg, *Man and Sin: A Theological View* (Notre Dame, IN: University of Notre Dame Press, 1984).

integral aspect of human formation. In expanding circles of influence, some sin of some world infects all human beings.[12]

John Haught can be understood within the parameters of a social interpretation. The substance of original sin, he writes, "is the culturally and environmentally inherited deposit of humanity's violence and injustice that burdens and threatens to corrupt each of us born in this world."[13] Evolution, however, has effected a twofold change in our understanding of this doctrine. It has completely destroyed belief in a past of pristine perfection. In so doing, evolution has undermined the grounds for all the themes "of reparation and expiation [that] have become so deeply entrenched in our cultures and our classical spiritualties."[14] At the same time, in reminding us that human existence falls far short of its possibilities and considering evolution and an unfinished creation, the doctrine urges us to look toward the future for the fullness of existence. This will become a major theme in the discussion of eschatology.[15]

---

[12] Like others, Stephen J. Duffy keeps the name but constructs a meaning for it today from materials at hand ("Our Hearts of Darkness: Original Sin Revisited," *Theological Studies* 49 [1988]: 597–622). In a first move he deals with the effects of original sin, not the original or originating sin itself, but the condition in which we find ourselves, "the ongoing sinful, human predicament" (611). And this he reconstructs in a way analogous to others by turning to three levels of phenomenology: (1) internal description of the self from a psychoanalytical perspective in a way analogous to emergent freedom; (2) a description of our social-cultural situation with a stress on how society shapes the individual; and (3) a turn to the future in an eschatological perspective as a way out, looking to Irenaeus as alternative to Augustine. In the end original sin has become a "rationalized myth" and its referent is our present situation of experiencing moral impasse in our lives. The original meaning of original sin that explained the origins of sin has been left behind. It is no longer a theological category; it simply describes but explains nothing.

[13] John F. Haught, *God after Darwin: A Theology of Evolution* (Boulder, CO: Westview Press, 2000), 139. "Original sin consists of all the forces that lead us away from participation in" God's creative intent for the world (138). These forces contaminate each person and society. It should be noted that evolutionary psychologists dismiss these social explanations of aggressiveness. They see individuals as born with all sorts of aggressive traits; they emerge into society from inherited personal qualities. See Steven Pinker, *The Blank Slate: The Modern Denial of Human Nature* (London: Penguin Books, 2002), 312–13. Rolston suggests a "dual inheritance system" in which some of our conscious lives are "culturally determined without significant genetic bias" while in other areas human reactions "can have steady genetic bias" written into human responses, like instinctive responses to perceived dangers. The two spheres of influence may strengthen each other or be at odds. See Holmes Rolston, III, *Genes, Genesis, and God: Values and Their Origins in Natural and Human History [The Gifford Lectures, University of Edinburgh, 1997–1998]* (Cambridge, MA: Cambridge University Press, 1999), 131.

[14] Haught, *God after Darwin*, 141.

[15] The phenomenology and spiritual impact of society on the individual, for the development of both vices and virtues, should not be underestimated in the construction of an integral anthropology. But the question here focuses on whether descriptions of the sin of the world merit the status of the doctrine of Christian faith called original sin. This chapter proposes that evolution builds on the response of history to that question (there was no originating sin) by providing an answer to the question of the origins of sin.

Robert Neville offers a distinctive interpretation of original sin in terms of ontological guilt. The tradition posed original sin as an ontological problem because, by inheritance, it infected the development of human being itself; human nature was deprived and debilitated. Neville, by contrast, finds guilt attached to human existence through an analysis of our actual situation. Human life is constituted in a web of relationships to oneself, to other individuals, and to many communities, each one of which involves responsibilities that together define the pattern of a single life. Each person constantly has to choose between alternative obligations that pull in different directions. "The result is that even making the optimum choices at all the choice points, we deeply fail the people whom we should have served better."[16] One can try to minimize the obligation connected with these relationships and the guilt involved in their neglect as simply a function of finitude and the limits of human energy. But to do so is to call into question the character of human responsibility, and thus the very nature of humanity as it stands in relation to the Creator who constitutes human existence in freedom.

Neville's analysis reveals the deeper problem at stake in the doctrine of original sin, or, in Neville's language, the predicament of obligation and guilt. It appears in the alternative of either recognizing obligation and guilt or ignoring or denying this dimension of human existence. He refers to the latter as "nihilism."[17] The question revolves around whether or not one recognizes ontological value that is rooted in existence or being. Thus, the question of sin and guilt finds its way back to creation. The moral character of the human constituted in relationships thus expands the anthropological question *What is wrong with us?* into something far greater than moral weakness. It entails the question of the character of being itself, of the very nature of the reality in which we participate. If value is written into creation, so that value exceeds a merely neutral existence and consists of more than human estimation, then we must add to the question of the source of being the question of what the demands of value are. We not only have to ask why there is something rather than nothing, but we also have to ask whether there are values, what they are, and what we should live for.

Stephen Pope also considers the doctrine of original sin in his large work on evolution and Christian ethics and offers a somewhat distinctive position where he seems to be fighting with "evolutionists" rather than working from within an evolutionary perspective. He resists sociobiological heredity of aggressive traits

---

[16] Robert Cummings Neville, "Guilt and Justification," *Philosophical Theology,* vol. 2, *Existence* (Albany: State University of New York Press, 2014), 116.

[17] Minimizing human obligation and rejecting guilt "deny the ultimacy in the human roles of being under obligation and also can go further to deny the ultimacy of the ontological creative act as the founding of the human self that can be guilty. Here is the way of nihilism regarding obligation" (Neville, "Guilt and Justification," 122).

because it seems to make God the creator of an evil human nature.[18] He does not want to drop the doctrine,[19] but he always uses the phrase "original sin" with quotation marks. This may be understood to mean that the term does not refer back to an original pair but applies to the present condition.[20] Constructively, he understands that the mythic symbol of Adam and Eve tells the story of every person: "We all participate in the same pattern of disordered choosing."[21] The doctrine, then, consists of a symbolic lesson about personal human freedom, beginning with its first act, emerging into a world fraught with moral ambiguity and becoming implicated in it.

Framework for Understanding Sin

The doctrine of sin cannot simply be disregarded; too much is at stake in a holistic understanding of Christianity, not to mention human existence itself, for any attempt to ignore it. And yet the plausibility of the common traditional understanding of the doctrine of original sin, which still controls the Christian imagination, has collapsed and is helping to bring a credible Christian vision down with it. As valuable as they are, the attempts at revising an understanding of original sin have not filtered down to people at large. The main reason for this remains the connection of "original sin" with "Adam and Eve." Moreover, their success actually undercuts a doctrine of faith that lasted for centuries because, in the end, they describe actual sin rather than original sin. These accounts are not objects of faith but phenomenologies of our situation. As such, they are fine, but they do not constitute the doctrine of original sin.

Before turning to an evolutionary account of the dimension of sin in a Christian anthropology, let us consider a framework drawn from the tradition that sets parameters for theological reflection on moral human existence. A tension between two sets of insight and conviction, those of Augustine and Pelagius respectively, determine principles that should guide any account of human sinfulness.[22]

On the one hand, Augustine appealed to what he thought offered credible evidence for the doctrine of original sin as he understood it. There must be something wrong with human existence to account for the prevalence of egoism and violence. For Augustine, the universal character of evil rendered individualist

---

[18] Stephen J. Pope, *Human Evolution and Christian Ethics* (New York: Cambridge University Press, 2007), 156. I will cite O. E. Wilson further on as an exact case in point.

[19] Pope, *Human Evolution and Christian Ethics*, 154n77.

[20] Pope, *Human Evolution and Christian Ethics*, 154.

[21] Pope, *Human Evolution and Christian Ethics*, 155.

[22] The analysis here is drawn from F. R. Tennant, *The Origin and Propagation of Sin: Being the Hulsean Lectures Delivered before the University of Cambridge in 1901–2* (Cambridge: Cambridge University Press, 1908).

accounts ineffective. It is not enough to say people sin. Augustine experienced a collective pervasiveness of sin that ran deep and was inherently destructive. He was overwhelmed by sin's scope, its consistency, and the strength of its hold on human existence. He draws evidence from "the existence of the power of sin as habit, and our inability, in spite of formal freedom, to do the things that we would; and, secondly, the social nature of man and the physical unity of the race."[23] These two experiences set up a field of plausibility for the doctrine of original sin: something had to have broken down to account for the depth and universal extent of moral failure. One has to admit that this situation involves God to some extent: "Responsibility for the *possibility* of moral evil and for the opportunities for its realization lies with God."[24] But the pervasiveness of actual human sinning required some further universal explanation.

On the other hand, in Pelagius's view, there can be no formal sin that entails guilt without knowledge, freedom, and intent. The idea of an original sin that was objectively transmitted and inherited makes no sense. For Pelagius, one could not characterize as sin something that did not flow from knowledge, deliberation, and freedom. "The actuality of sin is derived solely from the individual will influenced by its social environment: that is the truth which Pelagius abstracted from its proper relation to the solidarity of mankind in the non-moral material of sin."[25] "No natural impulse, then, is itself sinful, unless present through our volition, and therefore through our fault."[26] Pelagius thus recognized individual responsibility against any idea of inherited guilt and defended the inalienable rights and responsibilities of individual freedom. Formal sin correlates with freedom and responsibility. All sin is actual sin and more serious because of its actuality. This stipulation hardly contradicts the need for grace. "The existence of sin is the sufficient basis of the doctrines of grace and redemption, quite apart from the further question of sin's origin and mode of propagation."[27]

This is Pelagius's positive contribution, a recognition that for sin to be sin, it has to be a function of human freedom. Pelagius tended to atomize sin into individual choices, and thus he minimized the social dimension of human existence. He did not read the collective power of sin, as well as the power of sinful habit, that sometimes manipulates the individual. And, by contrast, Augustine, with his sense of sin as a universal infection of human nature, did not attribute to individual human freedom its proper ability of striving to become a responsible self.

---

[23] Tennant, *The Origin and Propagation of Sin*, 15. Tennant is summarizing and generalizing Augustine's and Pelagius's thought here.

[24] Tennant, *The Origin and Propagation of Sin*, 122.

[25] Tennant, *The Origin and Propagation of Sin*, 120.

[26] Tennant, *The Origin and Propagation of Sin*, 104.

[27] Tennant, *The Origin and Propagation of Sin*, 13.

These two convictions point to a condition that seems to be universal, and it restricts the formal idea of sin to a function of deliberation and freedom; the two together set up parameters for positioning sin. We need an understanding that preserves the tension between a universal power that Paul almost reifies and a sense of personal responsibility. The theology of sin has to reconcile these two dimensions: sin as a universal and seemingly inherent quality of the species and yet formally a product of freedom and responsibility in order to be sin.[28] In short, how can sin be universal and yet a function of human freedom? Evolution helps to understand this enigma.

Interpreting Sin in an Evolutionary Framework

Let us turn now to an evolutionary interpretation of sin in our world that is theologically alert to what the tradition once protected in a language that is now misleading and that provides a formula applicable to the Christian life in the world today. This does not purport to be a doctrine of faith but precisely a Christian naturalist construction. After dismantling the notion of original sin, I describe more fully a constructive way of understanding some of the things that original sin protected and elicit the dynamics of evolution positively. Two questions that are addressed here go to the heart of the matter: In the light of the previous discussions of creation and evolution, can we find an occasion and even an impulse to sin that is prior to human activity within the process of evolution? And can we assign the universal and deeply ingrained dimension of sin to the dynamics of biological life itself, not to mention the sheer difficulty experienced by human beings to follow the moral imperatives that they have experienced within themselves? These two questions can be answered positively, and the responses form the backbone of how we may understand the roots of sin.

Presuppositions

This patient methodical account of sin begins with some presuppositions that control the development. The first of these revolves around the interpretive framework that evolution demands. To understand human existence in an evolutionary context requires thinking in terms of a narrative. This means placing human existence within the story of our planet and our species emerging out of the past through an evolutionary development that presently remains unfinished and heading toward some future. One has to envisage the analysis and reasoning in the terms of a story; the explanation of human existence and sin, if it can be called explanation, occurs as part of a grand narrative. This is "not

---

[28] Tennant, *The Origin and Propagation of Sin,* 79.

a story of an unjust God inflicting collective punishment on the human race for the sin of one man, and then demanding his own son's blood in some kind of warped restitution; not a story in which sin, guilt, and punishment are the dominant themes."[29] The story of sin forms a small but significant part of an infinitely larger story of creation itself. The story of the unimaginable size and magnificent complexity of evolution across matter and time to life on our tiny planet and then the marvel of self-conscious and reflective human existence exercising some control of its own history provide the large context that embraces any analysis of emergent sin.

This story changes everything. The old myth, as significant as it may be as a symbol of our relationship with God, cannot serve as a framework for a realistic understanding of sin; in fact, it positively distorts it. The story of evolution shows that sin has not been introduced into reality by the action of a single person or group; it emerged out of matter, even as did human existence itself. Sin forms part, albeit a dark and injurious part, of human existence itself. Of course, we must consider sin an aberration of human responsibility, like an infection of an organism and terrible in its effects. But sin still remains a dimension of a much greater narrative that is positive in its initiation and goal. Using his theological imagination, Karl Rahner constantly reminds us that, in the tension between grace and sin, sin is not of equal force.[30] Using an evolutionary imagination helps us to locate sin that, even when it shows up and looks like a powerful force in history that elicits personification, remains concrete, specific, and a part of a much greater story.

Along with the supposition of an evolutionary framework of understanding, we need clarity about the meanings of the relatively commonplace terms *evil* and *sin.* Let us consider a working definition of evil as something that is injurious to life, especially human life.[31] This somewhat simplistic definition makes a point rather than being comprehensive. The meaning of *evil* frequently merges with moral wickedness and sin, but the move here distinguishes objective evil from sin and relates the application of *evil* to physical events that adversely affect life. For example: "A rock doesn't care whether or not it gets broken apart, but

---

[29] Daryl Domning, "Sin, Suffering, and Salvation: What Does Evolution Have to Say about Them?" *The Atom and Eve Project: Using Science in Pastoral Ministry* (Washington Theological Union, Nov. 10, 2012), 13, http://washtheocon.org/resources/using-science-pastoral-ministry/. It is always unfair to contrast theology and popular beliefs, but the unfair contrast makes a point. At the same time it begs the question of how prevalently a literal form of the mythic story can still be found operating beneath abstract theological reasoning.

[30] Karl Rahner, *Foundations of Christian Faith: An Introduction to the Idea of Christianity* (New York: Crossroad, 1994), 102.

[31] Robert Wright notes that the word *evil* does not really fit in a modern scientific worldview; things are the way they are. But, he adds, if "it will help to actually use the word *evil,* there's no reason not to" (Robert Wright, *The Moral Animal: Why We Are the Way We Are: The New Science of Evolutionary Psychology* [New York: Vintage Books, 1994], 368).

an animal does. Therefore, although rocks and atoms had been coming apart for eons before life evolved, it was only with the appearance of *life* that 'physical evil' came into existence."[32] From "the beginning" things have been breaking down and falling apart in the construction of new being. Earthquakes are part of the ongoing formation of the planet. Earthquakes only appear evil when, by degrees, they destroy life and kill people. The sequence of death and birth summarizes the process of natural selection, which is positive. Locusts are good until they wipe out the food people depend on. Evil, in the sense of physical or objective evil, exists relative to the destruction of life.

What is sin? People have been thinking about this question since the dawn of human morality, so we must be satisfied with a working concept. We may think of sin as morally sensitive, deliberate, and intentional egocentric behavior that injures the self or others. In the context of creation it goes without saying that this offends God. Immorality becomes "sin" linguistically in the context of a relation to God who is the guarantor of the value of the injured party. Sin becomes a collective social force in history when it becomes hardened into patterns of group behavior and social structures, as we saw in the previous part of this chapter. The intent of this particular definition, for there can be other formulas, aims at formalizing a notion of sin as a moral activity distinguished by knowledge and conscious intent in contrast to actions that are ignorant, spontaneous, unthinking, or unconscious of their effects. Abstractly, this distinction is relatively clear, but reflection shows that there are layers of awareness and ignorance and that self-consciousness always comes in degrees. This means that there are levels and gradations of sinfulness and guilt.[33]

The disciplines of ethics and moral philosophy and theology take for granted this distinction of formal sin, and thus responsibility and guilt, from injurious actions of human beings that are ignorant, uninformed, unintentional, spontaneous, or coerced. But the formal idea of sin can play a role in clarifying what is and what is not sin, or at least provide diagnostic markers for sifting through the evidence. With these distinctions in mind, and the large story of the evolution of life drawn across the broad canvas of time, how can we sort out the elements of the rise of what Christians call sin?

---

[32] Domning, "Sin, Suffering, and Salvation," 5.

[33] Social sin demands careful reflection. Its recognition depends on a social historical consciousness that understands how social structures depend on a collective will; social patterns are constructed, depend on human freedom, and can be changed. But right here the parameters of Augustine and Pelagius come into play. Use of the term *sin* requires careful parsing of how human freedom and responsibility come into play. Social sin is really sin, but is so by analogy with personal sin. Social ethicists wrestle with the levels of moral consciousness and responsibility. See Roger Haight, "Sin and Grace," in *Systematic Theology: Roman Catholic Perspectives*, ed. J. Galvin and F. Schüssler Fiorenza (Minneapolis: Fortress Press, 2011), 385–402. There, I equated original sin with social sin. The perspective of evolution offers a clearer, more nuanced view of the origin of sin.

Data and Principles

In the context of an evolutionary universe, and armed with relatively simple distinctions from moral philosophy, we begin a constructive analysis of the rise of what Christians call sin. This entails putting together certain data and principles to form a theological conception, not a doctrine of faith, of the source and place of sin within the human species.[34]

First, we begin by considering the process of evolution, with particular attention to the evolution of life as a whole. The concept of an evolving material universe includes an energy, instinct, or impulse in individual beings and/or groups to survive, to draw into themselves the resources of life, in order to expand and extend their existence. Evolution rests upon an elementary drive or striving that seeks survival of the self or the species and continued existence on the biological level. In a theological understanding, the power of creation undergirds this mechanism, and God accompanies and sustains the process of ongoing creation. Creative causality, even though it is unimaginable, should not be considered neutral or passive. It supplies the power of being and, as Presence, sustains and energizes the evolutionary process.

Domning goes behind the emergence of life to a dynamism that involves life and death, change through breakage and repair, where basic systems on the chemical level compete for resources. He describes how "the feedback loop [within chemical units] exhibits something called *centripetality*: it tends to suck into itself more and more of the material and energy that sustain the loop. And of course, individual loops will compete with one another for that material and energy wherever those are in limited supply."[35] This action of drawing into itself the resources of existence and actualizing a fundamental drive to exist seems to describe a pattern that works analogously across the spheres of chemistry and biology. This means that one finds analogues to the processes of life, to metabolism, mutation, natural selection, ecology, competition, cooperation, and reproduction, within the physical world. These processes reflect the analogous but elementary integrity of existence across the material universe.

These data stimulate Domning to generalize about the mechanisms of life across the board:

---

[34] This essay in constructive theology is dependent upon two thinkers, one hundred years apart, who interpret the doctrine of original sin in evolutionary terms. Frederick R. Tennant was a theologian who had been a scientist and worked within a Darwinian framework; Daryl Domning is a scientist who has for decades been interested in the doctrine of original sin. I borrow freely from both in constructing a synthesis.

[35] Domning, "Sin, Suffering, and Salvation," 7. Holmes Rolston agrees: "Every organism . . . must also be self-projecting, pushing itself forward." This self-assertion is not "selfish"; it is not suspect; it is the essence of life on earth. "Self-development, self-defense, is the essence of biology, the law of the wilderness." In the end "all organisms defend their lives" (Rolston, *Genes, Genesis, and God*, 40).

At least from the earliest appearance of living cells . . . there was, there-fore, a characteristic form of behavior: amorally *selfish* behavior, which is *necessarily* the most basic behavior of any living system. Life must always sustain it*self* by acquiring materials and energy, if necessary at the expense of other life, through competition and self-interested cooperation. This behavior is *necessarily* reinforced by natural selection: if you don't do it, you don't long survive, much less evolve. This is how life and evolution *have to* work, in any material world—including the one that the Creator pronounced "very good" (Genesis 1:31).[36]

As with the so-called selfish gene, the personification reinforces the point and should not be taken literally. The mechanism will have bearing by contrast when we consider intentionality. But we have to recognize the mechanisms of life that specify how the instinct for self-preservation manifests itself.

Second, one can chart a number of survival instincts that protect individual life and the life of the species on all levels. They reappear in human existence. Consider these basic human responses that have their hereditary roots in his-tory, reaching back into the early strata of animal and vegetative life: sexual drive toward generation and continuance of the species; aggressiveness in self-defense and seeking the resources of life; competition with other species for limited resources; constructive alliances for mutual benefit; greed leading to acquisitiveness and to hoarding the resources of life.[37]

These instinctual reflexes are not sinful. They refine more closely the drive for existence by specifying an elementary response to a threatening world in service of the project of survival. In short, they are positive instincts, part of a larger pool of developed responses in the portfolio of living beings. As Domning states: "Apes and humans (and by inference, their last common an-cestors) perform the same repertoire of actions; but . . . we don't impute 'sin' to them because we don't deem them to have a level of intelligence that would make them moral agents."[38] Tennant picks up the same thought drawn from a Darwinian framework: "According to evolutionary doctrine, man's constitution is at first simply animal. He inherits the tendencies of the stock, the original material of impulse and emotion out of which sin is soon easily made."[39] These impulsive responses form a set of nuanced, unreflective, non-sinful, common,

---

[36] Domning, "Sin, Suffering, and Salvation," 7.

[37] Patrick Amer traces the sources of several basic instincts from an evolutionary psycho-logical perspective. He focuses on violence, acquisitiveness, kinship altruism, and dominant-submissive hierarchical behaviors. See *The Five Commandments of Jesus: A New Approach to Christianity* (New York: iUniverse, 2009), 23–31.

[38] Domning, "Sin, Suffering, and Salvation," 8.

[39] Tennant, *The Origin and Propagation of Sin*, 117.

amoral or morally indifferent but object specific, inborn propensities that are part of nature and deemed good.[40]

Let me focus for a moment on just one of many human responses with a long hereditary lineage: aggression. Aggression takes many forms: "the defense and conquest of territory, the assertion of dominance within well-organized groups, sexual aggression, acts of hostility by which weaning is terminated, aggression against prey, defensive counterattacks against predators, and moralistic and disciplinary aggression used to enforce the rules of society."[41]

This aggressive instinct is not evil in its source or a flaw in human nature but an evolutionary trait that served the purpose of survival and still can be positively functional. In the present state of human nature it is a given; it is part of human makeup. Wilson sums up its status in pointed naturalistic terms:

> Human beings are strongly predisposed to respond with unreasoning hatred to external threats and to escalate their hostility sufficiently to overwhelm the source of the threat by a respectably wide margin of safety. Our brains do appear to be programmed to the following extent: we are inclined to partition other people into friends and aliens, in the same sense that birds are inclined to learn territorial songs and to navigate by the polar constellations. We tend to fear deeply the actions of strangers and to solve conflict by aggression. These learning rules are most likely to have evolved during the past hundreds of thousands of years of human evolution and, thus, to have conferred a biological advantage on those who conformed to them with the greatest fidelity.[42]

This description would be depressing if it were a full description of natural human behavior rather than natural instinctual response. It does not adequately describe even a facet of actual human behavior, let alone give an adequate account of human nature. But aggressiveness remains a pre-human instinctive reaction that lives deep in human personality and plays a role in human behavior

---

[40] Steven Pinker states it plainly: "Evolution is central to the understanding of life, including human life. Like all living things, we are outcomes of natural selection; we got here because we inherited traits that allowed our ancestors to survive, find mates, and reproduce. This momentous fact explains our deepest strivings" (Pinker, *The Blank Slate*, 52).

[41] Edward O. Wilson, *On Human Nature* (Cambridge, MA: Harvard University Press, 1978), 101–2.

[42] Wilson, *On Human Nature*, 119. Pinker concurs: human nature is no blank slate but a bundle of drives that are the product of evolution. "These personally puzzling drives have a transparent evolutionary rationale, and they suggest that the mind is packed with craving shaped by natural selection, not with generic desire for personal well-being" (Pinker, *The Blank Slate*, 54).

everywhere. It is but one of many such instincts that exercise various levels of pressure under different measures of control.[43]

Third, the recognition of a distinction between instinctual impulse and deliberate human activity lies implicit in the discussion of instinctual responses and the earlier definition of sin. We make it explicit because of its centrality to the argument here. The distinction correlates effectively with one made in moral philosophy between an *actus hominis* and an *actus humanus*, the first being an action performed without attention, perhaps spontaneously, in an unthinking, unintentional, and undeliberate way. So much of our lives runs on rote. This stands in contrast to the fully human act in the sense of its knowing, deliberate, intentional, and free character. This latter range of action defines the sphere of morality, responsibility, and potential sin. But how did evolution give rise to this distinction? By what stages of evolution did animal activity pass to moral human activity?

Like the ascent of the human species itself, so too must moral sensibility be a product of evolutionary development. We know the two ends of the development. In broad terms, they are *animal nature* as a point of departure and the *human nature* we know in its present condition. These rough terms do not take into account the continuity between these two stages of biological, psychological, and social development, which today would be understood as having occurred in a gradual, continuous, and nuanced way through evolutionary adaptations.[44] The point being made here is rudimentary. In the evolution of the human from its nonhuman and partly human ancestors, moral sensibility also evolved over a long period of time in a gradual process.

Tennant extrapolates in large abstract terms how that evolution to the point of moral intelligence occurred. The process began with the appearance of what can be considered humanity. This early form of human existence inherited the natural and essential instincts and impulses of its animal ancestors; as was already explained, these instincts were non-moral and should be reckoned appropriate, integrated, and functional rather than abnormal. But this means that voluntary

---

[43] One can find biological tensions at work on levels prior to the evolution of moral sensibility and consciousness. One cannot find a simple explanation for sin, not even in egoism, or a drive for self-preservation, or an evolutionary purpose to communicate the genes of the species. Those drives will always be in a potential tension with alternative tendencies toward reciprocity with others to achieve the same end, the strategy of building alliances or functional altruisms that are noncompetitive and reinforce the possibility of success in a common goal. Sin, aggressiveness, evil coexist in a tension with non-zero-sum or noncompetitive impulses. See Robert Wright, *Nonzero: The Logic of Human Destiny* (New York: Vintage Books, 2000), 325–27.

[44] Thus, for example, studies show that some animals elicit what appear to be moral actions, that is, they have some form of a moral sensibility and choice. The point being made here is not the total difference between the two ends of the development but the evolutionary continuity between them.

behavior appeared in the human species before a clear moral sensibility or consciousness of right and wrong. Tennant thus postulates a period in the history of humanity in which volitional evil conduct was innocent because unaware of a normative conscience and moral sanctions. In other words, sin had not yet emerged; moral sensibility and more acute moral sensitivity also had to evolve.

During this middle period moral laws were gradually conceived and sanctions constructed. Formal morality could not arise before a moral code or set of values was experienced, expressed, and internalized. Human beings must have a consciousness of right and wrong, of good and bad behavior, to have a sense of morality and sin. Tennant calls this period the time "during which moral sentiment is gradually evoked and moral sanctions are gradually constructed. Acts once knowing no law now begin to be regarded as wrong. The performance of them henceforth constitutes sin."[45]

The principle involved here corresponds with the supposition that no sin is possible without knowledge of right and wrong. The rise of moral sensibility supplies the basis for moral deliberation and a consciously moral decision. Philosophically, sin requires this knowledge. External actions can be right or wrong, but they need to be appreciated as such to raise them to the human level of responsible actions, of moral good and bad, that constitutes the sphere of sin. Tennant compares his position on sin to the words of Paul in Romans: "Yet, if it had not been for the law, I would not have known sin. I would not have known what it is to covet if the law had not said, 'You shall not covet'" (Rom 7:7). He takes the text of Paul, draws it into an evolutionary context, and reads it in a way that parallels the construction of gradual moral awakening on a social level. Thus, he notes, "sin does not, and cannot, exist at all without the law, and . . . the motions in man which the first recognized sanction condemned were natural and non-moral; not sinful, even in the sense of being abnormal or displeasing to God."[46]

Emerging out of innocence, actual behaviors are only gradually learned to be evil or wrong or sinful. In the earliest period human beings had only the vaguest knowledge of right and wrong, locally perceived and enforced; moral sensitivity gradually became clearer and more developed. Moral perception, conviction, and enforcement develops socially and not simply as a personal conviction, even though the two dimensions cannot be separated. Hence, the

---

[45] Tennant, *The Origin and Propagation of Sin*, xxii.

[46] Tennant, *The Origin and Propagation of Sin*, 94–95. *Law* here carries the meaning of knowledge of the difference between right and wrong, good and bad, and thus bearing moral sanction. The point refers to moral responsibility rather than objective results. For example, when a tiger kills a person, God does not impute sin to the tiger. But God should not be considered indifferent to human or any other kind of suffering.

language of social consensus and law.[47] One can envisage a social version of what Edward Schillebeeckx calls a negative experience of contrast as a fundamental logic of a developing moral perception. It begins with an immediate or direct perception of some situation or event as wrong; whether or not one can unravel its negativity, intuitive conviction says this should not be. This involves an implicit recognition of the way things can and should be. Such a positive perception is logically necessary for the negative valuation to exist, even though it may remain implicit before one can explain why the situation is wrong. This dialectical contrast provokes a desire that things be changed, that the wrong be righted and the situation redressed. This fundamental logic seems broad and deep enough to postulate something like it at work in the earliest moral perception of humankind.[48] Needless to say, the scope of moral responsibility expanded with social consciousness. "Today, in a global world, we can no longer be defined by tribal or ethnocentric consciousness. The 'we' that once involved only our own clan has now evolved to include the whole of creation."[49]

How should Tennant's construct be evaluated today? Pope looks at a variety of recent theories of how a sense of morality evolved in the human species, and he finds three types of theory. The first evolutionary explanation, adaptation, describes it as a biological behavior pattern that adapts the species to its environment for survival. Morality supports a stable environment and enables the group to fit and survive.[50] The second type of theory explains morality as a function of human consciousness. The evolutionary move involves the rise of reflective human consciousness, appreciation of value, and an ability to imagine alternative actions. Morality involves more than biological adaptation; the dawning of reflective consciousness operated to establish a "moral" sense above

---

[47] We do not have direct evidence of the development of moral sensibility and norms in nascent humanity. But Tennant sees an analogy in the birth and moral development of an infant growing into maturity. The closeness of such an analogy may be debated, but it highlights dynamism and a direction of development. He writes: "The earliest sanctions known to the race were but crudely ethical, and their crudity was but gradually exchanged for the refinement characteristic of highly developed morality. Similarly, the subjective sense of guiltiness, in the primitive sinner as in the child of very tender years would at first be relatively slight, and would increase *pari passu* with the objective holiness and severity of the ethical code" (Tennant, *The Origin and Propagation of Sin*, xxi–xxii).

[48] See Patricia McAuliffe, *Fundamental Ethics: A Liberationist Approach* (Washington, DC: Georgetown University Press, 1993), 1–38. Haught states it directly: "Awareness of [a] sinful state of affairs can occur to us only if we also already have at least some sense of what the 'ideal' (nonsinful) situation would be like" (Haught, *God after Darwin*, 139).

[49] Judy Cannato, *Field of Compassion: How the New Cosmology Is Transforming Spiritual Life* (Notre Dame, IN: Sorin Books, 2010), 72.

[50] Several authors fit this type of theory, and Pope reads them reductively: adaptation is "selfish" in the sense that the material development serves the individual and species (Pope, *Human Evolution and Christian Ethics*, 250–55).

pragmatic materialistic fit.[51] The third type of theory directly rebuts biological reductionism and sees culture as a factor in the evolution of moral sensibility; it involves the common recognition of values.[52] All three of these theories, without the reductionism of the first, help to explain with greater precision the large picture painted by Tennant. They show that Tennant presents little more than an early schematic outline. But all three of them fit into the broad structure that Tennant presents.

Another recent discussion of the structure of evolution may also shed some light on the development of moral sensibility, namely, niche theory. Stoeger described a niche as an ecology, "a rich interrelated network of conditions, processes, and entities. That ecology is not completely isolated . . . but its mutually beneficial and intimate internal interrelationships are normally much stronger than those with the exterior."[53] The term *niche* refers simultaneously to spatial and social relationships and behaviors of a species, "including shared skills, beliefs, and patterns of relationship and learning."[54] Niche theory complicates further the mechanics of evolution by showing that genes do not offer an exact blueprint for heredity, that "our central nervous systems interact with our social and physical environments,"[55] and that patterns of social behavior are learned from environmental necessity and can be gradually built into heredity. This has bearing on two dimensions of Tennant's theory of the evolution of a sense of morality and sin. It confirms continuing evolution within a species pushed by adaptation to environment and developing social relations. This represents human "nature" possessing a social dimension integrated into the biological organism. And it provides another way of distinguishing the human from earlier hominid forms. Gradually Homo sapiens developed a moral sense of freedom and responsibility that allowed it to establish some measure of control over spontaneous impulse. In other words, the human consciousness evolved from being "we are" to also being a "we should be."

Finally, where does this evolutionary development leave human nature? Nothing in this evolution provides reason to regard human nature in negative terms. Human beings have not "fallen" or been corrupted. If anything, the human species, in acquiring a moral sensibility and a sensitivity to moral value,

---

[51] Pope, *Human Evolution and Christian Ethics*, 255–57. This does not undermine continuity with earlier forms of consciousness.

[52] Pope, *Human Evolution and Christian Ethics*, 257–58.

[53] William R. Stoeger, "The Immanent Directionality of the Evolutionary Process, and Its Relationship to Teleology," in *Evolutionary and Molecular Biology: Scientific Perspectives on Divine Action*, ed. Robert John Russell et al. (Vatican City: Center for Theology and the Natural Sciences, 1998), 184.

[54] Julia Feder, "Directed toward Relationship: William Stoeger's Immanent Directionality and Edward Schillebeeckx's Mystical Eschatology," *Theological Studies* 78 (2017): 450.

[55] Stephen J. Pope, "Does Evolution Have a Purpose? The Theological Significance of William Stoeger's Account of 'Nested Directionality,'" *Theological Studies* 78 (2017): 467.

undergoes an enlightenment. Human beings retain the vestigial influences of past stages of evolution, but they cannot be born sinful. The theological tradition called some of these influences concupiscence and temptation, but that does not amount to sin. Rather, they still play their role in everyday life and in longtime human survival. In many cases the urges and desires of "nature" appear to push or pull in morally cruel or evil directions, but they can also support virtue and impel good action. In the words of Tennant, these instinctual responses to the world about us "belong to man as God made him."[56]

And how are we as God made us? Human beings are surely sinners. But evolutionary reasoning shows that the sins of which we are convicted are functions of our free and deliberate activity.[57] By extension, and as demonstrated so clearly by the sociology of knowledge, the culture and institutions we build are functions of human freedom. But our formal and thus sinful participation in sinful institutions, in order to be sinful, must in some measure be a function of our moral awareness and "buy in," however strong or attenuated that might be.

The elements of this view of sin in descriptive evolutionary terms may seem to have left us with a far too naive, positive, and even optimistic view of human nature. This evolutionary appraisal appears nothing like the dark picture painted by the cumulative experience of what appears all around us and in us. This portrait does not resemble the Christian tradition of a nature sometimes described as infected with the disease called sin. What happened to the evil within us? But why would one be convinced by such a conception? The reasons cannot be far from those of Augustine: the actual world we encounter and the unruly human nature we experience in ourselves. No other evidence exists. Temptation does not make the world a sinful place. But sinful social structures promote an active potential for acceptance of disvalues or basic convictions that corrupt moral sensibility and encourage injury of whole groups of people. We know them as racism, classism, sexism, homophobia, and other social sins. Sucked into these vortexes, acquiescent response, group opinion or pressure, and thoughtless impulsive action do enormous damage. Blind adherence to social patterns can and does kill at a distance. The actual sins by which we hurt others and are hurt by them need no other explanation than evolutionary human nature

---

[56] Tennant, *The Origin and Propagation of Sin*, 95. He sums up the present condition of evolved humanity in this way: "When we reflect that many of these propensities are inevitably strong because they are, or once were, useful or necessary to life, and were therefore through countless ages intensified by natural selection, there is no reason left for referring their clamorous importunity to an evil bias or a corrupted nature" (95).

[57] Robert Wright clarifies much of this discussion with his recalling the naturalist fallacy of confusing value and moral obligation with evolutionary mechanisms. Everything changes with the arrival of reflective self-consciousness and a consciousness of the social nature of the human. See Robert Wright, "Evolutionary Ethics," *The Moral Animal: Why We Are the Way We Are: The New Science of Evolutionary Psychology* (New York: Vintage Books, 1994), 327–44.

itself, both on biological and cultural levels. Social sin is real, but as a form of actual sin. "In this message, evil and sin lose none of their horror; but they find their true place as unavoidable features of a material creation—and even as essential tools of creation, in the cases of mutations and natural selection."[58]

Sins flow from deliberate human freedom, are solidified in patterns of behavior, and leave us in our finitude unable to measure up to our responsibilities. The modern phenomenologies of emergent freedom and social sin are drawn up into an evolutionary framework and not abandoned. The sin that accumulates in the world and in the life of each person seems more than enough to preserve us from an easy optimism and alert us to the need of forgiveness. In the words of Tennant: "Man, as a sentient being endowed with instincts and impulses, inevitably possesses propensities which belong to him not at all as a fallen and corrupted being, but as man, and which must of necessity involve him, from the time that his moral life begins, in a lasting series of struggles and efforts if he is to order himself as a rational being in accordance with the requirements of an ideal or a moral law."[59]

We conclude this central part of a description of sin in an evolutionary anthropology. Several distinctions together provide a new theological understanding of sin without resorting to notions of "original sin." The first embraces them all: we must think of the human species in terms of an emergent cosmology and an evolutionary understanding of life. Without that fundamental premise, nothing that follows falls into place. Within an evolutionary matrix our animal urges, sometimes referred to as our lower appetites, are not intrinsically bad but neutral instincts that can point the direction toward action that may be judged good or bad: they evolved to serve human life and not to be rooted out. These spontaneous urges, when they are confronted with values and norms distinguishing good and evil moral action, can become an engine of human development and creativity on both the personal and social levels.

These distinctions satisfy the two tensively related requirements for a theology of sin represented by Augustine and Pelagius: the strong grip that biological and cultural evolutionary mechanisms have on human behavior, for good and for evil, and the principle that human beings are responsible for their sins and can only be personally guilty as a function of the freedom supplied by reflection and intention. The dynamic interaction between material and social human instinct and moral sensibility universally structures human consciousness. It does not depend on but operates within different particular moral cultures. And the tension itself bears no personal guilt.[60] Rather, human beings, within

---

[58] Domning, "Sin, Suffering, and Salvation," 13. Note that the word *unavoidable* in this text has an evolutionary provenance and does not represent individual human choices.
[59] Tennant, *The Origin and Propagation of Sin*, 101.
[60] The situation described by Neville earlier does entail a kind of "objective" guilt in the sense that human beings are morally stymied by being implicated in multiple relationships that

themselves, resonate with the primitive evolutionary dimension of the human person. Moral struggle for order within oneself replicates the primordial process of reflective consciousness developing out of matter, recognizing instinctual and social reflexes within the self, and gradually embracing an order or discipline in life. Freedom's moral sensibility arises out of that very tension, so that each one must bear personal responsibility for personal sin.

Each one should also recognize social responsibility for social sin. An analogous process goes on in groups that achieve some measure of common consciousness. Social sin is real, even though personal responsibility is attenuated by the degree of personal power to change certain situations or extricate oneself from them. Objective institutionalized evil is sin because it ultimately depends on the corporate human freedom that holds it in place. Participation in so many instances of institutional sin requires elementary distinctions in order to label it sin and measure responsibility. On the one hand, one can be personally responsible for institutional or social sin in various degrees depending on one's personal responsibility for its existence. On the other hand, participation in larger objective institutions beyond one's personal control have to be measured by degrees as social rather than individual responsibility.

In conclusion, Tennant's hypothesis of a period between the evolution of Homo sapiens and the development of our moral sensibility shows clearly that human existence has evolved to a level that transcends the instinctual. Human beings have not left impulse and drive behind. Evolution is continuous. But humans possess a reflective ability to recognize the power of instinct within the self and in some measure to control it. This is another sign of the distinctiveness of the human: it possesses a moral sensibility and can, in various ways and degrees, be moral. And where is grace in all of this? As outlined in the previous chapter, it suffuses the whole course of existence. We are born in grace and sustained by it. It remains the inner loving accompaniment of divine Presence in the whole drama of being.

Spiritual Resonances

We conclude this chapter with a brief reflection on some of the spiritual resonances of this reconceptualization of the theology of sin in the light of evolution. The body of Christians worldwide may be divided into three parts. Many have so internalized the language of original sin and a fallen humanity that they cannot imagine a change in that language. This testifies to the far-reaching implications of how deeply a Christian language of sin and guilt has colored all

---

involve conflicting moral demands that they cannot escape. Whatever way one acts involves personal responsibility, but one can never escape the moral demand for doing more.

the other doctrines. A second group of Christians, after learning the doctrine of original sin and a fallen humanity, and after reflection on the many uses of the language of sin and guilt, have abandoned the doctrine. Depending on the hold the doctrine had on their imagination, this may have led to their abandonment of the church as well. The insistence of the first group on this language may easily lead the second to lose faith in the authority of the church that continues to use it. A third group, which is more or less active within the church, knows that the doctrine of an original sin and a fall does not make any sense in an evolutionary world.[61] We saw the incoherence of the doctrine at the head of this chapter.

Modern interpretations of the concept may seem to provide plausible rationales for the doctrine. Not so. The classic doctrine of original sin considered the Genesis narrative as if it were history; by contrast, modern interpretations explain it as a classic mythological symbol that can release relevant anthropological reflections about our relationship with God. Their logic consists of contemporary anthropological phenomenology. The language of original sin inevitably evokes the story of Adam and Eve and is popularly linked to history. As a myth about prehistory with historical effects, it inevitably weakens the positive character of creation, evolution, and human nature by portraying history in the dark terms of disease. In contrast to supplying a new rationale for an incoherent doctrine, the evolutionary story provides no warrant for the misleading language of original sin or a fall. Evolution allows no space for a primeval fall of the race, and if the first sin is simply the first of many and does not generate universal effects, it bears no universal significance.

The term *original sin* should be erased from the Christian vocabulary.[62] Some concepts cannot be internally reformed, because the language evokes a particular reference and a relation to other ideas by an intimate connection that cannot be broken. Such is the case with original sin. It cannot be dissociated from the Genesis account of Adam and Eve, and it always suggests an actual sin that generated universal deprivation of God's grace. Adult catechesis and basic theology often cannot begin without first clearing away that misconception.

This is not a radical theology of sin that tears this traditional language out of the Christian vocabulary by its roots. Surely that will be the opinion of people in the first group. But it does not stand up to scrutiny. The steady message of

---

[61] Much more should be said about this group. Theologians in this group are either silent about original sin, or substitute actual sin on a corporate or systemic level for it, or wish to drop the doctrine. Those who are not professional theologians frequently are left without commentary on the language of original sin that is so prominent in public worship.

[62] See Patricia Williams, *Doing without Adam and Eve: Sociobiology and Original Sin* (Minneapolis: Fortress Press, 2001). Jack Mahoney writes, "In an evolutionary theology there is no need for the idea of an early collective lapse of the whole of humanity from divine grace through an original sin of its protoparents" (Jack Mahoney, *Christianity in Evolution: An Exploration* [Washington, DC: Georgetown University Press, 2011], 52).

this chapter maintains that sin is real, prevalent, and often scandalous in its massive effects. For many, like Augustine, that is "proof" of original sin. But when that logic fails, as it has, the reality of sin does not disappear. The fact that sin can be described coherently within a framework of evolution does not lessen its power and/or the need of grace for salvation. We need to examine how that grace has been revealed in Jesus Christ, and how through him it comes to bear on the evolving human species.

6

Jesus of Nazareth

This chapter turns to Jesus of Nazareth. It dialogues more with history than evolution. It begins by explaining the difficulties involved in gaining anything more than a blurred but more or less historically accurate conception of Jesus's teaching. The chapter's center of gravity lies in Jesus's representing and acting out the rule of God. Considerations of evolution come up where they are relevant to the portrayal of Jesus's ministry.

Over the next two chapters we consider a theological understanding of Jesus Christ within the framework of evolution as it has been presented thus far. This project may be considered analogous to a process of inculturation. When Christianity spread north and west into Greek and Roman cultures, it took on many of the features that we now take for granted. Some regard this as the fall of biblical Christianity; others make a stronger argument that Hellenization preserved Christian faith for Western culture. In the process, scripture acted as a continuous normative critic of the development. In our time evolution presents a question analogous to the one posed to Jews and Gentiles who were Greeks and Romans: Can a person who accepts the description of reality that science offers also embrace the Jesus Christ of Christian faith?

The project of understanding Jesus Christ within the framework of evolution carries with it criteria whose explanation will help to clarify how these chapters unfold. For example, while the viewpoint is evolutionary, the subject matter derives from scripture. The method, therefore, must include appeal to and interpretation of biblical sources and also remain consistent with the tradition of Christian faith. But we consult these traditional sources of theology in response to new questions that are raised by evolution. Although scientific culture does not subsist above criticism, it imposes some methodological restraints.

One such restraint can be found in an approach to Jesus Christ *from below.* This term needs only an initial definition because it will be displayed in the chapter itself. It represents an approach to Jesus Christ that begins, but does not end, with Jesus of Nazareth. Jesus of Nazareth is the subject matter of Christology; all interpretations of him are precisely about him. The point of departure for faith's reflection on the theological significance of Jesus of Nazareth must begin with and, in some measure, be continually tied to the historical figure. The discipline of critical history bears on this chapter more than evolutionary consciousness. But at the same time, the interpretations of Jesus's ministry and person will be conscious of their relevance within an evolutionary context.

The requirement of a Christology from below explains the relationship between this chapter and the next that will reflect on the understanding of Jesus of Nazareth interpreted as the Christ. The term *Christ* did not arise as a proper noun or name, even though common language uses it this way, but as a title and interpretation of Jesus. The problem with using *Christ* as a name arises when one asks what this usage presupposes or entails.[1] Attention to Jesus of Nazareth at the start of reflection that seeks to understand him contains the conviction that all theology about Jesus Christ should in some way be tied to, but not limited by, the fact that he had a historical existence and that we can know something about him. To bypass this lets go of the reins on a theological imagination. In short, this chapter and the next are related as, first, a presentation of Jesus of Nazareth and, second, the interpretation of Jesus as the Christ.

But nothing in theology can be so simple. Because the four Gospels about Jesus were composed well after his death, and because they are not monographs but collections of stories about Jesus of different provenances, and because each story has its own original context and history of development, to capture Jesus "as he appeared to his contemporaries" names a delicate and complex task. Some of the stories offer extravagant representations of him that need to be understood culturally. It is thus difficult, some say impossible, to get a close picture of his historical appearance: not physically, not in his early life, not in the chronology of his ministry, not in his psychological self-understanding. Exegetical historians, moreover, bring different presuppositions to the task. They have left us a history of different perspectives on his teachings. To introduce the subtle dimensions of our historical knowledge of Jesus, we begin with two different approaches as a foil to set a straightforward but necessarily somewhat fuzzy standard for proceeding.

In the second part of the chapter we complicate the task by recalling the parameters that accompany an evolutionary context and show how they give

---

[1] For example, in the New Testament *Christ* is a Greek translation of the Judaic term for "Messiah," who generally speaking was not a divine figure; the one coming with the clouds of heaven (cf. Dan 7:13–14) was not Yahweh. In comparison, what does *Christ* mean in the history of Christology? It can refer to Jesus during his lifetime; or it can refer to the risen Jesus, or the person with two natures, or the preexistent Logos or Son, or the preexistent Jesus, or the divine Jesus, or the second Person of the Trinity. An approach from below helps to clarify the difference between a person and an interpretation of that person.

rise to the possibility of a religious interpretation of Jesus of Nazareth. Then the third part develops specific examples of what Jesus taught, how it was heard by his fellow Jews, and how it may make spiritual sense to people today. This will set the stage for a resume of how Jesus himself was interpreted by his followers in the course of the first century and beyond.

Negotiating an Approach to the Jesus of History

Negotiating an approach to a realistic imaginative conceptualization of Jesus of Nazareth in a short space requires simplifying a topic that has engaged Christology for a long time. The reasons for differences in the portraits of Jesus in the canonical Gospels are clear enough: the Gospels were edited in distinct communities, at different times, for different audiences, facing different problems; and the stories they used and sometimes shared had a developmental history unevenly going back to Jesus either historically or affectively. They were remembered in faith and used as vehicles for expressing it. Some years ago I illustrated the problem to which this distance between original events and later depiction of them gives rise in a contrast between the way Raymond Brown and John Dominic Crossan approached the passion narratives.[2] One framework for viewing the gospel texts sees them as events remembered, while the other views the gospel narratives as composed of events constructed. These are types of approach or mindsets rather than consistent descriptions of performance. Thus, Brown writes, relative to the passion narratives, that the early followers of Jesus "did remember basic items in sequence about the death of Jesus."[3] By contrast, Crossan emphasizes the perspective of the later communities who used these stories to communicate and explain their faith. "The individual units, general sequences, and overall frames of the passion-resurrection stories are so linked to prophetic fulfillment that the removal of that fulfillment leaves nothing but the barest facts."[4] This perspective accents the continuity of prophecy fulfilled and sees it as a process of construction to make a claim of faith rather than report an empirical event.

Another more fully developed contrast in approaches to Jesus of Nazareth is illustrated by the friendly dialogue between N. T. Wright and Marcus Borg. Wright lines up more with Brown, and Borg with Crossan. But we can let

---

[2] Roger Haight, *Spirituality Seeking Theology* (Maryknoll, NY: Orbis Books, 2014), 124–27.

[3] Raymond E. Brown, *The Death of the Messiah: From Gethsemane to the Grave* (New York: Doubleday, 1994), 17. But Brown is also critical and selective about what he accepts as historical according to accepted criteria.

[4] John Dominic Crossan, *The Birth of Christianity: Discovering What Happened in the Years Immediately after the Execution of Jesus* (San Francisco: HarperSanFrancisco, 1998), 521.

them speak for themselves on what history can say about three issues: the accessibility of Jesus, the content of his ministry, and his death?[5]

First, how can one form a picture or conception of Jesus as a historical figure during his public ministry? How did he appear to his contemporaries? Borg deals with this objectively as a historian. The main source for knowledge of Jesus are the Synoptic Gospels. But they contain two different kinds of stories, those based on memory, and those that are narratives retrojected into the story of Jesus by the later community to make a theological point. The name Jesus sometimes refers to the figure in history and sometimes to the living resurrected Jesus to whom the community actually related. In other words, the stories about Jesus in his ministry also represent a later relationship with and conviction about Jesus alive with God. Finding Jesus as a historical figure requires sifting through the texts and deciding what is historically plausible by using established criteria.

Unlike Borg, who works here as an objective historian, Wright operates from faith, inside the community, and addresses that community. There are two ways of knowing Jesus, by history and by faith. By history, we know about Jesus; by faith, we encounter Jesus. These two must be held together. He writes: "The more I find out *about* Jesus historically, the more I find that my faith-knowledge of him is supported and filled out" (26). On that premise Wright rebuts Borg by saying one cannot build a universally acceptable interpretation of Jesus step by step, because the methods and the steps used by exegetes are contested (21–23). All one can do is present a holistic interpretation that is simple, coherent, and compelling and allow it to take its place among others (23). Wright rejects at the outset a gulf between Jesus and the New Testament interpretation of him (24).[6] Essentially, we have fundamentally different methodological presuppositions that work in different proportions in all appreciations of Jesus.

Second, Wright thinks that if you adopt the perspective of a first-century Palestinian Jew, Jesus and his message will fall into place. The Synoptic Gospels give a fairly accurate historical portrait of Jesus. The kingdom of God that Jesus preached was mainly drawn from Isaiah; it would be a rule of peace and justice through obedience to God's will. Jesus "believed that the kingdom was breaking into Israel's history in and through his own presence and work" (37). Israel was to become the light of the world and the salt of the earth (43–44). Wright sees Jesus as a radical, against the system and against the revolutionaries.

---

[5] Marcus J. Borg and N. T. Wright, *The Meaning of Jesus: Two Visions* (San Francisco: HarperSanFrancisco, 1998). The numbers within the text in this section refer to pages in this text. For outside arbitration, see Terrence W. Tilley, *History, Theology, and Faith: Dissolving the Modern Problematic* (Maryknoll, NY: Orbis Books, 2004), 128–41.

[6] Wright sums up his view of Jesus this way: "He was a prophet, announcing and inaugurating the kingdom, summoning followers, warning of disaster, promising vindication, clashing symbolically with other agendas, implicitly claiming messiahship, and anticipating a showdown. He was, in other words, a thoroughly credible first-century Jew" (51).

His healings and his message of social justice formed a new agenda of God's rule that can be read in all the symbols of Jesus's words and actions (42–47). In sum, Jesus "believed he was Israel's messiah, the one through whom the true God would accomplish his decisive purpose" (50).

By contrast, Borg approaches Jesus's ministry more objectively and analytically. He does not believe that Jesus conceived of himself as messiah, that this was a later interpretation (54). Borg describes Jesus as a Jewish mystic, not a biblical term, to make Jesus intelligible today. It refers to one who is open to transcendent reality, a person of Spirit. Analytically, Jesus had a calling, probably associated with John the Baptizer, and then set out on his own as a teacher of unconventional wisdom, as a healer and exorcist, and as a social prophet who preached the kingdom or rule of God. Borg notices different meanings of the kingdom of God drawn from gospel texts rather than from comparison with Isaiah. But in the course of his ministry, Jesus preached the kingdom of God and did not preach himself.

Finally, both authors have definite views about Jesus's death, and they differ quite noticeably. One can appreciate at this point how their different suppositions yield significantly different interpretations. For example, Borg is a Christian working as a historian to discover the Jesus of history, and Wright is a Christian examining how his faith corresponds with history. The one, Borg, does not see Jesus as conscious of being messiah or highlighting his own person but as focused on the rule of God; the other, Wright, recreates in his imagination the way to understand contextually the integral picture that especially the Gospel of Mark dictates. For Borg, Jesus was called to ministry, through the Baptist, and preached and acted out the rule of God as teacher, healer, and social prophet. He was a witness to the kingdom of God and died as a martyr to the cause of the kingdom. Later, after Easter, the community interpreted Jesus as the messiah. For Wright, before he began his ministry, Jesus internalized the prophets (especially Isaiah) and the tradition of Israel's suffering as the road to victory. He thus assumed the role of messiah in pursuing his ministry and was conscious that, through God's power, his death would usher in the rule of God.

This dialogue between two established New Testament scholars illustrates significantly different frameworks for interpreting Jesus of Nazareth. Most biblical scholars and theologians recognize that the logics of these "counter" positions and others will influence every attempt to describe the ministry of Jesus of Nazareth. But are these differences that make a difference? Without deciding on one over the other, or adapting a third exegetical stance that claims objectivity, what follows are three broad principles summarizing a mediating position that reflects a cautious constructive theological stance.

First, although the sources do not give us a sharply focused image of the person of Jesus of Nazareth, we can construct an indistinct but historically accurate portrait of his teachings and ministry. Much of the controversy about whether or not we can reconstruct the Jesus of history depends on expectations about the results. We can know more than that he existed and less than anything like a biography. The gospel stories provide a substantial view of his teachings and ministry that can be deemed historical without claiming that he used these words or thought this way or that. For example, it seems impossible to answer the question of whether he thought of himself as messiah. We cannot get inside Jesus's personal self-consciousness; there are too many different ways of being conscious of something; and there are too many different meanings of *Messiah*.

Second, to appreciate Jesus historically, he must be located in the world of first-century Jewish Palestine and Galilee. This means allowing the historians of the period to set up a context that differs widely from everyday life in today's world, whether in non-Western cultures or the developed West. Jesus was a Jew and not a Christian; his teachings were ancient Jewish teachings and not less true for being so.

Third, this first interpretation of Jesus of Nazareth has to respect his human existence. At this point some of the ideas introduced earlier in this work come into play. The emergence of our material world, the integrity of the evolution of life, and the theological understanding of creation and God's action in the world do not permit us to think in terms of interventions of God into our sphere of life as a secondary cause. The more faith projects God at work in Jesus in the empirical terms of nature miracles or works that seem to challenge the patterns of nature, the more his historical reality is compromised. The divine power at work in Jesus does not take empirical form; it is not itself created agency. The more interpreters credit the historical Jesus with Newtonian-era "miracles," the less is Jesus truly human and one of us as the core of Christian faith maintains and his universal relevance demands.[7]

Therefore, modesty in our expectation of what the historical drive to understand Jesus can deliver will, in turn, reward us with a firm historical focal point for Christian faith.

An Evolutionary Appropriation of Jesus of Nazareth

After considering how the Gospels can yield some measure of basic knowledge about Jesus of Nazareth, we can say more about a process by which Jesus may be appropriated as Christ and savior in an evolutionary context. How can this knowledge form a starting point, if not a basis, for developing a formal Christology? This question can be understood in terms of inculturation. Imagine the

---

[7] Docetism was the early Christian view, deemed heretical, that Jesus was God and only "appeared" to be a human being. This viewpoint and conviction has far-reaching residual manifestations today.

many questions posed by Greek culture to the new religious movement during the second and third centuries.

Analogously, how can people thoroughly committed to an emergent universe and the evolution of life appreciate Jesus of Nazareth as savior? We address this question formally and abstractly as a matter of method that provides a map for what follows. It is not *the* method but an approach to Christology. It generates an understanding that rearranges certain conceptions that, from an evolutionary perspective, appear to be distortions arising from anthropomorphic thinking or mistakenly construing God as a secondary cause.

There are at least four dimensions in an encounter with and appropriation of the teachings of Jesus that the New Testament calls salvation. The description of these does not constitute an argument but a phenomenology of disclosure. We note, here, that God does not "intervene" into Jesus's life or into the world through him because God is already there. The analysis, therefore, positions Jesus as one whom people encountered as a mediator of God, so that even today the stories of his teaching and healing introduce people to God as Presence and mystery. This revelation of God constitutes the salvation from God mediated by Jesus that can be further characterized in the language of the New Testament as enlightenment, liberation, and new life.

God's Presence in History

An evolutionary premise does not remove the delicacy of the historical task of providing a realistically plausible portrait of Jesus of Nazareth. But it undermines the idea that we can read the sophisticated stories about Jesus from this distant culture as straightforward communications about events, like a newspaper article. All the stories about Jesus had a context and a historical development before they were included in the canonical Gospels. The historical problems of the first part of this chapter are compounded by the conclusions drawn in earlier chapters about the transcendent being of God, God's creating causality as distinct from what was called secondary causality within finite systems. At the same time the positive view that one can identify God's creating causality with the language of Spirit and grace correlates well with the vocabulary of the New Testament, always with the proviso that these analogies are attempts at bridging worldviews that differ widely.

The understanding of creation proposed earlier entails the following general injunction: God's transcendence is absolute, even though it sustains created reality in being and thus implies presence. God's transcendence corresponds with God's radical immanence to the created sphere. God suffuses all reality as the pure energy of its being and as such should not be imagined as a finite cause in a creaturely way. The panentheistic view of God thus remains paradoxical and filled with tension; God as Presence is not an empirical reality. This view correlates in some respects with suppositions of Jesus's own time. It does not seem plausible for anyone to have looked at Jesus going around doing what prophets and healers did and to have said that Jesus is Yahweh. The sense of Yahweh's transcendence, as distinct from various godly spirits, was absolute. In some sense the workings of Spirit and Wisdom could be likened to incarnation, but early Christianity could not envisage the idea that the creator God could be incarnate the way an implicitly subordinate surrogate could. One can speak of God's incarnation in the Jewish scriptures, but the language is not technical and can be read as intending God's presence or immanence.[8]

If one accepts the conflation of the concepts of God's primary or creative causality, of Spirit, and of grace or gracious Presence, the correlation between God's immanence and the language of how God was operative in Jesus's person and ministry gains traction. What we find across the Gospels generally takes on systematic coherence in Luke's portrayal of Jesus. God as Spirit, or simply the Spirit, activated the begetting, the life, the calling, the power, and the resurrection of Jesus. That same Spirit animated the disciples and energized the Jesus movement in Luke's theology. Of course, Luke's narrative often represented the presence and power of the Spirit as intermittent actions of an agent. But revising that feature of his theology in an evolutionary world to refer to God's direct Presence to all reality and especially human beings in their intentional activity interprets and adjusts the synoptic tradition smoothly.[9] An evolutionary context thus changes the framework of ancient conceptualization and thinking, but it does not alter the theological vision.

Jesus as Medium of Transcendence

Chapter 3 reviewed possible "names" of God for our time. Among them was absolute Mystery. Frequently people confess this particular designation of God and then, forgetting it, move on to speak about God as a known entity. For example, in the context of a dialogue with science, scientists who reject the idea of God sometimes speak of God in terms that imply information about an object. "God is up in heaven" is the same kind of statement as "the cat is on the mat" or "Caesar crossed the Rubicon." Sometimes Christian theologians fall into the same intentional misconception when they speak of Jesus Christ

---

[8] Terrence E. Fretheim shows that the references to God entering into and acting through the created order are quite broad and fluid. In other words, "incarnation" is metaphor with wide application to the ways God "appeared" acting in the world. See "Christology and the Old Testament," in *Who Do You Say That I Am? Essays on Christology*, ed. Mark A. Powell and David R. Bauer, 201–15 (Louisville, KY: Westminster John Knox, 1999).

[9] Chapter 4 herein shows how scriptural Spirit language often represents God's action within a person as intermittently working from outside a person or beyond their natural powers and how that language can be interpreted today. I return to this issue in the following chapter.

as having two natures that bear a comparable formal meaning of a "kind of being." But the idea of a divine nature points to an absolutely incomprehensible mystery that materially cannot be compared with any finite nature. We will return to that statement.

At the same time, every experience of transcendence occurs in a moment of time and in a particular place. That particularity includes the concrete circumstances that lend a description to the experience. Frequently, a religious experience clings to a specific object or event that either mediates the experience or gives it distinct or even unique contours of meaning. The object of religious experience would remain incommunicable without specific symbols and language to provide meaning to its content.

The object of a strictly religious experience, that is, one that presents itself as transcendent, cannot be separated from its particular expressed form or medium. Together they possess a dynamic tensive inner relationship, an ineffability inherent in its transcendence and a relatively commonsensical meaning that mediates the experience or expresses its content. On the one hand, without such a linguistic or otherwise symbolic form of mediation, an experience of transcendence would have no discernable content; it would appear as a diffuse feeling or impression without reflective substance. On the other hand, the transcendent dimension of an authentic religious experience breaks open the ordinary meaning of attempts to encompass its transcendent content.[10]

Historically speaking, the source of many religious traditions lies in just such a primal religious experience. The idea of religious experience is used very broadly here in contrast to accepting objective data or ideas—for example, a subjectively resonant experience, of the founder, or the person or people who entertained a foundational spiritual experience, or the first people to whom they communicated it. Comparative religion provides innumerable examples of concrete sacred places, persons, and events that have functioned as apertures of transcendence, the focal points of a religious imagination, and the starting point of a religious tradition. Jesus of Nazareth takes his place in this history of religion as a presupposition for understanding him and the Christology that developed within the Jesus movement.

Jesus of Nazareth provides the focus of Christian faith. Jesus was the point of departure of what became Christian faith in God that was mediated by him; through the communities he left behind and the Gospels especially, he still grounds and constitutes that faith and the religious experience behind it. As an

---

[10] Analogous conceptions of religious meaning, symbolism, and predication can be found in many religious thinkers in different ecclesial traditions, for example, Pseudo-Dionysius, Thomas Aquinas, Friedrich Schleiermacher, John Smith, Karl Rahner, John Zizioulas, and Paul Ricoeur. The point of all these thinkers is that religious language communicates on the basis of a distinct epistemology that is variously explained in terms of analogy, mystical mediation, iconic ascent of the mind, symbolic mediation, or some other tensive system.

analytical fact this assertion obscures its narrative character. This did not happen all at once; it still goes on as a series of events. It will be made clear that Jesus Christ has a longer story than did Jesus of Nazareth, so that a person can easily object that a fixation on Jesus will not accommodate the many ways and the various guises defining the way Christians relate to Jesus Christ. But at the same time Jesus was a concrete historical person, and the various interpretations of him and his message can neither simply disregard nor explicitly contradict certain features that can be established about him by history. Jesus of Nazareth is the primary mediating and thus constitutive factor of Christian faith.

From Narrative to Reflection

The structure of religious experience and the way worldly objects or events mediate its specific content raise the pointed question of how Jesus opens up human consciousness to the character of God. Can a critical analysis of common religious experience clarify how one should approach the portrait of Jesus found in the Gospels? Christians with a scientific and evolutionary consciousness have to struggle with this issue of how anthropomorphic stories about Jesus acting with divine power can be understood as mediating a critical appropriation of God. We consider now a constructive response to this question.

To begin, people who read the Gospels thinking that Jesus was a theologian may be disappointed. He was a preacher, teacher, healer, and prophetic critic of life. The sum of his teaching lies embedded in the little stories and the larger narrative. But how does one move from the stories about Jesus and the stories he told to a constructive summary of the content of his ministry? As a first response to this question, Paul Ricoeur suggests that a way for understanding this process has a model in Jesus's parables: he told stories to teach about God and human life within the framework of God's rule. These stories inevitably made a point—frequently a surprising or even shocking point—that poked his listeners. They were meant to disorient those who heard him before they reoriented them.[11] The parable is a narrative that functions as a metaphor or simile; the kingdom of God is like this story. As a narrative it reveals something dynamic, not a sacred thing or condition; it presents a metaphorical process that opens the listener to transcendence.[12]

One should look upon Jesus himself as a parable of God. This comparison of Jesus and his ministry with a parable sets the context for presenting how he operated and the process of learning from him. The premise allows us to read Jesus in the terms that our sources provide: vignettes about his doings and

---

[11] Paul Ricoeur, *Figuring the Sacred: Religion, Narrative, and Imagination* (Minneapolis: Fortress Press, 1995), 281.

[12] Ricoeur, *Figuring the Sacred*, 147.

sayings. Through them we can form a holistic perspective on his message without slighting specific teachings. This approach interprets Jesus and his teaching as directed toward communicating or opening up human imagination to God and God's ways. Jesus's teaching was not about himself.

The perspective for reading the story of Jesus as a parable of God should not in the first moment be argumentative. Jesus offers no proof of the existence of God or his own status but addresses the faith of his Jewish people in terms they could understand. Whatever the perspective of the editors of the Gospels, Jesus's faith was Jewish; his teachings were Jewish; and he addressed Jews. Today the ministry of Jesus should best be read within the context of faith in the creator God.[13] Another world opens when one considers Jesus within the context of being in a vital relationship with God. Recognizing that relationship leads to asking about its nature and allowing Jesus to shed light on it more generally, even to the point of being a representative of God. The parable that is Jesus opens up the human imagination to new possibilities of life, to new values, and to a new goal or purpose of living. The process is cumulative. For example, a particular parable of Jesus says this or that about God, and another parable stresses something else about God. In an analogous manner one may look upon the whole trajectory of Jesus's ministry and the sum total of what can be reconstructed of his story, and ask about the ways Jesus represents the Presence of incomprehensible mystery. More will be said about the answer to that question in terms of content; here we are talking about process.

Interpretation of God through the ministry of Jesus also requires an active, analytical, and constructive imagination in order to be faithful to his teaching. As in a parable, so too with Jesus's ministry, one can say God is like this or like that on the basis of the Jesus story. But the narrative imagination has to take account of its metaphorical dimension. This move stops the action, so to speak, and opens up comparison and analysis in order to seize a truth within the story and subject it to reflection. The stories and the story of God mirrored in Jesus's teaching and action give rise to propositions that can and should be held up for meditation or analysis, especially considering the transcendence of God and the "supernatural" character of many of the gospel stories that form part of a distant culture. In this process a critical and constructive imagination reaches back into the New Testament stories of Jesus and brings forward their analogous relevance for life lived in a culture-shaped evolutionary consciousness. In the end the revelatory moment occurs in the convergence of narratives; the story of Jesus must fuse with my personal story within the present story of

---

[13] People read the Gospels from any number of perspectives. One can certainly read the Gospels simply to learn the moral teachings of Jesus. The point of this analysis is to show how Jesus illumines an already formed commitment to God and to situate the distinctiveness of the revelation he mediates.

the world.[14] This task never ceases because the world constantly changes, we change in it, and the living correlations have to grow with it.

To sum up this point, picking up the gospel text and reading Jesus's portrayal of God describes a completely spontaneous action of a Christian. But prior commitments and implicit premises and reflexes feed into that operation. These become sharply evident when a critical scientific imagination encounters a supernaturalistic anthropomorphic story of God's intervention into nature. The resolution to that problem can be an equally spontaneous use of an interpretive imagination; it realistically situates Jesus in his culture and draws forward from his teaching and action his representation of the absolute mystery of divine Presence adapted to our present-day environment. The common field of communication in this dialogue consists in the encounter with transcendence.

Revelation Is Salvation

Even though historians use various principles to encourage objectivity, one does not approach Jesus of Nazareth without some personal questions. One of these concerns a way of understanding salvation in an evolutionary context. Evolution sets some boundaries on the imagination. One of them revolves around the autonomy and integrity of nature. Scientific method does not reckon on God intervening in the processes of evolutionary becoming. Creation theology understands God's constant creative causality as another way of speaking of God's immanent Presence as a ground of finite being. Assuming a historical perspective also militates against imagining that Jesus of Nazareth had a prior existence before he came to be in time. Jesus did not come from another sphere with a verbal message about that other order of reality. As one of us, a human being, Jesus reveals a God who is present to him: his consciousness, thought, affections, and commitment. Jesus mediates God's self-revelation in and from the presence and power of God as Spirit within him.

In terms of content Jesus reveals to his fellow human beings in his distinctive way something that human beings already bear within themselves. As we have seen, God is present to all created reality. But a consciousness of this surely does not affect all people, all the time, and in the same way. This raises the question of the dynamics of revelation. In the language of H. Richard Niebuhr, although revelation occurs in a particular event mediated by an external medium, it consists of coming to a new expansive consciousness; it bears a relevance that encompasses one's whole existence because it puts us in relation to ultimacy. Christians relate to Jesus as revealer of God when what he communicates to

---

[14] "Such 'meaning' is not confined to the so-called inside of the text. It occurs at the intersection between the world of the text and the world of the readers. It is mainly in the *reception* of the text by an audience that the capacity of the plot to transfigure experience is actualized" (Ricoeur, *Figuring the Sacred*, 240, see also 242).

them defines their being in relation to God. Jesus Christ is the one "in whom we see the righteousness of God, his power and wisdom. But from that special occasion we also derive the concepts which make possible the elucidation of all the events in our history. Revelation means this intelligible event which makes all other events intelligible."[15]

Such a profound and comprehensive conception of revelation, far different from a communication of information, defines a meaning for the symbol of salvation. Salvation has to make sense within the evolutionary conditions that describe and circumscribe our human reality. Understood within the context of revelation, salvation does not imply a change within God or God's relation to creation; it is not a new act of God, and not an intervention of God into the created sphere. But one should regard Christian salvation as being mediated by the act of Jesus or a series of acts that brings to awareness a condition that was either previously unknown or opened up, clarified, and thematized by the person and his ministry. Salvation as revelation carries a new transformed conscious relationship between the creature and the creator that Jesus and his ministry effects inside the person who encounters it. This chapter and the next develop this salvation in terms of an enlightenment, a liberation, and a new life. Jesus as the medium of Christian revelation actualizes Christian salvation in those who encounter it.

What Jesus Communicates in His Ministry

The dialogue between Borg and Wright shows deeply held coherent but divergent convictions on how and what we can know about Jesus. Nevertheless, an apologetic approach to Jesus in our day must engage the historical figure. Jesus of Nazareth mediates salvation by communicating the object of Christian faith. But we have no physical description of Jesus and no certainty about his exact words in specifically determined circumstances. And we cannot get into his head psychologically. How, then, do we proceed?

The portrayals here do not describe Jesus as would an eyewitness recounting what he or she saw; they represent a rather abstract image of the person and an interpreted portrait of his teaching in word and action. Behind it lies the world

---

[15] H. Richard Niebuhr, *The Meaning of Revelation* (New York: Macmillan, 1962), 93. John Haught sees special revelation analogously as a concretization of general revelation giving it specific content and tying it to history. Revelation is a manifestation of mystery in a special occasion giving rise to concept and symbol. "By 'special revelation' I mean a concrete symbolic disclosure, culturally and historically conditioned, of the universal and eternal mystery of God" (John Haught, *Christianity and Science: Toward a Theology of Nature* [Maryknoll, NY: Orbis Books, 2007], 30).

of the Jewish faith tradition.[16] The important point here is that the portrait refers to the Jesus of history. Schubert Ogden accurately described this portrait as belonging to the "existential historical" Jesus, that is, to the way he impressed those responsible for the reports, as distinct from an empirical descriptive account.[17] Those who told these stories also used their imaginations in the telling; one cannot know anything without imagination. It also worked for those who constructed the Gospels from the stories, and we too should use it not as an obstacle but as a vehicle for understanding. This explains why there are many different interpretations of Jesus, all of which may bear some truth, just as it was during his actual ministry.

A contrast demonstrates what I am looking for here. In *Jesus Symbol of God* I sought to recreate the historical meaning of *prophet, healer,* and *teacher* in a Jewish context in order to capture objectively how Jesus presented himself. Here, we are looking for the salient characteristics of the concept of God that Jesus communicated and still communicates today. I have chosen six stories from the Gospels to structure the reflection. What follows involves interpretation that stays attentive to two things at once: how people were affected in his day, and how we, in a very different cultural and scientific world, can absorb the same teaching from the same mediator but in a distinctive linguistic form that is comprehensible in an evolutionary world.

Physical and Moral Healing (Mark 1:21–39)

> They went to Capernaum; and when the sabbath came, he entered the synagogue and taught. They were astounded at his teaching, for he taught them as one having authority, and not as the scribes. Just then there was in their synagogue a man with an unclean spirit, and he cried out, "What have you to do with us, Jesus of Nazareth? Have you come to destroy us? I know who you are, the Holy One of God." But Jesus rebuked him, saying, "Be silent, and come out of him!" And the unclean spirit, convulsing him and crying with a loud voice, came out of him. They were all amazed, and they kept on asking one another, "What is this? A new teaching—with authority! He commands even the unclean spirits, and they obey him." At once his fame began to spread throughout the surrounding region of Galilee.

---

[16] Limitations of space have precluded a helpful description of first-century Palestinian Judaism drawn from historical studies such as Sean Freyne, *Jesus, a Jewish Galilean: A New Reading of the Jesus-Story* (London: T and T Clark, 2004). See, for example, Lisa Sowle Cahill's setting of Jesus's context in *Global Justice, Christology, and Christian Ethics* (Cambridge: Cambridge University Press, 2013), 82–94.

[17] Schubert M. Ogden, *The Point of Christology* (New York: Harper and Row, 1982), 41–63.

As soon as they left the synagogue, they entered the house of Simon and Andrew, with James and John. Now Simon's mother-in-law was in bed with a fever, and they told him about her at once. He came and took her by the hand and lifted her up. Then the fever left her, and she began to serve them.

That evening, at sunset, they brought to him all who were sick or possessed with demons. And the whole city was gathered around the door. And he cured many who were sick with various diseases, and cast out many demons; and he would not permit the demons to speak, because they knew him.

In the morning, while it was still very dark, he got up and went out to a deserted place, and there he prayed. And Simon and his companions hunted for him. When they found him, they said to him, "Everyone is searching for you." He answered, "Let us go on to the neighboring towns, so that I may proclaim the message there also; for that is what I came out to do." And he went throughout Galilee, proclaiming the message in their synagogues and casting out demons.

This passage from the first chapter of Mark's Gospel depicts a day in Jesus's ministry. It was probably constructed by Mark from distinct stories, and it serves a literary function analogous to an overture. It sets out a framework of a typical time, place, and scenario of actions in which to imagine Jesus's ministry in Galilee. It tells by narrative what he did. He taught and he healed or performed exorcisms; healing and teaching went together.

The narrative begins with Jesus teaching in the synagogue. Capernaum was on the shore of the northwest sector of the Sea of Galilee, and it served as the center of Jesus's Galilean activities. On a Sabbath the service would have included "prayers, Scripture readings, and teaching. Anyone of sufficient learning could be invited to teach."[18] The Gospels do not tell us what his credentials were, but they testify to his inner spiritual authority. His teaching was Jewish teaching. It dealt with people's relationship with God and their moral relationship with others and in society. The mind can distinguish these two relationships but they cannot exist authentically apart from each other. They run together. There is no connection with God independent of social relationships; interaction with people define our relationship with God. Jesus's consistent teaching reflects his double relationship and most people understand why.

His healing struck people as "amazing" and "wonderful." Later, in certain contexts, especially with the rise of science, Jesus's amazing deeds were considered

---

[18] Daniel J. Harrington, "The Gospel according to Mark," *The New Jerome Biblical Commentary* (Englewood Cliffs, NJ: Prentice Hall, 1990), 600b.

"miraculous" or "demonstrably" enabled by a divine power.[19] It would be more reasonable to look upon Jesus as a healer who acted within a context of faith and who was motivated by an experience of God as Spirit within him. Conclusions about what Jesus actually did and how he did it are largely speculative because these things cannot be known in specific detail. The consensus says that Jesus healed "by faith," but that does not yield precise knowledge. One has to situate what he did within a context in which other healers too were at work in Palestine around the same time. But that he attracted crowds by his healing falls neatly into place.

Marcus Borg, as we noted, called Jesus a charismatic figure. This deliberately vague generic designation opens the imagination to an appreciation of Jesus that could describe the impressions of his contemporaries and of people today. A charismatic figure carries an inner resource that gives the person authority; it does not flow from office. This refers to religious authority that appealed to the freedom of his listeners, a spiritual sensibility in a religious context. People came to hear him and be made whole in different personal ways. We might say that his authority contrasted with other kinds of religious teachers at the time.

Jesus's authority and his power to heal come from the same source. The Gospels attribute them to the power of the Spirit. One needs imaginative effort to enter into the cultural and spiritual outlook of the gospel world to appreciate this. Within the sphere of empirical events a world of demons worked their evil intentions. Human behavior could be controlled by these external forces working within, and Jesus's healing was often seen as an exorcism, channeling the power of God as Spirit in a victory over Satan.[20] This story dramatizes a comprehensive worldview when it represents the evil spirit talking to Jesus. The dialogue illustrates what amounts to a cosmic struggle between the forces of the rule of God and the forces of evil.

The story presents Jesus as acting out of a dynamic existential relationship with God; to call it intimate would suggest that such conscious relationships tend to be intensely personal. He went out early to collect himself, to be "alone" with God. He moved from prayer to action. His relationship to God drove him to action and existentially supported his ideas about the rule of God. The stories of Jesus's ministry illustrate the correspondence between his teaching and his

---

[19] Jesus's miracles define a place where evolutionary consciousness comes into play. The premise for reading an overt display of divine power entails taking a given story at face value as a descriptive account of events as they unfolded. It also depends on a mechanistic understanding of the laws of nature. On the one hand, Jesus's wondrous actions have strong historical warrants: he did something that amazed people. On the other hand, descriptions of what Jesus actually did are speculative: we do not know. An evolutionary consciousness supplies negative criteria for the discussion. John P. Meier, offers a thorough discussion of Jesus's miracles in *A Marginal Jew: Rethinking the Historical Jesus,* vol. 2, *Mentor, Message, and Miracles* (New York: Doubleday, 1991), 507–1038.

[20] Harrington, "The Gospel according to Mark," 600b.

actions. All these general statements can be supported by imaginatively recon-structing what lay behind the texts.

Jesus has an open and universal appeal rooted in his humanity, shared with others of our species, and marked by values that are found in other religions as authentic human values. That we find aspects of Jesus's message in other religions does not minimize but provides evidence of its classic character. Yes, Jesus was a product of his Jewish tradition, but he put his mark on his message, and people yesterday and today resonate with its authenticity.

Gerhard Lohfink sums up what can be discerned historically in this imagi-natively constructed typical day of Jesus's ministry. One point has to do with Jesus: people were amazed at his authority in teaching, and this inner quality also displayed itself as power over the demonic sphere. We have no reason to doubt that Jesus had these qualities. The passage shows Jesus introducing order into chaotic lives; the inner demons and those of society working in people were overcome; many perceived God's power of salvation working in this typical daily ministry. On another more general or abstract level Jesus's ministry was associated with the rule of God. His ministry supported and mediated God's values. The point, yesterday and today, rests in the phrase "the rule of God" and how Jesus's ministry related to it.[21] More about this later.

The texts that follow were chosen to lift up important elements of Jesus's daily ministry that made a profound impression on his audiences, especially his followers, and that can still appeal to people today who are looking for a spiritual worldview.

Illumination of Consciousness of God (Matt 20:1–15)

"For the kingdom of heaven is like a landowner who went out early in the morning to hire laborers for his vineyard. After agreeing with the laborers for the usual daily wage, he sent them into his vineyard. When he went out about nine o'clock, he saw others standing idle in the marketplace; and he said to them, 'You also go into the vineyard, and I will pay you whatever is right.' So they went. When he went out again about noon and about three o'clock, he did the same. And about five o'clock he went out and found others standing around; and he said to them, 'Why are you standing here idle all day?' They said to him, 'Because no one has hired us.' He said to them, 'You also go into the vineyard.' When evening came, the owner of the vineyard said to his manager, 'Call the laborers and give them their pay, beginning with the last and then going to the first.' When those hired about five o'clock came, each of them received the usual daily wage. Now

---

[21] See Gerhard Lohfink, *Jesus of Nazareth: What He Wanted, Who He Was* (Collegeville, MN: Liturgical Press, 2012), 7–9.

when the first came, they thought they would receive more; but each of them also received the usual daily wage. And when they received it, they grumbled against the landowner, saying, 'These last worked only one hour, and you have made them equal to us who have borne the burden of the day and the scorching heat.' But he replied to one of them, 'Friend, I am doing you no wrong; did you not agree with me for the usual daily wage? Take what belongs to you and go; I choose to give to this last the same as I give to you. Am I not allowed to do what I choose with what belongs to me? Or are you envious because I am generous?'

This is a parable about the rule of God, the equivalent of the kingdom of heaven. The phrase *the rule of God* refers to God's will or the way things would be according to the values of God.[22] The title of this reflection, "Illumination of Consciousness of God," directs attention to how this parable can influence conceptions of God and one's life in society. Jesus intended some of his parables to do that by a shocking metaphor that contradicts conventional wisdom, interrupts the way things are, and dislocates everyday life with the implications of a distinctive concept of God and God's rule. This reversal of expectations creates a space to reconsider and find a new understanding of a larger world. The parable of the workers in the field provides a good example. Everyone in the story and those who hear it expect that the landowner would pay a just wage, that is, equal pay for the amount of work done. Few people will completely accept the rationale of the generous landowner. It is good to be generous, but the fabric of society consists of delicate balances and an overall requirement to follow the rules. Personal resentment easily turns social.

This story has many facets and yields many interpretations. One thing is sure, if it is a parable of Jesus, it cannot be interpreted with negative Jewish stereotypes.[23] With that negative guide, whose story is this? If the story is about the landowner who owns a vineyard, it is about God and Israel; if it is a story about a householder who pays a living wage to all who work, it may be about a community in which all workers and their families are cared for. It may be about both of these. For Levine, the focus of the story is the householder, landowner, and owner of the vineyard,[24] who represents God by his action. But the parable does not exclusively refer to God and salvation. It also has a broader message of how the rule of God should affect a community in everyday life, including economic well being.

---

[22] The rule of God receives more-focused attention later.

[23] Amy-Jill Levine, *Short Stories by Jesus: The Enigmatic Parables of a Controversial Rabbi* (New York: HarperCollins, 2014), 202. "When Jewish practice or Jewish society becomes the negative foil to Jesus or the church, we do well to reread the parable" (211).

[24] "The householder has the last line just as he was featured in the opening verse, and so it is his perspective that the parable foregrounds" (Levine, *Short Stories by Jesus*, 214).

Levine's interpretation of the point of the parable seems unforced and right. It should not be read as an allegory but as a reaffirmation of God's will from Jewish tradition. The householder's action provides a model for life according to the rule of God, for followers of Jesus, and for people who pay salaries.[25] They should pay what is just, and wherever they can, they should pay a living wage that supports all workers. The rule of God means that a community of the people of God takes care of its members. Jesus is following Deuteronomy: "Since there will never cease to be some in need on the earth, I therefore command you, 'Open your hand to the poor and needy neighbor in your land'" (Deut 15:11). In other words, over and above the contracts that govern a just wage, the landowner and the whole community are responsible for all its members.[26]

This reading of the parable accommodates several elements that preserve the reversal but also fit seamlessly with other teachings of Jesus. On the one hand, the shock of the payment and the complaint of the first workers and the reader of the story make sense from an individualist perspective. The work of those hired early and late is unequal. On the other hand, the rule of God is *like* heaven, but it is here on earth; it includes communitarian existence. Here, the rule of God confronts the whole community and invites behavior that is responsible to one another. In short, Jesus asks the community as a whole to think not only in contractual terms but also to adopt "a sense of justice keyed into what people need to live."[27]

One cannot accept a teaching of Jesus like this as revelatory of God by simply reading the words on the page. The story must address a question about ultimate reality and communicate the stark contrast between human ways and the ways of God to which the scriptures bear witness. Karl Barth makes this contrast the revealed basis of his theology.[28] When one enters the world of scripture, or is drawn into it, God reveals God's self as radically other than the demands of human and moral logic. God's self-revelation breaks open human thinking and draws it into another divine sphere. This suggests Jesus's intent and shows how his parable interprets us prior to us interpreting it. The parable criticizes, judges, unveils another way, and promises "fuller measure," the overflowing

---

[25] Levine, *Short Stories by Jesus*, 217.

[26] Levine, *Short Stories by Jesus*, 218. Levine supplies several stories in the Jewish tradition that make the point in a way analogous to the parable. The realistic meaningfulness of this interpretation of the parable requires different appropriations in different social economic systems. Although the shock of the gratuity implied in the story remains, one can imagine systems that actually appropriate its meaning by deploying means that promote the welfare of the community.

[27] Levine, *Short Stories by Jesus*, 218.

[28] Karl Barth's testimony to the priority of God, of revelation, of the biblical Word to all human self-understanding is represented as compelling spiritual experience in *The Word of God and the Word of Man* (New York: Harper and Row, 1957).

of life, the gift that exceeds expectations, the grace and generosity of God that negates the negative and gives in abundance.[29]

From an evolutionary perspective this story of God's will for human community does not describe two worlds that run parallel to each other; nor is one laid on top of the other. These two spheres of meaning have ontological dimensions that subsist within each other. God's love is always there as judgment and invitation. As volcanic energy only appears occasionally, so too God's dynamic love is just below the surface of all human life. But this parable continues to be disturbing because it reveals human resentment at God's generosity. The more some are lifted by generosity, the more resentment builds against those who receive it. The parable addresses everyone.

Personal Rebirth and Liberation (Luke 15:11–32)

Then Jesus said, "There was a man who had two sons. The younger of them said to his father, 'Father, give me the share of the property that will belong to me.' So he divided his property between them. A few days later the younger son gathered all he had and traveled to a distant country, and there he squandered his property in dissolute living. When he had spent everything, a severe famine took place throughout that country, and he began to be in need. So he went and hired himself out to one of the citizens of that country, who sent him to his fields to feed the pigs. He would gladly have filled himself with the pods that the pigs were eating; and no one gave him anything. But when he came to himself he said, 'How many of my father's hired hands have bread enough and to spare, but here I am dying of hunger! I will get up and go to my father, and I will say to him, "Father, I have sinned against heaven and before you; I am no longer worthy to be called your son; treat me like one of your hired hands."' So he set off and went to his father. But while he was still far off, his father saw him and was filled with compassion; he ran and put his arms around him and kissed him. Then the son said to him, 'Father, I have sinned against heaven and before you; I am no longer worthy to be called your son.' But the father said to his slaves, 'Quickly, bring out a robe—the best one—and put it on him; put a ring on his finger and sandals on his feet. And get the fatted calf and kill it, and let us eat and celebrate; for this son of mine was dead and is alive again; he was lost and is found!' And they began to celebrate.

"Now his elder son was in the field; and when he came and approached the house, he heard music and dancing. He called one of the slaves and asked what was going on. He replied, 'Your brother has come, and your

---

[29] Lohfink, *Jesus of Nazareth*, 243.

father has killed the fatted calf, because he has got him back safe and sound.' Then he became angry and refused to go in. His father came out and began to plead with him. But he answered his father, 'Listen! For all these years I have been working like a slave for you, and I have never disobeyed your command; yet you have never given me even a young goat so that I might celebrate with my friends. But when this son of yours came back, who has devoured your property with prostitutes, you killed the fatted calf for him!' Then the father said to him, 'Son, you are always with me, and all that is mine is yours. But we had to celebrate and rejoice, because this brother of yours was dead and has come to life; he was lost and has been found.'"

This story could begin with the proposal that "the rule of God is like," because it is a teaching of Jesus. It has three main characters, the father and two sons. Does the rule of God appear in reading the story through the overly generous father, the rebellious and repentant son, or the loyal but resentful son? We can understand this story as involving all three interacting but from the perspective of a loving, forgiving, and reconciling creator God. Calling the parable "The Prodigal Son" is inaccurate, because all the relationships and interactions take on integrated meaning in the light of the father.

This story depicts God in human terms as pure overflowing love and acceptance. The father embodies the cliché that God loves the sinner, not the sin. His love appears restless and active; a longing love lies buried in his watching and running to greet the repentant and remorseful son.[30] But the first reversal in the story appears in the over-the-top act of reestablishing the young man in a newly enhanced former position. The older brother is right; it exceeds all limits. This depiction of God succeeds in communicating an excess of forgiving love. Is there any way of breaking through the anthropomorphism of the narrative? We can insist that God completely supports and reestablishes fullness of life, wholeness, integrity, abundance, and fulfillment in spite of everything. But do we need to? Nature itself proclaims excess. The exegete Lohfink bursts out in scientific evolutionary terms: "A whole universe is squandered just to beget more and more extravagant life forms on one tiny planet and make a place for the human spirit."[31]

Some think this compassion of God stands in dynamic tension with the justice of God's rule over history: mercy versus justice, compassion versus judgment. But setting up these polar opposites as equals flies in the face of Jewish tradition and Jesus's teaching. God's judgment does not oppose compassion but is

---

[30] The son's reasoning seems rather pragmatic, but the text has him confess to himself and then to his father: "Father, I have sinned against heaven and before you."

[31] Lohfink, *Jesus of Nazareth*, 244.

rooted in it. God's judgment flows from compassion for the injured and aims at protecting the victim. The still deeper strain of constructive love appears in the third part of the story, after the departure and the return.

Some exegetes read this parallel as a judgment on the self-righteous. But is not the older brother rightfully resentful at the excess of the father, especially when his loyalty goes unrewarded?[32] This idea is reinforced by the contrast between the two parts of the story. But God's judgment of the brother takes the form of pleading and cajoling; he draws out a petulant failure to recognize the exalted position the brother already occupies. The father's judgment, in other words, is two-pronged; it flows from a sadness at what happened to the younger man, but the father always hoped and looked for change. The same constructive judgment is operative in a different way for the older son. The saying of the father to the older son contains a stunning manifestation of love that he actually takes for granted: "All that is mine is yours." God's judgment arises out of creative love and compassion and adjusts to each situation.

When one reads this Jewish story with a Lutheran lens, it reflects in perfect narrative form the maxim of justification by grace through faith, where the effect of grace is intensified by need. Both Luther and Ignatius of Loyola were clear on the logic that the deeper one feels a sense of sin and alienation, the stronger will be one's faith and gratitude for God's love and acceptance.[33]

Not enough attention is given to the depth and length of the effect of this experience of being loved and accepted by God. Ideally, it transcends the level of an immediate, actual, and existential engagement with God. The acceptance by God despite sin or any other physical, moral, or spiritual deficit can effect a "rebirth" or a "new being" equivalent to a transformation of the self. Such an experience can literally give to a person a new self-conscious identity. It may sustain a courage to live in the face of threats that reach the boundary between life and death. It can become a source of a lifetime of gratitude. One cannot imagine the young man, who was dead and then made alive again, as ever forgetting his rebirth. If the older brother could hear the words of his father, his resentment would begin to dissipate. Levine reads the point of Jesus's story as reconciliation. It gives us "hope for our own reconciliations, from the personal

---

[32] Robert J. Karris, "The Gospel according to Luke," in *The New Jerome Biblical Commentary*, 707b.

[33] For Luther, human existence is ensnared in a sinfulness from which it cannot escape except through God's forgiveness that effects a new freedom. Each experience intensifies its opposite (Martin Luther, *Commentary on Galatians (1535), Luther's Works*, 26 [St. Louis: Concord, 1963], 126–27). In Ignatius Loyola the same dynamic appears at the end of the first week of his *Spiritual Exercises* in a tension between consciousness of one's sin and gratitude for God's mercy and forgiveness (Ignatius Loyola, *The Spiritual Exercises of Saint Ignatius*, ed. George E. Ganss [Chicago: Loyola Press, 1992], nos. 61, 71.3, pp. 44, 47). These do not exhaust the ways of experiencing God's acceptance, but they are personally powerful.

to the international."[34] God is the source and power enabling the possibility of that reconciliation.

Finally, this story of Jesus is not "christological" but a Jewish story of the rule of God. The justification by grace refers to the love and compassion of the creator God. In the rule of God, God rules because God creates, and all depends on God. But God rules out of love and compassion; God sustains human freedom; God welcomes the lost who return; and God reconciles the alienated. Such is the character of God ruling, and such is the pervasive character of the sphere of God's rule. It should generate in like measure a spirituality of gratitude.

The Rule of God (Matt 6:9–13)

> "Pray then in this way:
>> Our Father in heaven,
>> hallowed be your name.
>> Your kingdom come.
>>> Your will be done,
>> on earth as it is in heaven.
>> Give us this day our daily bread.
>> And forgive us our debts,
>>> as we also have forgiven our debtors.
>> And do not bring us to the time of trial,
>>> but rescue us from the evil one."

This passage depicts Jesus teaching his followers how to pray; it contains Matthew's revisions of an earlier version of the Lord's Prayer found in Luke. This passage highlights the idea of the rule of God in Jesus's teaching. Scholars are generally agreed that this is a comprehensive idea, like a center of gravity, that helps to organize and situate Jesus's many teachings and actions. Understanding what Jesus intends by this multilayered conception helps to interpret particular texts. We can understand the rule of God as the object that Jesus communicates, the broader framework of his specific teaching, and thus the driving passion underlying his ministry.

One of the problems for determining the meaning of the rule of God stems from Jesus's practice of referring to and describing the rule of God with images, especially the narrative metaphors or parables. The problem arises when one cannot determine the exact point that Jesus's comparison illumines. Jesus possibly presupposed that his Jewish hearers knew exactly what he was talking about. To what does the rule of God point, name, or refer? Matthew answers this question in a most unambiguous way: "your kingdom come, your will be

---

[34] Levine, *Short Stories by Jesus*, 70.

done, on earth as in heaven." The parallelism between kingdom and the will of God on earth effectively means that they are synonyms: "The kingdom means the will of God on earth."[35]

Envisioning what the rule of God does not mean helps to reveal its positive meaning. The rule of God is not a place in the way a kingdom might be understood. Consequently, the term *rule* is preferable to *kingdom,* because the active subjective sense of God's intention being enacted replaces a static objective condition. The primary sense is God ruling, so that things unfold according to the will and intention of God.

The rule of God refers to God's will for things on earth: "The kingdom of God is primarily and above all on earth."[36] The rule of God that Jesus preached intended an ordering of human life and society that is grounded in the sphere of the creator God. The rule of God is not heaven but a world that conforms to God's will. The rule of God is indeed "within you" (cf. Luke 17:21), but this does not narrow God's will for human life to an individualist relationship with God. God's will spans individual, community, and society producing organic human integrity and development.

A deeper understanding of the Jewish resonances of the rule of God shows that its classic character can readily be appreciated today outside Jewish tradition. Some exegetes accept the logic of interpreting the rule of God not in the tradition of a Davidic model for the ideal king, but in the context of Torah, the law of the people of God from the transcendent One. The idea of God's kingship or rule derives from Torah, the first commandment, the sovereignty of the Creator and Ruler of the universe: "The creed that 'God rules as king' constitutes the center of the Torah."[37] God's law is God's will for reality. This sense of the sovereignty of God is enshrined in the psalms: "The Lord is king, he is robed in majesty" (Ps 93:1).[38]

Jesus's preaching does not situate him in the place of David as a new manifestation of the kings of Israel. He plays the role described by Isaiah: "the messenger who announces peace, who brings good news, who announces salvation, who says to Zion, 'Your God reigns'" (Isa 52:7). Moreover, the content of the rule of God is also drawn from Isaiah. Luke hammers that home in the story

---

[35] On Mark 6:10: "This request stands in strict parallelism with 'thy will be done.' God's will is for peace and justice (Rom 14:17). The prayer presupposes that the kingdom is not yet here in its fullness and thus represents a future eschatology, *as in heaven so on earth:* The prayer expects an earthly, this-worldly realization of God's will. It presupposes a certain analogy between heaven and earth" (Benedict T. Viviano, "The Gospel according to Matthew," in the *New Jerome Biblical Commentary,* 645a).

[36] Lohfink, *Jesus of Nazareth,* 25.

[37] Lohfink, *Jesus of Nazareth,* 174.

[38] See also Psalms 96–99.

of Jesus's return to Nazareth, where he stood up in the synagogue and directly applied the language of Isaiah to his ministry:

> to bring good news to the poor . . .
> to proclaim release to the captives
> and recovery of sight to the blind,
> to let the oppressed go free. (Luke 4:18)

Jesus is the messenger, servant, and representative of the rule of God.

"Thy kingdom come," Jesus prayed. The ministry of announcing and demonstrating the rule of God implies that it is not there or not in its fullness. This tension is not a simple alternative used to interpret texts; it involves the quality of time itself, always moving toward some unknown future. The rule of God, available now, promises a future at the same time; God as Presence promises a future. For all its practical bite and stinging reversals, the rule of God contains a promise of abundance and fulfillment. God is the alpha and omega.[39]

What kind of response should the rule of God as Jesus represented it elicit? What kind of reception or acceptance correlates with the message of Jesus? Treating Jesus's message of the rule of God like this in isolation, focusing on its basic meaning and logic, shows it to be an object of deep spiritual faith. The portraits of Jesus's ministry that emerge from the collected stories show an absolute commitment to God and God's rule as the core object of faith itself, both Jewish and Christian. Judging from the Gospels, for Jesus, the rule of God was the rule of his entire life and ministry. He lived for the rule of God with complete passion, and he proposed it to his followers. What Jesus holds out to the readers of the Gospels reveals objectively the very substance of Jewish and Christian faith: life lived within the sphere of creator God's will. One responds to the rule of God by acting within it. And we measure the authenticity of faith or trust in the rule of God by one's activity; one's action defines the integrity of one's faith.

Finally, one finds a correlation of the rule of God with people of God; the rule of God lives historically in the people who internalize and actualize it. It then begins to look like a historical movement and becomes reduced to or located within specific communities, if not territorially. But this objectification contradicts the most penetrating qualities of the creator God's rule. Surely many

---

[39] I do not discuss the apocalyptic language of the New Testament here. Lisa Cahill defines this as a language that "projects a radical intervention of supernatural origin that suddenly supervenes upon the world as we know it" (Cahill, *Global Justice, Christology and Christian Ethics*, 91). See her discussion of whether Jesus had an apocalyptic consciousness at pages 99–101. My reservation on this point concerns the literal interpretation of apocalyptic language that is applied to people in the first or twenty-first century. Apocalyptic language can be figurative and powerful at the same time.

people in many different traditions are striving to live according to values that are analogous to those of the rule of God in Judaism and Christianity, and just as surely the rule of God is within them.

Social Responsibility and Liberation (Luke 6:27–36)

> "But I say to you that listen, Love your enemies, do good to those who hate you, bless those who curse you, pray for those who abuse you. If anyone strikes you on the cheek, offer the other also; and from anyone who takes away your coat do not withhold even your shirt. Give to everyone who begs from you; and if anyone takes away your goods, do not ask for them again. Do to others as you would have them do to you.
>
> "If you love those who love you, what credit is that to you? For even sinners love those who love them. If you do good to those who do good to you, what credit is that to you? For even sinners do the same. If you lend to those from whom you hope to receive, what credit is that to you? Even sinners lend to sinners, to receive as much again. But love your enemies, do good, and lend, expecting nothing in return. Your reward will be great, and you will be children of the Most High; for he is kind to the ungrateful and the wicked. Be merciful, just as your Father is merciful."

Love, justice, and personal and social accountability are large subjects. This commentary does not match that expansiveness but focuses on the meaning that Jesus's consistent teaching on radical love can have for people today. Is there a meaning that Jesus intended for his audience that is relevant today? He proposes no national policy for international affairs or laws for business ethics in these teachings. But Jesus does address a fundamental spiritual disposition or attitude toward life that challenges all people today.

People call these teachings of Jesus radical in that they refer inward to the sources and roots of the motives that impel people to act. We are dealing with the groundwork for spiritual and moral activity. Jesus calls for what seems to be such ideal behavior that only very rarely do we find anyone acting this way, and, when we do, we wonder about its normalcy. These moral commandments call human beings out of a pervasive set of axioms and consistent ways of behaving justified by theory and practice. We are to love those who love us and treat our enemies in the same way. The world runs on love of family, friends, community, and even nation, and it should respond in measured reciprocity, and occasionally with a preventive "more," to all aggressive acts from outsiders. Jesus's teaching represents either radicalism or an impossible idealism in reference to general society.

Against a background of quid pro quo, Jesus proposes a wholly different set of responses. He commands love of neighbor and then folds enemies into the sphere of those who have a moral purchase on our good will. Some see this as impossible as a normative ethical response and not applicable in social reckoning. I want to find its social implications. Others say it proposes an impossible utopian ideal for eschatological times rather than a realistic moral directive. I want to describe a way in which it can be operative in human life today.

Jesus's teaching transforms the moral sphere itself; this too makes this teaching radical. Jesus consistently broke open the existing boundaries of value; in relation to common practice he changed the persons who were worthy of moral concern. Jesus taught love of the others, the enemies and the outsiders who were made into enemies. And he acted this out. Jesus associated with tax collectors and prostitutes. With this teaching Jesus is challenging the basic conceptions of the moral sphere that were and still are in place in everyday life everywhere.

There is reason to believe that Jesus learned this "new" moral sphere of the rule of God from the Torah. Leviticus taught love of enemies within the Jewish community. "You shall not take vengeance or bear a grudge against any of your people, but you shall love your neighbor as yourself" (Lev 19:18). Exodus commands that people should come to the aid of their enemies when they are in need (cf. Ex 23:4–5). But Jesus saw clearly that all people are neighbors within the sphere of the rule of God, that is, in absolute terms. As Lohfink paraphrases it: "Love of neighbor includes the enemy and precisely in its treatment of the enemy demonstrates itself as genuine love."[40] In the rule of God we see the moral imagination breaking out of tribalism and recognizing the implications that reside in the very idea of God as creator. We also have a concrete norm for measuring the authenticity of love and moral concern.

Another feature of love of enemies is necessary for it to make any sense at all in present-day culture. Love does not mean liking one's enemies but rather responding to their need (cf. Ex 23:4–5), and Jesus's teaching of the Good Samaritan exemplifies it. Love does not refer to a spontaneous impulse. "Love is not a feeling, but a freely chosen attitude. Only so does the command 'Thou shalt love' make sense. No one can command us to feel one way or another. Feelings are simply not subject to commands."[41]

One more point helps to make Jesus's teaching on the inclusive character of the love of neighbor come alive as an always-new foundation for living. This happens when love of neighbor transcends the status of a moral principle, or a universal law that regulates behavior by its application, or even an objective formula that defines the moral scope of the rule of God. When inclusive love of neighbor becomes internalized, it defines a person's fundamental spiritual outlook on the world. A fine example of how this disposition can be awakened is found in the spiritual exercise to attain love of God proposed by Ignatius of

---

[40] Lohfink, *Jesus of Nazareth*, 199.

[41] David Steindl-Rast, *Gratefulness, the Heart of Prayer* (Mahwah, NJ: Paulist Press, 1984), 174. In the words of Lohfink: "Love in the Bible is not primarily deep feeling and unwilling emotion but effective help" (Lohfink, *Jesus of Nazareth*, 198).

Loyola. In a meditation on creation faith, one comes to the internal realization that all is grace; that is, that reality, including oneself, is gift, and that gratitude has to describe a fundamental spiritual attitude or disposition toward being itself.[42] From this source all response to the world flows from a disposition that regards the world itself and one's being in it as gift.

To conclude the analysis of this radical element in Jesus's teaching of the rule of God, we have to explain what must seem like the long route to social responsibility and the impulse to participate in the liberation of people in society. The human race is presently at a loss in its historically conscious and pluralist world to find a ground for social responsibility. If it is to be Jesus's view of the rule of God, one must show how his teaching transcends a sectarian view and applies to the whole of human existence itself. Once again, now through Jesus himself, we are driven back to creation theology and stewardship. We are to love our enemies because they are fellow human beings created and loved by God; we are to love the earth for the same reason. As Calvin stated clearly: "Earthly blessings . . . have all been given us by the kindness of God, and appointed for our use under the condition of being regarded as trusts, of which we must one day give account."[43]

Hope, Purpose, and Courage (Luke 16:19–31)

"There was a rich man who was dressed in purple and fine linen and who feasted sumptuously every day. And at his gate lay a poor man named Lazarus, covered with sores, who longed to satisfy his hunger with what fell from the rich man's table; even the dogs would come and lick his sores. The poor man died and was carried away by the angels to be with Abraham. The rich man also died and was buried. In Hades, where he was being tormented, he looked up and saw Abraham far away with Lazarus by his side. He called out, 'Father Abraham, have mercy on me, and send Lazarus to dip the tip of his finger in water and cool my tongue; for I am in agony in these flames.' But Abraham said, 'Child, remember that during your lifetime you received your good things, and Lazarus in like manner evil things; but now he is comforted here, and you are in agony. Besides all this, between you and us a great chasm has been fixed, so that those who might want to pass from here to you cannot do so, and no one can cross from there to us.' He said, 'Then, father, I beg you to send him to my father's house—for I have five brothers—that he may warn them, so that they will not also come into this place of torment.' Abraham replied, 'They have Moses and the prophets; they should listen to them.' He said,

---

[42] Ignatius Loyola, *The Spiritual Exercises of Saint Ignatius*, nos. 230–37.
[43] John Calvin, *Calvin: Institutes of the Christian Religion*, 3.10.5 (Grand Rapids, MI: Eerdmans), 443–44, available online.

'No, father Abraham; but if someone goes to them from the dead, they will repent.' He said to him, 'If they do not listen to Moses and the prophets, neither will they be convinced even if someone rises from the dead.'"

This story of Jesus deals with practical matters of social justice in Israel. It begins with, focuses upon, and ends with the concerns of the rich man, but his story involves Lazarus, the poor man at his gates. In many ways it is a story of reversal: the rich have their reward in this life but they will suffer in the afterlife; the poor suffer in this life, but they will be drawn into eternal comfort in the afterlife. It is a practical story whose purpose is to warn and challenge Jesus's hearers and the gospel readers today. Does the story have any implications today for people who are conscious of living in an evolutionary world?

The parable revolves around the rich man. He is a construct and has no name. The story mentions no evil deeds. But he did not attend to the poor Lazarus at his gates as a Jew should. In this neglect of his duties he stands condemned by the law and by the prophets. People in Jesus's time knew the texts. The Book of Deuteronomy states: "If there is among you anyone in need, a member of your community in any of your towns within the land that the Lord your God is giving you, do not be hard-hearted or tight-fisted toward your needy neighbor. You should rather open your hand, willingly lending enough to meet the need, whatever it may be" (Deut 15:7–8). And in response to the question of what God wants of us, Isaiah states:

> Is it not to share your bread with the hungry,
>   and bring the homeless poor into your house;
> when you see the naked, to cover them,
>   and not to hide yourself from your own kin? (Isa 58:7)[44]

Despite the dramatic reversal of the fortunes of the rich man and Lazarus, the point revolves around the rich man and whether others will recognize their responsibility, notice the consequences of neglect, and act. The narrative leaves no doubt that the rich man's brothers are headed for the same destiny. But they cannot be contacted, and, if they were, they would be no more moved by a new witness than by the law, the prophets, and the whole Jewish tradition. The story, therefore, in its first and most direct meaning, provides a practical message that communicates a moral and spiritual message of covenant responsibility for the weak and marginalized members of the community. It bears a warning and a challenge because one's eternal destiny is at stake.

One can find a deeper meaning in this story that does not represent its primary intent of practical action but lies embedded in its logic. The question of

---

[44] See Levine, *Short Stories by Jesus*, 270–71.

ultimate justice resides in the contrast between the rich man and the poor man, Lazarus, and in beliefs about eternal reward and punishment in an afterlife. These convictions function as a groundwork for morality; they "provide a sense of justice for those who see the uncaring rich prosper and the poor suffer."[45] In our time overt injustice ranks with innocent suffering as a major challenge to belief in a friendly God; it attacks a hopeful spirituality. "Justice has to be found somewhere. If not in this life, then where? Then when?"[46]

The story of the rich man implicitly responds to the question of ultimate justice. The answer it offers forms the background of the story. It affirms that our universe and our world share a just moral structure. Punishment awaits those who fail to listen and to act according to the responsibilities of the covenant that in Jesus's presentation, the rule of God symbolizes. An ultimate destiny of comfort and fulfillment awaits those whose lives seem meaningless because they are consumed by suffering.

Jesus lived in a coherent world created by God, the ultimate guarantor of justice. Jesus presumed this, and the story appeals to it and reasserts it. He asserted it directly in Luke's version of the Beatitudes. These aphorisms explicitly contrast the fates of the poor and of those rich who neglect the poor. "Blessed are you who are poor, for yours is the kingdom of God" (Luke 6:20). "But woe to you who are rich, for you have received your consolation" (Luke 6:24). The neat correlation of the same teaching in two different forms shows this represents a deeply internalized conviction.

This story of Jesus that entails the order of the universe takes on a third existential meaning in our time when it is confronted with the randomness of evolution. As we noted earlier, when the universe presents itself as a narrative, randomness seems to attack its basic purpose. Although he was not an evolutionist, Jesus thought in the context of time; his vision about life in this world included the past and an absolute future. A stable will of God for justice and human flourishing guided the people of Israel, Jesus, and his later Christian followers. But just as randomness presents new demands on coherence, the framework of evolution releases themes in Jesus's teaching that address present-day self-understanding.

The parable presupposes human freedom and places considerable responsibility upon human agency. The world continues to be created with history; it is not predetermined but consists of a dialogue between God and the people of God. The rule of God is *of God*, but it does not prescind from human participation. The parable also implicitly affirms that human agency has a role in human destiny and the outcome of life. The rich man got what he chose, although it would be

---

[45] Levine, *Short Stories by Jesus*, 265.
[46] Levine, *Short Stories by Jesus*, 265.

monstrous to rejoice in his fate.[47] The parable captures brilliantly the tension between agency and outcome. In response to questioning, it implies that human beings can produce meaning within chaos and thereby participate in creation.

The parable carries a message that is both personal and social; the figures are symbolic and bear collective relevance. The parable supports the concerns of the law and the prophets. The rule of God has a social dimension. The message reminds us that social patterns and the laws of society also have a moral dimension, and they may coordinate with or inhibit the rule of God in history. These questions raised by an evolutionary consciousness affirm, in fact, the liberationist themes of Jewish tradition and give them a cosmological standing in a religious imagination.

To conclude this reflection, the themes of hope, purpose, and courage do not lie on the surface of this story; they subsist within the narrative and its outcome. They can only be released by meditation, by seeking the religious vision hidden within the events and letting it illumine our spiritual dilemmas today. Hope is a fundamental moral disposition of openness and acceptance of existence. It trusts life despite reasons for surrender or despair. Hope always looks for and finds purpose; purpose supplies energy for a healthy life. And, as noted earlier, life cannot actively move forward without courage. This fundamental dynamic of life implicitly affirms a coherent and just universe even though it cannot muster empirical evidence to prove it.

Jesus as Representative of the Presence of God in History

We conclude this chapter with a holistic statement about how Jesus represented the presence of God in history. At this point in the conversation we understand Jesus as *representative* in ordinary or non-technical terms. Anyone who speaks of God represents God. It should be clear, too, that it is impossible to give an adequate summary of how Jesus represented God. The mode of his testimony, not to mention the subject matter and our sources, all prohibit it. Jesus himself still remains a shadowy figure; we have no physical description. Because we cannot understand without our imaginations, we spontaneously supply an image.[48] While this statement may not provide a portrait of the representative, Jesus of Nazareth, it alludes to his representation in a schematic, holistic way. Everyone

---

[47] Levine, *Short Stories by Jesus*, 265.

[48] This can and should at least be chastened by histories of the period and place of Jesus's ministry. As mentioned earlier, this is one among several shortcuts this presentation was forced to take. Notice, too, that I criticized "representative" language about God as being naive. So too, Jesus as representative of God has to be understood in a critical dialectical way.

will do this differently, because every interpretation implicitly listens to immediate contemporary relevance. But there are some common data in the Gospels.

During his relatively short ministry Jesus went around doing good. Mark feeds our imaginations with a typical day in which he taught in the synagogue, exorcised someone possessed, and healed many others who came to him. He healed people morally, spiritually, and physically. To ask how Jesus healed in scientific terms misses the point that he acted in his culture with a religious authority that people found amazing.

Many of Jesus's parables introduced shocking reversals of common conviction. This made them an apt vehicle for representing the rule of God. By dramatizing God's ways as unlike human ways, they provide possibilities for people to be "struck" by that sudden recognition. Such illuminations call assumptions into question and provide a new way of looking at every conceivable human dilemma. We have to notice here how thoroughly the new picture of the universe has contributed to expanding physical horizons. God expands the horizon of life in a different way, beyond the immediate, the empirical, the contractual, and the historical.

The story of a father with two sons attempts to illustrate a God of excessive love and superabundant grace. That appropriately translates into the intimate interpersonal sphere of each one's relation to God in terms of real rebirth and new being. But there is more. That new being mediates liberation and provides a personal platform to engage the world without ultimate fear. It allows a person the freedom to regard the other not as competitor and without resentment but as a friend of God. God grounds the moral imperative for social engagement and reconciliation. It is much deeper than pragmatic reciprocity.

If the rule of God that Jesus represented means the way God intends the world to be and it will be when all is said and done, many of his teachings fall into place. That abstract description only offers a formal and not a material designation. But it helps to locate the phrase *the rule of God* within God's mystery, within the world, and within human hopes. When it first finds lodging in the human imagination, the rule of God gives Jesus's teaching and ministry a holistic framework. This rule of God truly motivated him. We only have fragments of Jesus's teaching, but they fit together within the rule of God, and they apply to everyday life across human history.

Love of enemies directly communicates the radical countercultural character of the rule of God. Impossible! But Jesus is not the first or the only one to recognize all humans as worthy of respect in some absolute way. The Golden Rule abounds across religious traditions. Something metaphysical underlies this categorical imperative. It flows from Jesus's understanding of the rule of God, but anthropologically it may also provide a signal, not a proof, of the existence of God whose Presence is behind it.

The rule of God entails a moral universe. One probably has to add to this proposition the phrase *despite all the evidence to the contrary.* That was always relevant for personal life in the face of setbacks: God guarantees justice in the end. The rule of God also applies directly to a judgment of society. And it becomes still more important metaphysically in an evolutionary world, a theme to be discussed in the final chapter. We need basic trust in existence in order to open the human spirit to the absolute future; we need the courage that hope provides to live with purpose in a world we can only accept as ultimately purposeful by faith. We need confidence that our investment in the world counts. The symbol of the rule of God packs all of this into itself.

These elements of Jesus's teaching and acting out the rule of God add up to a coherent message that does not lie prisoner to an ancient culture. That does not mean that all will understand Jesus's message in the same way, let alone commit to it. But it provides a framework of intelligibility that allows conversation. Most of what Jesus offers as God's representative appeals to universal human aspiration, whether it satisfies or not.

After Jesus's death and the recognition by his followers that he was alive by the power of God and within the sphere of God, attention slowly began to bend back on the revealer or the messenger of God. Gradually the term *representative* took on new metaphysical meaning. Thus was born the theological project of Christology: understanding Jesus as the Christ. The following chapter engages that question. The context of evolution will have greater impact on that formal theological discipline.

7

Christology from Within

This chapter addresses the interpretation of Jesus of Nazareth as the Christ and a formal Christology. Creation entails the immanence of God, and evolution shows the seamless integrity of nature across time. God, as the power of being and Spirit, sustains and accompanies evolution in the direction of greater complexity. Can Jesus as divine savior be drawn into this framework? The chapter treats Jesus's resurrection, the salvation he mediates, and his divinity, and at the same time preserves christological tradition.

We continue the project of understanding the person and role of Jesus Christ in Christian faith within the context of evolution. This began with early chapters that laid out a new context for theology. The following chapters added new premises for thinking about Jesus Christ. For example, as the doctrine of original sin assumed great importance in Western Christianity, so too did the idea that Jesus entered into this world from outside it to accomplish an atonement with God. But an evolutionary world has no place for an original sin.[1] We introduce this chapter, then, by setting the stage for a theological development of christological thinking that attends to our evolutionary context and still keeps close to the sources and tradition. Christology "from within" does not deny the merits of Christology "from above" (the otherness of God) and "from below" (recognizing Jesus's human status) but rather refocuses those accents into a way of thinking suggested by evolution.

The premise for reflection on Jesus Christ in an evolutionary world was set in Chapter 3, namely, the Presence of God within all reality. We should not think of Jesus Christ as an intervention into the universe, our world, or our humanity. Cletus Wessels expressed this well: "God does not act as an external cause of

---

[1] "There is need for a savior, but it is not because of an original sin and a fallen nature. Thus, there is no need for Jesus as our savior to redeem us objectively and ontologically from such a sin and its consequences" (Cletus Wessels, *Jesus in the New Universe Story* [Maryknoll, NY: Orbis Books, 2003], 188).

the universe, but as an internal cause of the unfolding of the mysterious web of relationships found everywhere . . . in the entire universe. And *how* does God act in this emerging universe? All the evidence leads us to a sense of a God acting and unfolding from within as the immediate inner source of all that is."[2] This view takes us out of a mythological understanding of a distinct Word of God "up there" coming down and going back again. We have to break out of that imaginative framework, exploit the gains of creation theology, and think in terms of God within.

The large issues for Christology should be placed on the table at the beginning of our reflection. They are many, but I will concentrate on three that contain a theological structure for understanding Jesus's salvific role and person. Following a presentation of Jesus's ministry, a first question concerns the resurrection. Unfortunately, Jesus's resurrection came to be understood as an empirical event that appeals to the imagination. In fact, we find no portrayal of the resurrection in the New Testament. Rather, we have stories of apparitions and testimonies that people "saw" him. In an evolutionary context these still seem like miraculous interventions.

A second basic issue centers on salvation. The experience of salvation that disciples felt and still feel supports various interpretations of Jesus, but a wide variety of metaphors are used to express what salvation means. What did Jesus do for human salvation? Can we draw out what people experienced as salvation in readily accessible terms that can be appropriated in an evolutionary consciousness? This remains the keystone of Christology; the basis and the coherence of affirming the divinity of Jesus depends on how one understands Jesus being savior. We already have a start on that from consideration of Jesus's ministry.

A third issue lies embedded in the confession of the divinity of Jesus. This doctrine developed through an extended and exceptionally complicated debate during the early centuries of Christianity, obviously prior to evolutionary consciousness. It continued to develop even though classic formulas remain in place. But critical historical consciousness now recognizes that the "classic" language is culture bound and, in fact, misleads. We need new language to preserve its original meaning.

This reflection on Christology in an evolutionary context is structured around three significant affirmations that respond to these questions. The first asserts that Jesus was raised by God from death. That conviction has to be discussed in terms of the experience that originally gave rise to it and still does today. The second affirmation states the universal relevance of Jesus Christ for the world today with the term *salvation.* But how does one explain that? Many christologies dot the landscape of the New Testament, the history of theology, and our present situation. All of them derive from the experience of salvation that Jesus

---

[2] Wessels, *Jesus in the New Universe Story*, 58.

mediated. How may we understand that salvation as a common generative experience that also makes sense in an evolutionary world?

The third affirmation addresses the formal christological problem and holds the divinity of Jesus Christ. But how should we understand it? Can Christians maintain the divinity of Jesus in a way that does not appear absurd on the face of it, makes sense in a context of evolution, and stays faithful to the intent of the classic formulas while not denigrating other religions? An appropriation of these three traditional christological questions in an evolutionary context is the basic task of this chapter.

The Experience That Jesus Is Risen

We begin this understanding of Jesus Christ with a consideration of the resurrection. The resurrection lies between the followers of Jesus laid low by the event of his execution and their proclaiming his being alive with God and taking up his preaching of the rule of God with him as its mediator. The idea of resurrection means that in death Jesus was received into God's power of life; he did not cease to exist as a person but lives within the sphere of God. After death Jesus continues to exist by the power of the creator God. Like creation, the event of entering this new sphere of being cannot be imagined; dying into the incomprehensible mystery of God lies on the other side of empirical evidence and completely transcends our power to know positively. One can approach this unimaginable mystery, however, through a consideration of the experience that generated the conviction. Edward Schillebeeckx calls this the "Easter experience," that which gave rise to the affirmation that Jesus is alive.[3] Before the Easter experience the followers of Jesus had to deal with the crash of their hopes in what his ministry promised. Yet sometime later—we do not know how long afterward or when or where it got started—his followers proclaimed that Jesus was alive and that he inspired their mission.

How was this Easter experience generated? We do not know, but exegetes and theologians offer various theories. Some take the stories of Jesus's appearances at face value, but such interventionism is not plausible in an evolutionary context. It is more reasonable to read the stories as conceived after and within the Easter experience and written to communicate or bear witness to the object of faith: Jesus is risen. The coming to an awareness and conviction that Jesus

---

[3] Edward Schillebeeckx, *Jesus: An Experiment in Christology* (New York: Seabury, 1979), 379–97. The Easter experience and the resurrection are not the same. The one was an experience of the disciples; the other happened to Jesus. The Easter experience was the epistemological event that enabled the disciples to affirm that Jesus was raised. What follows is not a reduction of Jesus's real resurrection to experience of him or his memory but an attempt to understand how we can affirm Jesus's real resurrection.

lives can be understood as a gradual process that transpired within the community of followers. The appearance story offered by Luke of a daylong coming to such an awareness by two disciples as they traveled from Jerusalem to Emmaus, however, has a beginning, a middle, and an end. The story can be read as an allegory for the process by which Jesus's disillusioned followers came to recognize his dying into eternal life within the sphere of God.

The story has a straightforward development to its conclusion (cf. Luke 24:13–35). Two disciples of Jesus are on their way to Emmaus. They are joined by another to whom they confess their loss and disorientation. The story informs the reader that the fellow traveler is Jesus himself, but he remains unrecognized. The incognito Jesus then explains to the travelers how the Hebrew scriptures contain the explanation for Jesus's being handed over and killed. At the end of the journey the three travelers share a meal, and the two recognized Jesus in the breaking of the bread, at which point he disappears. They returned to Jerusalem to announce that Jesus is risen. Taken as an allegory, in which the two travelers represent the community of the disciples of Jesus, the story presents a plausible scenario for the gradual genesis of the Easter experience for which meals together provide a context of remembering stories of Jesus, recalling scripture, and sharing experience.

The story within the story, at least in its structure, also seems possible and even probable.[4] It represents a conversion, and the narrative tells how it happened. The story tells of those who were so moved by Jesus's ministry that they could be counted as followers. It begins with the destruction of their hopes. But the followers did not simply disband; they formed a group that tried to understand what happened. The entire New Testament shows that to do this they turned to the Hebrew scriptures. The story proposes that these Jewish Jesus people assembled for meals not unlike those shared during Jesus's ministry. At and through the sharing of meals together in the memory of Jesus, they recognized he was alive; "he had been made known to them in the breaking of the bread" (Luke 24:35).

In *Jesus Symbol of God* I formulated four elements that add up to an abstract account of the Easter experience of the earliest followers of Jesus.[5] These four dimensions can also be found in the conviction of Christians today, if they affirm the resurrection on the basis of more than external authority. The first element

---

[4] I rely on Hans Dieter Betz, "The Origin and Nature of Christian Faith according to the Emmaus Legend," *Interpretation* 23 (January 1969): 32–46. I focus on an allegorical structure to make a plausible historical speculation where few exist. But the Emmaus story on its own qualifies as a religious and literary masterpiece.

[5] For a fuller analysis of these dimensions, see Roger Haight, *Jesus Symbol of God* (Maryknoll, NY: Orbis Books, 1999), 140–46. Peter Carnley offers an analogous theory of the structure of resurrection faith (*The Structure of Resurrection Belief* [Oxford: Clarendon Press, 1987]). For a brief comparison of this account with Carnley's, see Haight, *Jesus Symbol of God*, 146–47n54.

consists of a public memory of Jesus of Nazareth. He is the object, or subject matter, of the resurrection. In the case of Jesus's disciples, they shared a vivid recent memory; for later Christians, the Gospels and the church preserve and communicate the memory of Jesus. The content of Jesus's ministry to the rule of God forms an essential part of this scenario. The second element is stipulated as an existential given: attention to Jesus presumes a predisposition of interest that constitutes an initial faith and hope. Spiritual and religious seeking entails a personal engagement distinct from mere curiosity about human behavior. The story of Jesus's ministry draws one in. A conviction about Jesus's resurrection entails the self, in the present and oriented toward the future. Third, the experience or conviction that Jesus has been raised comes as a grace or an enlightenment. The theological term *grace* was explained in Chapter 4. It indicates how the insight and conviction come to the self rather than being generated by the self; it involves God as Presence; the Easter experience includes a moment of grace, a gratuitous intuition into the way things are. And, fourth, these epistemological dimensions of the experience of hope and faith are prior to the accounts of appearances and visions that are found in the Gospels. The stories communicate the "fact" of Jesus's resurrection as testimonies of hope and faith rather than supply objective evidence for it. In other words the spiritual experience that Jesus lives with God accounts for the stories that, in turn, communicate the conviction. The tight structure of the Emmaus story makes it a concise vehicle for preaching these basic ideas.

With this theory in mind we turn now to the question of whether it opens up the resurrection of Jesus to the demands of an evolutionary conception of our finite world. The previous chapters form the background of this discussion. As a first reflection this view of Easter faith removes the overt supernaturalism of the accounts of Jesus's appearances to his disciples and others after his death. There was a time when these stories were considered objective historical descriptions or reports of events. As such, they provided motives for believing in the resurrection of Jesus. The disciples saw him alive and had interchanges with him. In later times of historical criticism and scientific criticism, these stories were gradually transformed into obstacles to faith; they helped make the resurrection appear to be fantastic. In short, literary, historical, and scientific criticism help to show more realistically the status and function of the gospel stories.

More explicitly, as Chapter 3 on creation in an evolutionary framework showed, God's proper action of creating can be neither perceived nor even imagined accurately. God's action in the world cannot be depicted in worldly terms as a finite agency that is part of the material or empirical system of interaction. So too, Jesus's resurrection cannot be an empirical event; it is precisely a passing out of materiality, as we know it, into the sphere of God that transcends the finite world to which the human remains are returned. For the New Testament writers, to be solidly true, the finite world had to be material and tangible; not to be so would not be real.[6] Jesus alive had to be depicted sensibly.

From a critical theological perspective one should not imagine the recognition of Jesus's resurrection and, more generally, of the resurrection of the dead, as a material or sensible perception, but a spiritual conviction that was and is mediated though a host of external and interior motives. This judgment, however, requires nuance, because all human cognition comes mediated through the material world and engages the human imagination. In principle, however, material evidence alone cannot produce faith in Jesus's resurrection; it requires a complex commingling of external testimony, internal concern for one's origin and destiny, and the divine creating Presence of God within called Spirit and grace.

Finally, in this view the place of Jesus's resurrection within the larger context of the meaning of Jesus Christ for Christian faith takes on profound significance. We have already seen how the new conviction that Jesus was raised transformed the disciples and accounts for a new phase of the Jesus movement. After the Easter experience a richer and more expansive interpreting of Jesus began. The logic of this experience ultimately carried Christians beyond the conviction that Jesus was the messiah. Generally speaking, the messiah was a human being, or a creaturely agent of God, rather than a divine figure.[7] So deep was the experience of salvation mediated by Jesus that divine qualities began to be associated with his person. The Easter experience and belief in Jesus's resurrection called forth a new appreciation of Jesus's connection with God. And because he was a human being like us, he presents a model for the hope that we will explore in the next chapter.

The Universal Relevance of Jesus Christ

The religious relevance of Jesus Christ lies in the salvation he mediates to the world. Theological interpretation of the Christian beliefs about Jesus Christ have their roots in the experience of God's salvation that he represents and communicates. How can we conceive a salvation mediated by Jesus Christ that

---

[6] The stories of Jesus's appearances offer strong evidence for this impression. John has Jesus inviting Thomas to stick his finger into Jesus's wounds (John 20:27) and eating with the disciples (John 21:12); Luke has Jesus floating up into heaven (Acts 1:9–10). The physicality ensures the reality of resurrection.

[7] The earliest tradition is much more complicated than this, because the universe was populated with various beings between God and finite human beings. For example, Jesus was associated with a "divine" Son of Man. See the works of Daniel Boyarin, *Border Lines: The Partition of Judaeo-Christianity* (Philadelphia: University of Pennsylvania Press, 2004) and *The Jewish Gospels: The Story of the Jewish Christ* (New York: The New Press, 2012). The Son of Man was a divine figure, but he was not Yahweh. Jesus was also interpreted as an angel. In brief, much depends on the meaning of a strictly divine figure.

is faithful to the tradition, universally relevant, and respectful of the autonomy of other faith traditions that in their own way also offer salvation?

A first step in understanding salvation in Christian terms consists in forming a relatively simple abstract preconception of salvation as a working definition. Gustavo Gutiérrez offers a short but comprehensive and accurate conception of salvation as the communion of people with God and the communion of people among themselves.[8] Despite the expansiveness of this conception, it possesses practical merits. It speaks from a concrete historical perspective. For example, it readily encompasses the work of Jesus during his ministry; his preaching and his faith healing affected people in a salvific way. The rule of God entails this salvation now and in the future. It intends an actual relationship with God and promises fulfillment. The salvation offered by Jesus Christ cannot be reduced to an imaginary transaction that occurred above history. Salvation consists of an existential reality and not something that happened apart from us. It refers to something that occurs in history in such a way that it can be experienced now as "the pledge of our inheritance toward redemption as God's own people, to the praise of his glory" (Eph 1:14).[9]

The requirement that we keep our understanding of the experience of salvation tied to history raises two questions: the first asks for a closer inspection of what salvation refers to as something that Jesus did and we receive; the second probes the genesis and status of the many different conceptions of salvation found in the scriptures and the history of Christian thought.

Regarding the first question, and in keeping with earlier theological moves of this book, understanding salvation within the sphere of revelation helps to simplify its dynamics. Salvation as a form of consciousness consists of coming to an awareness of God's relation to us and the contours of that relationship. In this view, promoted by John's Gospel,[10] Jesus saves by revealing God; he bears the Word of God. To clarify by contrast, the universe is not divided by a before and after Jesus, nor is God changed by the particular Jesus events in Palestine. Rather, Jesus's ministry effected a new revelation of God; continuous with Jewish religious history, it shares much in common with it and with other religious

---

[8] See Gustavo Gutiérrez, *A Theology of Liberation: History, Politics, and Salvation* (Maryknoll, NY: Orbis Books, 1973), 151.

[9] In keeping with Paul's text, we speak of the experience of salvation mediated by Jesus to people in this world in this chapter and a rather apophatic theory of the objective condition of everlasting life in the next.

[10] The author of John's Gospel writes toward the end of it that "these [signs] are written that you may believe that Jesus is the Christ, the Son of God, and that believing you may have life in his name" (John 20:31; also 21:24–25). The stress on belief suggests that the point of Jesus's ministry is a revelatory appeal to faith in its salvific relevance for each person. This view of salvation as revelation requires more theological reflection that cannot be entertained here on various forms and levels of conscious revelation, including terms like *implied consciousness*.

traditions. This particular revelation of God in Jesus is true and meant for all of humankind because it is true.[11] This revelation also qualifies as effective; it causes the experience of God's salvation within human lives.

The second question asks how we should understand the different conceptions of salvation in Christian tradition. We may look for an answer in the history that followed the Easter experience. The story remains somewhat speculative because we have so little direct evidence of the earliest years of the Jesus movement. But these abstract data seem to be certain. The followers of Jesus continued to meet in the context of temple and synagogue, to remember Jesus, confess their experience of him, tell stories about him, and generally try to figure out what had happened in the Jesus event and its implications. Resources for this included the Hebrew scriptures. From these creative gatherings, firmly anchored within Judaism, came the first conceptions of what God was doing in the events of Jesus's death in the new light of his being alive with God. One can readily imagine followers of Jesus engaged in a process of reflecting on the scriptures and how, out of their existential question, they found many references that seemed actually to describe his ministry and its climax or were used creatively to interpret it. Jesus was Isaiah's Suffering Servant, the Son of Man, the Pascal Lamb, the Wisdom of God, the Word of God.

In this story the status of the various "theories" of salvation or redemption generated in the extended conversation begin to fall into place. They put words around the basic revelatory experience mediated by Jesus: how people stand in relation to God and to one another, not only as persons but as groups, and the promised meaning of existence itself in the light of Jesus's resurrection. We should not confine this experience to a time in the past; people within the movement continued to encounter him because Jesus was alive and the community related to him. As the Jesus movement spread, the metaphors and conceptions of a divine logic behind the mediation of Jesus were multiplied. The New Testament provides a large number of "transcendent conceptions of salvation," that is, supra-historical rationales of what was going on: Jesus freed us from captivity to sin; Jesus redeemed us; Jesus reconciled us with God; Jesus suffered for our sins; Jesus was sacrificed for us. These saving actions gave him various titles: Jesus was the final high priest; Jesus was the Lamb of God; Jesus was the Word of God; Jesus was the son or servant of God, or the divine Son of Man; Jesus was the final prophet; Jesus was redeemer;

---

[11] This truth does not undermine the truth of other religious revelations. On the basis of the conclusions of Chapter 3 and Chapter 4, we are not operating here in a competitive sphere. God, and thus God's love and grace, define the being of all humans and other creatures as well. The view of God's revelation breaking through to human consciousness through various mediations helps explain the exclamation of Peter: "I truly understand that God shows no partiality, but in every nation anyone who fears him and does what is right is acceptable to him" (Acts 10:34–35). We return to this theme at the end of the chapter.

Jesus was Lord.[12] These titles and the projected scenarios behind them arose out of the continued experience of God that was initially mediated in Jesus's ministry. They should not be reckoned as revealed scenarios in the sense of information about transcendent goings on. They represent grace-filled projections based in a spiritual or religious experience constructed by the cultural tools that were at hand.

The objective salvation story told by Anselm at the end of the eleventh century offers a classic example of this process. He wrote in the theological tradition of Augustine but put such a sharp, clean point on Jesus's suffering to achieve divine "satisfaction" that his theory completely dominated the Western theological imagination. Adam's sin offended God infinitely, so the scales of cosmic justice could only be restored by a human who was the guilty party and a satisfaction that was infinite and equal to the offense. This accounts for the divine plan of a God-man whose self-sacrifice accomplished both simultaneously. Elizabeth Johnson patiently exposes the current unintelligibility of this conception and replaces it with scriptural witness that essentially describes the experience of a Christian who has internalized the message of Jesus of Nazareth.[13]

The salvation that Christians profess comes from God through Jesus of Nazareth requires several qualifications to prevent misunderstanding. One of these may be stated absolutely: God's salvation preexists the appearance of Jesus in history. As was made clear in earlier chapters, God is present to and exists within all of God's creation from the very beginning. In the words of Cletus Wessels: "In every race and every religion and wherever and whenever reconciliation, healing, and liberation are found, there is salvation. This salvation unfolds from the loving presence of God within us."[14] Jesus and his ministry did not constitute but revealed the availability of salvation and, as our scriptures testify, not for the first time. With his ministry Jesus revealed salvation in his distinct way. Jesus appeared within the historical context of God's self-revelation to Israel over centuries, and that revelation provided the substantial content of his ministry. But Jesus was a particular revelation of God as Presence as it appeared in his ministry. This tension of the particular and universal dimensions in Jesus's mediation of salvation

---

[12] These and other conceptions of God, of Jesus as God's revealer, of the process of salvation, and of Jesus as savior are expanded in Schillebeeckx's magisterial exegetical study of Jesus and salvation that covers all the books of the New Testament: Edward Schillebeeckx, *Jesus: An Experiment in Christology* (New York: Seabury Press, 1979) and *Christ: The Experience of Jesus as Lord* (New York: Seabury Press, 1980).

[13] See Elizabeth A. Johnson, *Creation and the Cross: The Mercy of God for a Planet in Peril* (Maryknoll, NY: Orbis Books, 2018), 1–30.

[14] Wessels, *Jesus in the New Universe Story*, 187. He adds: "In terms of the emerging universe, salvation can now be described in new terms such as restoration, transformation, reconciliation, and renewal, and it is possible to transfer these new ideas to the social, political, and religious spheres."

clarifies many of the problems that seem to be a source of endless confusion in Christian faith. Jesus's mediation of God's salvation distinctively witnesses to and communicates a salvation that has gone on from the beginning. Appropriation of this in Jesus's name constitutes *Christian* salvation.[15]

The particularity of Jesus's ministry means that he and his ministry were an essential part of his mediation of salvation. Christian salvation is Christian because it consists of Jesus introducing people into God's Presence, just as Jewish salvation means that Torah and prophetic witness communicate it. Jesus constitutes the distinctive character of the Christian experience of God's salvation. Jesus's revelation does not refer to an idea that he let loose so that it could float around detached from his memory. His ministry constituted this revelation as an actual consciousness of the people he addressed; Jesus communicated his own witness and mediation of God's salvation out of his own "consciousness of God."[16] His person constituted his revealing of the message of salvation; *he* delivered his message or revelation; as mediator, he mediated, embodied, and symbolized salvation. But Jesus's distinctive God-consciousness need not be thought of as exclusive; it does not compete with God's being present to and arising to consciousness through and within other faith traditions. This later Christian appreciation has only recently emerged and been made public by interfaith dialogue, Christian theology of religion, and comparative theologies within a more general historical and pluralistic consciousness. The development fits neatly within an evolutionary worldview.

How may we understand the Christian doctrine of the finality of Jesus Christ in this context? On the one hand, this conviction appears to be intrinsic to the encounter with God in Jesus's person and ministry. The stability of faith finds its roots in Jesus's representation of God. On the other hand, the belief seems threatened by an equally strong persuasion that God's Presence operates in other faith traditions. These two commitments, however, can coalesce in a recognition of where the finality lies, its basic logic. Jesus bears a particular, historical revelation of the universal rule of God. What is "final" refers to the rule of God that Jesus preached. Rather than looking at finality as one of a set of public doctrines about Jesus that can be compared with the teachings of other religions, one should consider how finality applies to Jesus's teaching

---

[15] It may not be redundant to notice here that this view of Jesus saving corresponds with what Jesus did during his ministry. This counters a trend that moves beyond Jesus's ministry and uses it as an occasion for theological speculation. The result often takes the metaphors for appreciating Jesus's saving ministry and literalizes them into transactions going on above history instead of keeping the object of interpretation in focus.

[16] The phrase, usually translated as "God-consciousness," is drawn from Friedrich Schleiermacher, *The Christian Faith* (London: Bloomsbury T & T Clark, 2016). But with specific reference to our point here, see his thesis #100: "The Redeemer assumes believers into the power of His God-consciousness, and this is his redemptive activity" (Schleiermacher, *The Christian Faith*, 425ff.).

and what his teaching means when it has been internalized by his followers. Jesus's finality means he reveals a pattern of life that matches the rule of God as being operative in and open to all.[17] We can reclaim the idea of the finality of Christ when we recognize that "the claim entails both recognition of God's decisive action in Christ and the decision to embrace Jesus's command: "Love one another as I have loved you" (John 15:12)."[18]

Before considering the understanding of the person Jesus Christ in an evolutionary context, it is helpful to portray the depth entailed in salvation construed in terms of revelation. John's Gospel presents salvation in revelatory terms. When the Prologue declares that God's Word of power, revelation, and communication became incarnate in the material of this world (cf. John 1:1, 14), the process assumes an ontological character. Clearly, this text had Jesus in mind, but the majesty of the image extends still further to creation itself. One cannot imagine a more magnificent and yet more intimate formula of incarnation than creation: created actuation by pure being itself and involving its personal Presence. Creation provides the basis for God within. Creation, affirmed in the context of an immense universe and a quiet experience of God within the self, provides the foundation for the meaningfulness of the term *incarnation* today. This idea of incarnation, rooted in creation, provides the ground and the sacrality of an autonomous secular universe, world, and culture. These images help to draw out the meaning of Jesus's rule of God for our time.

Another aperture opened up by creation theology for viewing and appreciating the meaning of salvation in our day doubles back to enhance our estimation of the human. This constant theme has no better defender than Karl Rahner, unless it is Irenaeus.[19] The depth of our estimation of human existence itself can be measured by our appreciation of God as incarnate. Like John's Gospel, Rahner thinks of incarnation as measured by the case of Jesus, but what he intends becomes a deeper and more magnificent vision when it takes the shape of creation itself. Human existence forms a part of the pictures of the universe that telescopes today are able to capture. While our imaginations cannot begin to

---

[17] "Rather than a 'totality of meaning,' the claim to finality says that in Jesus we discover the key to God's salvific action in human affairs. By calling his community to move beyond tribal forms of identity and exclusion, Jesus reveals God's desire for us to share in God's universal reconciliation of the human family by entering into the kinds of relationships that Jesus modeled." Christiaan Jacobs-Vandegeer, "The Finality of Christ and the Religious Alternative," *Theological Studies* 78 (2017): 364.

[18] Jacobs-Vandegeer, "The Finality of Christ and the Religious Alternative," 368.

[19] Irenaeus, the Greek-speaking bishop of Lyon in France in the late second century, wrote these words that continue to inspire: "For the glory of God is a living man; and the life of man consists in beholding God. For if the manifestation of God which is made by means of the creation, affords life to all living in the earth, much more does that revelation of the Father which comes through the Word, give life to those who see God" (*Against Heresies,* Bk IV, chap. 20; translation from www.newadvent.org).

sort those images out, and comparative demonstrations leave us in sheer wonder, God's active Presence sustaining the whole of creation both saves us from utter insignificance and ratifies the self-importance that all should feel about themselves. In his difficult prose Rahner states that human existence "comes to be when God's self-expression, God's Word, is uttered into the emptiness of the Godless void in love." He then follows this up: "When God wants to be what is not God, man comes to be. This of course does not define man in terms of the flatness of the ordinary and the everyday, but introduces him into the ever incomprehensible mystery. But he is this mystery."[20] In short, belief in the incarnation entailed in creation constitutes faith in human existence as something substantial and grounded because it has been created by God as the climax of evolution. Looking back, Jesus's preaching of the rule of God encompasses much of this.

Christology in an Evolutionary Context

We proceed to a consideration of formal Christology, the examination of the status of the person of Jesus Christ as the mediator of Christian faith. The following is little more than an outline in the face of the history and current discussion of Christology. Nevertheless, some pointed goals govern this analysis. We intend to preserve the essential message found in the New Testament and the classic doctrines and draw them forward in a way that renders them intelligible within an evolutionary world. The strategy to accomplish this first directs attention to understanding the experience that generated the sources of Christology and then represents this experience in present-day language attentive to evolution.

It must be presumed that readers appreciate the complexity of the theological discussion of Jesus Christ. It is virtually impossible to make any substantial claim that is not contested. This situation requires clear statement. The exposition, therefore, is structured with an overt logic that carries the reasoning. It moves from a statement of method, to the distinctive problems that evolution has raised, to the Pauline metaphor that guides the construction, to a consideration of the divinity of Jesus and a way of expressing it. The conclusion of this chapter reviews how the proposed Christology preserves the meaning of Christian tradition while fitting the evolutionary character of reality.

Method and Criteria

A theological conclusion on a given subject matter often depends on the presuppositions and method used to address it. This suggests that method bears more significance than conveyed by the often dry, formal, and abstract discussions

---

[20] Karl Rahner, *Foundations of Christian Faith: An Introduction to the Idea of Christianity* (New York: Crossroad, 1994), 224, 225.

of it. Theological positions cannot really be understood without attention to the logic underlying and producing the assertions. The correlational method used here consists of interpretation. First, it seeks to find an existential meaning in the sources of theology, that is, the kind of insight that motivated the given witness. But, second, to enable current understanding one has to bring what is understood as the early foundational experience forward into a different context and reframe it analogously within a present-day setting. The history of theology proves that this process does not yield a mathematical precision. But some objective and existential criteria control excess.

Consider this formula:

Content x in the context of X = Content y in the context of Y

On the objective side one has to consult exegetes and historians who reconstruct original meanings of our sources in their context $(x$ in $X)$.[21] And in the dialogue with present culture, we have to rely on various scientific descriptions of the world in which we live (a constructed y in Y). Both of these parameters influence but do not finally determine interpreted meaning. By definition the sameness of the past confessions and present-day confessions cannot be identical as in literal repetition; repetition itself generates new meaning in new contexts. Therefore, one cannot find an exact one-to-one transfer of meaning across different cultures and languages; translation always yields an analogy where the interpretation produces something partly the same and partly different. More exactly, the different expressions, although not exactly the same, are proportionate relative to the particular context. For example, the idea of creation expressed as evolutionary development communicates to faith today in a way that is proportionate to the way a mythological form functions in biblical consciousness.[22]

Another existential criterion helps to authenticate the proportion of the analogies between the conceptions of different cultures. The objective criterion addresses whether the statements of faith are intelligible in terms of what we know about reality. But one has to turn to an existential criterion to determine whether proposals support and empower Christian spirituality. Do they resonate with experience and enhance the meaningful character of everyday life? Do they make spiritual sense, not in terms of the language of the past that has been reinterpreted, but in terms of life today in relation to God and to our actual world? For example, in the previous discussion of salvation, that term really makes no sense without some appeal to spiritual experience. Some people resent the very idea that some religion offers them salvation. An existential criterion

---

[21] These meanings are often quite different than reading them off the page suggests.

[22] Edward Schillebeeckx explains this clearly in *Church: The Human Story of God* (New York: Crossroad, 1990), 40–43. The idea of biblical consciousness does not refer directly to the consciousness of authors but to the meaning that is preserved in the world of the texts.

moves beyond notional coherence and an intellectual conviction of the truth and reality of salvation; it operates with respect to an actual internal resonance. It follows that a basic criterion for the meaningfulness of christological doctrines lies in some experience of salvation from God mediated through Jesus. This existential criterion accounts for the genesis of doctrines in the first place, and it determines whether the truthfulness of theological construction is effective.

Formal Christological Issues Raised by Evolution

Christology deals with a host of questions that are either perennial or specific to a culture. The evolutionary point of entry highlights three issues that put a finer point on formal Christology, which deals with the status of the person of Jesus. The first of these arises simply by attending to a new scientific worldview; it consists of the challenge that an evolutionary world poses to ordinary christological speech. It is commonplace to think of Jesus as an incarnation of God: God has come down and assumed earthly human flesh. Jesus Christ becomes the archetypal intervention of God into history; God becomes an actor in history, and the world is different before and after Jesus Christ. But evolution challenges this established Christology, and the challenge cannot be accommodated by an interventionist view. Evolution must be treated as an a priori part of the situation that asks the christological question; evolution has to be the premise from which the understanding begins to take shape. Evolution thus shapes the discussion from a perspective that calls into question a *descent* Christology in which Logos or the Son appears to be an intervention into history. It leads the discussion toward a Christology understood in terms of an *internal dynamic* that is aligned with creation itself and the working of Presence as Spirit within.

The second issue, in some ways, transcends the focus on evolution. The classic formula of the Council of Chalcedon held that Jesus Christ was one person with two natures, thereby asserting that Jesus was both human and divine. But reflective consideration calls this language into question. The technical meaning of *nature* was undecided and contentious at the time of the council, and the common sense meaning of the term when predicated of God refers to absolute incomprehensible mystery that in no way corresponds with finite natures. The formula of two natures implicitly affirms something absolutely unknown of Jesus as if it were accessible and even comparable to human nature. The formula has a linguistic provenance generated by an analytical philosophical perspective—not a bad thing. But it took over the imagination and left the narrative perspective of Jesus's ministry behind. In the end, "one person with two natures" says nothing more than what experience of salvation tells us: God's Presence was shown or manifested to us in the person and ministry of Jesus. A second problem in Christology, then, consists of revising the two-nature theology, and evolution may help us here.

The third issue flows from our culture today, which has encouraged a new positive openness to other revelations and other faith traditions. It does not read Christianity or Jesus Christ in exclusive terms as the only savior or even in inclusive terms as the absolute savior who effects the salvation of all whether they know it or not. More Christians than ever before have a particularist notion of Christian salvation as one among the media and forms of other faith traditions. The classical world has been shattered by historical and pluralist consciousness, and many can no longer embrace a competitive conception of religious worldviews. The question here is fairly precise: Can one overcome relativism and offer a universally relevant understanding of Jesus Christ that fits this culturally evolutionary world and still retains the substance of traditional faith?

Jesus as Second, New, and Final Adam

We begin a constructive interpretation of Jesus Christ with a New Testament Christology that is dear to Paul. Usually called a "second Adam" Christology, it, like others, attributes distinctive qualities to Jesus. The primal character of this metaphor resonates with Paul's experience. This Christology focuses on the ministry of Jesus and his destiny, places these in the massive context of creation and the length of human history, and then opens up the theme of human destiny in resurrection. Its classic statement occurs in Romans 5:12–21.[23] The following verses provide the core comparison and contrast between Adam and Jesus:

> Therefore just as one man's trespass led to condemnation for all, so one man's act of righteousness leads to justification and life for all. For just as by the one man's disobedience the many were made sinners, so by the one man's obedience the many will be made righteous. (Rom 5:18–19)

This is one among a large number of New Testament christologies.[24] A brief commentary on this important example sets a framework for further constructive interpretation. Paul is writing to Jewish Christians and explaining to them who Jesus is in terms of their tradition. He focuses on Jesus of Nazareth, the human being, and his ministry, abstractly in terms of obedience. This is Paul's interpretation, but it allows Jesus to be his own witness by the pattern of his

---

[23] It also appears in Paul's 1 Corinthians 15:21–23, 45–49. For an analysis of this Christology, see Haight, *Jesus Symbol of God*, 156–59. That work also examines Mark's view of Jesus as Son of God, Luke's Jesus as prophet and healer empowered by the Spirit, a number of passages that depict Jesus as the Wisdom of God, and the classic statement in the Prologue of John's Gospel that Jesus is the Logos or Word of God (*Jesus Symbol of God*, 159–78).

[24] See Frank Matera, *New Testament Christology* (Louisville, KY: Westminster John Knox Press, 1999).

ministerial obedience. This appears clearly in the contrast with Adam. Against the background of the symbol Adam and all his disobedience stood for, Jesus's ministry represents fidelity to the will of God, to the rule of God. The contrast of opposite consequences is equally dramatic. Adam's disobedience led to death and destruction in history, whereas the righteousness of Jesus's obedience to the rule of God led to his resurrection and promises life for all. The contrast and implicit replacement of Adam with Jesus as a new paradigm of human existence releases forceful, pointed meaning for Paul's readers.[25]

Note the reflective and expansive horizon that this straightforward contrast offers to an understanding of Jesus Christ in an evolutionary context. Although the metaphor of a second, new Adam involves a simple functional contrast between disobedience and obedience, it says much more by implying a metaphysical or visionary framework. Adam is primal: the first created human and father of the race. Paul thus proposes that Jesus has become the new source of a faithful humanity. Paul's imagination encompasses all creation and the whole of human history. But he does not leap into the sky and appeal to a son of man coming from heaven or an incarnation of a personified word of God. Paul, here, appeals to Jesus's obedience and implicitly to the meaningfulness of his ministry to the rule of God. This particular Christology of Paul provides a good model for approaching an interpretation of Jesus that will stay close to history in order to see how the power of God has become manifested within the events of history. This does not imply any minimization of other New Testament christologies; they do not compete with one another. But this constructive metaphor of Jesus as a new Adam can readily absorb others into itself.

Thinking about the Divinity of Jesus

The Christian conclusion that Jesus of Nazareth was a divine figure resulted from a discussion that lasted about three hundred years. The debate included contrary positions in a step-by-step logic that depended on cultural assumptions and a literal kind of reading of scripture as proof texts, as if it contained transcendent information.[26] It also included sound instincts and commonsensical reasoning that still apply today. This section is titled "Thinking about . . . " because a full discussion of Jesus's divinity is not possible in a short space.[27] What follows

---

[25] I assume that Paul thought Adam was a real or historical person and thus compared two human beings. From our perspective the interpretation of Jesus as a "second Adam" presents Jesus as a new paradigm of human existence before God and within the rule of God in contrast to a literary type and religious symbol.

[26] To be semantically clear, I mean "transcendent information" as a paradox or implicit contradiction. If something is *transcendent,* it is a matter of faith and not available to inspection; *information* refers to empirical data that can be verified.

[27] I have offered such a full discussion in *Jesus Symbol of God,* 424–66.

is a series of considerations in the light of the problems raised by evolution that warrant an approach to Jesus's divinity that can help make sense of the doctrine, as distinct from the reality that it points to, which remains wrapped in the mystery of God. The discussion seeks to understand why this doctrine was affirmed, why it should not be slighted, even though it cannot be understood in the language of the past, and how one might entertain it as newly meaningful in an evolutionary context.

Recalling the ministry of Jesus offers a good place to begin a discussion of boundaries to the affirmation of the divinity of Jesus Christ. Jesus was a human being who was born and died in Palestine in the first century. The doctrine formulated at the Council of Nicaea in 325 affirmed that the Word of God that was incarnate in Jesus of Nazareth was strictly divine, not less than the creator God. The council was able to speak this way because earlier in the historical discussion the personification of the "Word" of God was hypostasized or reified and thought of as having enough individuality to be distinct from the creator God whom Jesus called Father and be incarnate in Jesus.[28] The use of words and propositions from scripture, used as warrants, enabled this way of thinking. For example, John's Gospel says that "the Word was God" and "the Word became flesh" (John 1:1, 14). It has Jesus saying, "The Father and I are one" (John 10:30). In the development of Christology, the "Word of God" and the "Son of God" were conflated, became synonymous, and functioned as the subject matter of the debate. We may recognize the difference between Jesus and an interpretation of him, or between Jesus and God at work in him, but such distinctions were frequently not operative. Jesus became simply the preexisting Word of God, Christ, the Son of God; the distinction between the historical figure, Jesus, and the metaphorical interpretation disappeared. The prevalent interpretation of the doctrine of one person with two natures proposes Jesus as a truly divine entity, the Word of God, who has assumed a human nature.

This analysis of the debate leading to the quintessential Christian doctrine of the divinity of Jesus at Nicaea does not debase the doctrine but shows its historical logic in order to insist that an evolutionary context requires a different approach. The language of Christology will have better traction if it begins by fixing the imagination on the human person, Jesus, as he went about his ministry, and finds there, especially in his message, but not independently of his person, the opening to transcendence and a particular revelation of God as Presence. Actually, existential and spiritual reasons supported the procedure of proof texting. People continued to relate to Jesus as a mediator of salvation from God, and that seemed to presuppose that God dwelt within Jesus in such a way that

---

[28] An implicit subordination of the Word of God to God the Father was implied in this discussion, because it remained unthinkable that the creator God could have been incarnate in matter and flesh. The incarnation of God as Father was raised along the way but judged to be unimaginable. A latent anthropomorphism affects this whole discussion.

God could be encountered in and through him. In other words, faith's conviction that Jesus of Nazareth introduced one into the Presence and saving power of God was continuous from his first disciples to the framers of the Nicene Creed and the doctrine of the Council of Chalcedon that authorized the phrase "one person with two natures." The constant in the development operated beneath the language. People encountered Jesus as representative and mediator of salvation from God, and that implies that the divine Presence resides within him in a way that accounts for the experience of salvation mediated through him.

We have seen in Chapter 3 and Chapter 4 that Israel had various ways of speaking about the immanence of God to the world and within the human person. Yahweh remained unspeakably transcendent. The notion of God expands in the course of Israel's history from the God of Israel at war with other Gods to become more and more universal as the God of the universe. In the course of that history one finds many conceptions of how God actively operates in the world. Much scriptural language still resonates with an aesthetic appreciation of the universe and nature. Creation, in effect, wrote God's "Wisdom" into nature itself. Psalm 104 is a hymn to the interconnectedness of the intricate functions of the world and how they support living things. Israel did not ignore the wonders of nature that still amaze people today. They attributed the finely tuned organic web of nature to the personified Wisdom who accompanied God's power (Prov 8:22–31). We have seen how *Spirit* pointed to God's active being present especially in marvelous things; it was the unseen but efficacious agency of God. God's *Word* symbolized the spontaneous power of God to accomplish efficaciously whatever God wished; that is, creator God spoke, and it was done according to God's Wisdom (cf. Wis 9:1–2). These terms manifest a fundamental recognition that God does not subsist in a solitary state cut off from the world. People discerned God as the immanent power and transcendent intelligence and wise designer of all things. Yes, the transcendent one communicated with angelic messengers, but God was also encountered by Moses directly as a wondrous physical event. Incarnation applied to Jesus was not an entirely new idea.

These reflections lead to a first conclusion that the divinity of Jesus refers to the Presence and power of God within him. The language that most directly communicates this actually dominates the Synoptic Gospels and can be also found in John. In Luke, the Spirit of God empowers Jesus's life from beginning to end. It appears at this juncture that, within the framework of scripture and the account of Jesus's ministry in the New Testament, we already have a portrait of the historical person being sustained and empowered by the Spirit of God within him.

This first conclusion, however, leaves us with a theological problem. On the one hand, God working within Jesus thus understood leaves him looking much like every person. As we saw in Chapter 4, the convergence of Presence of

God by primary causality in all creatures, and the Spirit of God, as well as its experienced graciousness revealed in Jewish scripture and the ministry of Jesus, together mean that what is true of Jesus is true of all people. On the other hand, Christians do not relate to Jesus as to other people, but to one in and through whom they encounter God. Jesus thus bears within himself a distinction from all others. That distinction does not lie in Jesus's unique individuality alone; neither can it be reduced to his personal energy and striving. A distinctive Presence of God to him makes him the Christ. Is there a way to understand this distinctive divinity or Presence of God within him and at the same time insist that Jesus, as a human being, is one of us?

Revising Two-Nature Language

On this precise point the language of classical theology breaks down. The ideas of natures, essences, hypostases, substances, and beings do not match the fluidity of reality. They lack the inner flexibility needed to correspond with the intrinsic movement and becoming that underlie space-time and the evolutionary process. The boundaries of "essences" and "natures" correlate poorly with the inherent dynamism and interconnectedness of the physical world that science portrays.[29] This does not dismiss a whole linguistic structure, any more than quantum mechanics completely undermines Newton's mechanics. But it encourages other ways of thinking to appreciate a clearer relevance entailed in the divinity of Jesus.

A good example of the limitations of classical categories can be found in the two-nature formula of Chalcedon. On the face of it the doctrine introduces number into the person of Jesus with two "natures" side by side.[30] It fails to express how the divine relates to Jesus of Nazareth, making him divine. Thinking in terms of defining the boundaries of natures and metaphysical hypostases or subjects will always create a competitive either/or relationship between the divine and the human. In this context each nature competes with the other to

---

[29] Evolutionary psychologist Steven Pinker defends a universal but complex human nature that involves the human mind that "is equipped with a battery of emotions, drives, and faculties for reasoning and communicating, and that they have a common logic across cultures, are difficult to erase or redesign from scratch, were shaped by natural selection acting over the course of human evolution, and owe some of their basic design (and some of their variation) to information in the genome" (Steven Pinker, *The Blank Slate: The Modern Denial of Human Nature* [London: Penguin Books, 2002], 73).

[30] This was the charge of the Alexandrians against the Antiochenes. In some measure it is true. One has to be able to imagine Jesus as a single integral human being like everyone else. We've already seen that placing these two "natures" side by side incoherently places primary causality side by side with secondary causality.

command the imagination.[31] Creation theology can resolve this christological issue. But it requires reflective adjustments from traditional essentialist categories and a cautious application of some basic principles from the structure of creation and Christology itself.

First, Jesus cannot be conceived as essentially different from other human beings. More positively affirmed, Jesus has to be regarded as a human being like all other human beings. This constitutes the historical basis of Jesus's universal relevance, and it requires that God relate to him the way God relates to all human beings. Without this principle Jesus cannot be universally relevant, the second or new Adam, and the potential savior of all humankind. All of these points require putting more emphasis on the scriptural and ecclesial teaching that Jesus resembles us "in every respect," sin excepted (Heb 4:15). The very point of every Christology is salvation offered to all. No understanding of Jesus's divinity that lifts him out of or above the human race passes this first test.

Second, when we consider how divinity can enter the discussion of Jesus, an evolutionary worldview urges us to think of God as within reality and not outside it or coming in from outside. The imagination gets in the way when we think of God in anthropomorphic terms as a big person outside the sphere of creation rather than its inner ground of being. At this point the catechism is accurate when it answers the question "Where is God?" by "God is everywhere." God is the within of reality itself. God in relation to created reality is incarnate.

Third, this relationship of God to reality has been well expressed, but not described, as one between a completely mysterious primary causality and the secondary causality we know through our finite empirical existence. These forces of being are utterly different, the one unimaginable pure being itself, the other consisting in the finite forms and actions of everything, from subatomic particles to black holes and galaxies. But they are not over against each other or side by side; they are not two. In the actual world neither exists without the other. Together, infinite being and finite beings make up all created reality.

Fourth, these distinctions are sufficient to provide a way of thinking about how God was and is present and at work in Jesus. God relates to Jesus as the ground of Jesus's being. That Presence to Jesus, however, bears a distinctiveness from other human beings on two counts: we can describe one on the basis of Jesus's individuality and the other on the basis of intensity or degree of God's Presence. The so-called uniqueness of Jesus can be accounted for by his individuality. Jesus as an individual is completely unique, and that includes God's

---

[31] This was the charge of the Antiochenes against Cyril's Alexandrian Christology; in the end, it leaves a divine subject and "nature" assuming a human nature and not a human person. This scheme departs from the narrative of the Synoptic Gospels and leaves us to imagine and relate to "God as Logos" as an actor in history. This results in the kind of mythic thinking that cannot find a place in an evolutionary historical world.

Presence to him and his historical revelation of God. God's Presence is unique to each creature. The question of intensity of presence involves a more difficult problem. A more intensive presence of God to Jesus cannot be imagined any more than God's creative causality can be. It remains postulated. But we might expect such a postulate on the basis of the language of faith. Faith in Jesus being a revelation of God saving that is relevant to all human beings already entails an enhancement of God's Presence in him as primary cause, Spirit, and grace. Any Christian relating to him as the revealer of God implicitly accepts the postulate. God's enhanced presence to Jesus also means that Jesus is both saved and savior, the receiver of revelation and the revealer, not on the basis of his own power, but through the power of God as Presence within him and us.[32]

The Problems of Christology Today

We return to the issues that an evolutionary world poses to a traditional understanding of Jesus Christ. The distinctions brought forward to address Jesus's status as revealer and his divinity render this Christology faithful to the tradition of Jesus as the Christ while accommodating the world as we find it.[33]

The first problem involved imagining Jesus Christ as an intervention into history in a world influenced by science that does not accept that language. This poses a serious problem for general Christian consciousness because our ordinary Christian language is interventionist; that is, it directly conveys an "entering into" our condition. Theology often speaks of Jesus's entry in empirically miraculous language. More reflectively, theology has also proposed that God has intervened into a history of sin to redeem it, to change it, to heal it, and to make it whole again. If that language does not offend, it will be difficult to change it. But for those who have internalized an evolutionary worldview, it seems unreal to portray God's transcendent relation to human existence in such matter-of-fact transactional terms.

The structure of the God/world relationship established in creation theology provides a directly relevant way of thinking christologically. The problem begins with an illicit projection of God in anthropomorphic terms that ignores the

---

[32] This defines a way of thinking that does not claim to resolve the mystery of God's Presence to the world or to Jesus. A moment's reflection will show that this language only describes the mystery rather than pierces it.

[33] Applying the voice of Karl Rahner to this point, Judy Cannato writes: "It is clear in Rahner's teaching that the experience of the Incarnation is not a break with evolutionary history, not an event standing outside of space-time, but a natural development in the universal bestowal of grace that leads to humankind's conscious acceptance of God's self-communication. It is essential that the Incarnation, embodied in the person of Jesus, is part of the entire experience of God's self-communication to the world" (Judy Cannato, *Field of Compassion: How the New Cosmology Is Transforming Spiritual Life* [Notre Dame, IN: Sorin Books, 2010], 53).

difference between God and finitude, between creator and creature.[34] It can be resolved with a conception of God as transcendent creative Presence within the finite order. This does not refer, here, to God found in our interior consciousness; it is rather a cosmological conviction directed at the fabric of created reality itself. God as creator subsists within reality, and all reality subsists within the power of God's creativity. Yet, in this non-pantheistic view the created world is real and not God at the same time that it subsists in the power of God, who supports its autonomy.

In this "grace-filled naturalism" the collocation of those two ordinarily opposed categories sets up a tension. From one perspective we perceive a world that is empirically naturalistic in its laws and processes and thoroughly secular in its trajectory across time. From another perspective we understand the world as creation by the power of a personal God that cannot be imagined anthropomorphically as *a* person and cannot be reduced to less than what the empirical world has itself produced: reflectively self-conscious personhood. The natural world is contained within the embrace of an infinite serendipitous creativity that in the pure act of immaterial Spirit creates with a benevolence that Jesus called love. Creator and creature are not at odds cosmologically.

We have already considered a response to the second and more directly christological problem contained in the language of one person with two natures. This abstract form of understanding gives rise to debates when mistaken as an explanation rather than pure confession that God was at work in Jesus. These debates almost always leave Jesus back there in the day-to-day ministry that Mark described. The abstractness of the concept of nature misleadingly seems to designate and circumscribe the reality of the creator God. The dynamism of reality and its emergent and evolutionary drift cannot be accurately contained by the clear distinctions that "nature language" sets up.[35] By contrast, grace-filled naturalism refers to a dynamic union of forces or vectors within inorganic and organic beings that analogously are alive. The mutually entwined and dynamic complementarity of created and creating energies entails motion and change in the interplay of contingent and fluid reality across space-time. God does not

---

[34] A strong affirmation of this difference does not imply their separateness; creation cannot exist without a creator. Frequently the ideas of difference and unity are held together in tension. Likewise, distinction can be accompanied by non-separation. The idea of differences within a unity of being and intelligibility has many examples from everyday life.

[35] I want to affirm something more than "this is not the language employed by science." That is clearly the case; the explanatory categories of science blend measured time and motion into inherently functional language that is only metaphysical by larger interpretation. Beyond that I want to assert that substance language implicitly ignores (abstracts from) the dynamic energy that constitutes reality, and each entity's reacting to a perpetual bombardment of random forces from outside. We cannot communicate without common language, and that makes stable meanings attractive, but essentialism restricts attention being given to individuals and detailed circumstance.

have a nature; God is the unnamable ground of being and the infinite horizon of all that is. The language of creative Presence in all created activity offers a structure for understanding Jesus Christ that is general in the sense of universal but also intimately concrete, fluid, flexible, and dynamically interrelational in every instance. God was present within Jesus's natural life with a Presence that made him revealer of God and savior.

The third issue, christological exclusivism, has a long tradition in Christianity, and christocentrism still persists among the majority of Christians.[36] But considerable cultural pressure urges reflective Christians to look positively on other autonomous faith traditions. The core of the problem lies in the lack of a language that preserves the absoluteness of a Christian faith commitment with a recognition that other traditions too bear truth that has satisfied peoples' absolute spiritual commitment over millennia. Dealing with this problem will help define further the way we may conceive the Presence to Jesus that makes him divine.

The first step in that direction consists of setting the question in a larger framework. How can we understand Christian revelation so that it honors the autonomy of other religious traditions?[37] To do this we have to widen the framework for dialogue from the particularist historical frameworks of individual faith traditions to a more universally recognizable framework of understanding. For the Abrahamic religions this is found in the dynamics of creation. Other faith traditions will have fundamental frameworks that are functionally analogous.[38]

A resolution to this problem for Christian theology lies in holding together two fundamental convictions so that they may chasten each other. The one consists

---

[36] By christocentrism, I mean a worldview that conceives the ultimate relationship of all reality to God as constituted by Jesus Christ. It is distinct from theocentrism, which understands all reality as related to God as creator. The first conception involves a notion of Christian "supremacy," whether or not it accepts salvation outside the Christian sphere. A theocentric worldview still understands Jesus Christ as the center of Christian faith in God. Such is the position represented here. The change of conceptions bears some structural analogy to the passage to heliocentrism.

[37] I am indebted to Edward Schillebeeckx for this way of framing the question of other religions from a Christian perspective: "How can Christianity maintain its own identity and uniqueness and at the same time attach a positive value to the difference of religions in a non-discriminatory sense?" (Schillebeeckx, *Church*, 165). Framing the question in competitive either/or terms cannot generate a productive response.

[38] Paul Tillich deeply influenced the language of comparative religion with his categories of "ultimate concern" and an "ultimate" or "ultimacy." The distinction allows for an undifferentiated human anthropological constant of existential ultimate concern that has different historically mediated ultimate "objects." Creation theology explicitly draws the Christian imagination into a sphere of ultimacy that will be expressed differently in other faith traditions. "Functional analogy" refers to an analogy between functions rather than between concepts or things. For example, one will have a hard time showing that the actual concepts of the ultimate in Buddhism and Christianity are analogous. But one may fruitfully examine how they function analogously in Buddhist and Christian spirituality.

of a form of theocentrism that is rooted in creation theology.[39] The other lies in recognition of our historicity. Historical consciousness acknowledges that all our knowledge, including our deepest cultural convictions, are perspectival, and that other cultural mediations and perspectives bear truth. This does not involve relativism, because one can know something to be absolutely true even though one grasps it from a certain perspective and in a partial way.[40] Together, these two convictions open the possibility of a genuine contact with absolute truth that is both limited and culturally conditioned so that all our convictions about it fall short.

On the one hand, the conception of creation offered in Chapter 3 proposes that God is within and present to all reality. From a Christian perspective, being directly dependent on God means that God can appear in human consciousness through various forms of mediation that give rise to revelation. Christians should expect to find in other religious traditions traces of the same Presence that lives in their own, even though such consciousness sometimes takes a radically different form due to its historical mediation. On the other hand, no religious tradition can profess to know all there is to know about ultimate reality. Christians who recognize the incomprehensible mystery that is God can scarcely maintain that God does not exceed the revelation contained in their own tradition.

For Christians, a dynamic evolutionary view of God and of all of God's creation does not restrict God's being; it opens up the human imagination. God the creator of all is Presence to all. God is not *a* being but, as creator of being-in-time, God supplies incessant energy and the enduring support of what is. From a Christian perspective God can erupt into human consciousness in any place and in many different guises. It is wrong to envisage transcendent conceptions of ultimacy in direct competition with one another.[41] They all have a source and a logic. On that understanding, in a sphere not easily defined because it consists of an openness to transcendence, interfaith relationships can generate exchange,

---

[39] I have to reassert here that it is very difficult to discuss this issue in a short space; it involves a long conversation that has become intense and polarized over the last decades. I cannot offer a fully expanded discussion here, but these reflections indicate how creation theology and evolution offer resources for a response to the issues and a noncompetitive fidelity to the tradition.

[40] See Karl Mannheim, *Ideology and Utopia: An Introduction to the Sociology of Knowledge* (New York: Harcourt Brace, A Harvest Book, 1985 <1936>). Mannheim speaks of "relationism" rather than relativism. "Relationism does not signify that there are no criteria of rightness and wrongness in a discussion. It does insist, however, that it lies in the nature of certain assertions that they cannot be formulated absolutely, but only in terms of the perspective of a given situation" (283).

[41] To construct propositions from different faith traditions that stand in direct opposition or contradiction with one another misses a fundamental point: the principle of contradiction rests on the premise of all things being equal, and they never are and cannot be in such comparisons. The systems of thought are different and the "objects" are transcendent.

dialogue, and then conversation; hostile debate almost always will come from less than religious motives, because ultimacy always reveals itself as mystery. Jesus and his revelation of God do not compete with other savior figures but confirm their possibility and provide Christians with a groundwork for exchange.

This conception helps us to be clear about what is meant by the confession that Jesus is divine. It cannot mean that Jesus the creature is not a creature. It means that God, and not less than God according to Nicaea, was present to and determinative of Jesus's being. This same God is present in other media of God's revelation, not in the same way, but in the way that makes them, in some measure, true revelations of Presence. We cannot conceive of God's Presence to creation in competitive terms, but we can talk about our real differences.

Conclusion

This chapter aimed pointedly and positively at the effects that internalizing an evolutionary worldview would have on Christology. It presupposed that evolutionary consciousness demands some changes in the way we imagine, speak about, and conceptualize Jesus's role and place in Christian faith. Jesus and his teaching constitute the object of christological interpretation. And the single major factor that influenced the way the earliest followers interpreted Jesus after his death lies in some form of an Easter experience by which they encountered Jesus alive and with God.[42] This Easter experience can be shared analogously by all Christians. It describes the structure of a faith conviction that what happened to Jesus at the end of his life transcends history and occurs in God's sphere.

The second part of the discussion answered the question of how Jesus, who has determined the contours of Christian faith in God, has universal relevance. The usual response to this question lies in a conception of human salvation and how Jesus mediated it. What does it mean to say that Jesus is savior of the world? The answer often comes from one of many different conceptions of salvation that are found in the New Testament and the history of Christian self-understanding. The kernel of the response offered here finds its place within the context of revelation or mediation of an awareness or consciousness of God. The message of Jesus is found in the church, its scriptures, and the tradition of their interpretation. Jesus bears universal relevance because of the consciousness of God he mediates to Christian faith and potentially to all. It is important to see that Jesus's message, which was learned from his tradition, was communicated by his teaching it and acting it out. Jesus as mediator became part of the message.

---

[42] This deliberately ambiguous statement could mean that the disciples came to the recognition *that* Jesus was alive, or it could mean that they psychologically encountered Jesus alive. Or it may have been both at the same time, because to realize *that* Jesus was risen would have been existentially transforming.

The third part took up the traditional idea of Jesus's divinity, which seems particularly difficult to conceive in an evolutionary framework. The formula of one person with two natures confesses Jesus's status, but it collapses as a theological explanation and easily invites dismissal as anthropomorphic myth. But a shift to the framework of a theology of creation opens possibilities of understanding the human person Jesus being supported and sustained from within by the Presence of the creator God in a way analogous to all creatures and especially human beings. At the same time, because the creative act of God is always also particular, God was present as the ground of Jesus's being in a unique way because of his particular identity and in special way because of its intensity. People who receive God's revelation in and through him have a sense of God's special Presence to Jesus.

Scripture and the history of theology have given various names to the way God's Presence accompanied Jesus in a special way: Spirit, Word, Wisdom, Glory, and divine Power stand out. But certain qualities of this language become prominent in an evolutionary context. God's Presence in Jesus is a presence within and not from outside or above; God's Presence is aboriginal to human existence itself; it is analogous to God's Presence to all; and it can certainly be manifest outside of Jesus and within other religions. In this way we are driven back to what was called panentheism according to the pattern of creation theology. Salvation consists of consciously being introduced into God's Presence, and Jesus is truly divine in a way that does not exclude other mediations being true divine revelations of ultimacy.

The divinity of Jesus so understood as the grounds for the salvation that he proffers to human existence opens up the question of the future: What can we hope for?

8

What Can We Hope For?

Eschatology (consideration of the end of time) forms the bookend opposite of protology (creation). Together they encompass an emergent or evolutionary understanding of reality from the perspective of faith. Creation responds to the question of why there is anything at all. Eschatology responds to the same question, but usually in terms of where it will lead and what we can hope for ultimately. The chapter uses this topic to sum up this work on Christian faith in an evolutionary context.

Evolution offers a new framework for understanding Christian faith relative to the worldview at the time that the basic doctrines were formulated. It provides a context for an appropriation of the doctrines that corresponds with our age and culture. During the hundred years after Darwin's *The Origin of Species by Means of Natural Selection*, evolution met constant resistance from Christians, even though many theologians incorporated it into their understandings of doctrinal commitments. Today, beginning with children in grade school, people regard evolution simply as a description of how our world came to be as it is. And some theologians, sometimes quite enthusiastically, write from the standpoint of evolution in a way that does not retrieve significant components of traditional doctrines. Others accede to more doctrinal detail than the legitimate constraints of science allow.

This situation leaves us with some basic questions. For example: Does evolution make faith more difficult or provide constructive intelligibility to the Christian vision? Is the present interpretation of Christian teaching a defensive move, a tactical retreat in the face of an invasion of science? Or does a new worldview invite theological insight to reappropriate what Christian faith offers our contemporary world? The Christian doctrines of the end times open these large questions as well. The randomness of natural selection challenges purposeful direction in the movement toward the future. What are we talking about when we use the language of eternal life? More important, how do we justify our language?

This chapter has two main objectives. It takes up and responds to the question of what we can hope for in an evolutionary worldview. That question puts the larger theoretical issues of purpose and destiny into the concrete terms of faith language. The second goal is to bring this constructive statement to a close. By considering what we can hope for, we formulate a response that includes the principles developed in the earlier chapters.

The chapter begins by recalling basic principles from the evolutionary understanding of the world that shape the context of our thinking. It then considers the tradition to find elements of a theological language that help to formulate a context for talk about the absolute future. It recalls elements of creation theology, introduces eschatology, and underlines the resurrection of Jesus Christ. The chapter concludes by offering principles for spirituality, a shorthand term for the Christian life, because our basic hopes guide the way we live.

Evolution: Reality as Narrative

When Darwin introduced evolution into nineteenth-century consciousness, it appeared to threaten the doctrine of creation; the randomness that plays an intrinsic part of its dynamics seemed to undermine purpose in the universe. These problems still linger among many Christians.[1] Our response to the question of what we can hope for, therefore, begins with a more positive view of what evolution holds out to the human imagination. This first section, then, reaches back to the early chapters to highlight principles that may set a context for our hope. These principles do not constitute the source of Christian hope; that privileged position belongs to scripture and, in particular, Jesus Christ. But because evolution appeared for many as a negation of faith and hope, I want to show by contrast how evolution offers support for Christian conceptions of an absolute future. The three principles of becoming, the autonomous integrity of the universe, and directionality oversimplify massive scientific data and reflection into general statements, but together they help make the point that evolution can provide a friendly matrix for hope in the future.

Reality Is Becoming

All finite being exists as being in motion across time. Immediate perception fails us at this fundamental level because it tends to represent all things within

---

[1] This remains a lively conversation among theologians. For example, see Stephen J. Pope, "Does Evolution Have a Purpose? The Theological Significance of William Stoeger's Account of 'Nested Directionality,'" *Theological Studies* 72 (2017): 462–82.

the context of the moment. By contrast, evolution evokes the temporal character of created reality; finite reality consists of material space-time and not as object within a container of time. In a contrast with Aristotelian metaphysics, science transforms "prime matter" into factors of pure energy, the motion of electrons, photons, and other particles in motion. Everything that exists swims from a past in a moving present into a future. The image of a static reality deceives; what is captured in a moment has already passed the point of its capture. Everything is temporal; duration belongs to its being. Time, the constant movement of temporal beings, means change. *Changing* offers another name for *becoming;* the two terms are almost synonymous. Reality, one can say, is change, incrementally from the perspective of the human eye and imagination, but at bottom unimaginably quick.

Appropriating this evolutionary perspective requires a reorientation of fundamental conceptions of reality on a metaphysical level.[2] For example, the idea of unchanging reality, or unchanging ideas and descriptions of them, can only be accepted cautiously because both the knower and the known are always in motion, always changing perspective. This applies especially in the sphere of ideas and values. If something has been a value from time immemorial, it may be outdated. Process and change should affect settled opinions and convictions about things. Nothing remains stable; everything changes.

Recognition of new comprehensive points of view may cause discomfort, but they also promise a new and deeper appreciation of old truths. The fact that reality is a narrative, that the human species has been striving for intelligibility and understanding for 200,000 years, and that we have come up with an unfinished story moving through time into an unknown future, opens up striking new potential for appreciation of the human condition. Evolution does not merely describe reality as intrinsically developmental, which is clear on the surface of things. It calls also for an adjustment of how we understand reality itself and ourselves in it.

The Integrity of Autonomous Finite Reality

The idea of the universe points to a massive system of interactive and interrelated forces of immense complexity. Having emerged from an initial starting point and bonded by a continuous process through space-time, the universe remained consistent in itself. The Big Bang symbolizes the beginning of the time and reality of our universe. This reconstructed starting point contained

---

[2] By metaphysics, here, I mean a set of principles—explicitly acknowledged or implicitly at work—that makes up a horizon of consciousness and thus a subjective context for understanding. It may or may not require a philosophical system. It filters and arranges the data into a priori perceptions or categories that form the presuppositions for finding units of intelligibility corresponding to our language or that make new demands on our language.

within itself, either actually or potentially through temporal creativity, all our present world needed to become itself. Reality developed through the interaction of forces within: All reality consists of "the quantum field theory of the quarks, electrons, neutrinos, all the families of fermions, electromagnetism, gravity, the nuclear forces, and the Higgs [field]."[3] Scientifically speaking, the theory of how these elements interacted accounts for all we experience. From the perspective of science one has to respect "the formational and functional integrity and relative autonomy, of nature."[4] At every level of reality "there are self-ordering and self-organizing principles and processes within nature itself" that allow a description and explanation of the world. "No outside intervention is necessary to interrupt or complement these regularities and principles at this level."[5] "There are no gaps in the secondary causal chain."[6]

Initially, this view seemed to contradict an interventionism everyone took for granted. God possessed free range of action within the sphere that God creates. In anthropomorphic language one easily thought of God as able to interrupt the order of the material world and history as the sovereign of creation itself. But this failure to respect both science and the transcendence of God's creating leaves us with a flat-out unresolvable problem of theodicy: God can but does not respond to suffering. Chapter 3 presented a different conception of how God acts in history: God does not act in the world as a finite creature or secondary cause, but as a Presence that sustains the autonomous action of nature.[7] This may not completely resolve the mystery of God's relation to what humans perceive as evil, but it opens up a new positive conception of God's relation to the world.

---

[3] Recalling Sean Carroll, *The Big Picture: On the Origins of Life, Meaning, and the Universe Itself* (New York: Dutton, 2016), 176. It should be understood that Carroll's statement is contentious because, from the perspective of self-consciousness itself, value theory, philosophy, and theology, not to mention other disciplines, there is more to reality than the empirically measurable.

[4] William R. Stoeger, "Conceiving Divine Action in a Dynamic Universe," *Scientific Perspectives on Divine Action: Twenty Years of Challenge and Progress*, ed. Robert John Russell, Nancey Murphy, and William R. Stoeger (Berkeley, CA: The Center for Theology and the Natural Sciences; Vatican City: Vatican Observatory Publications, 2008), 220.

[5] William R. Stoeger, "Describing God's Action in the World in the Light of Scientific Knowledge of Reality," in *Chaos and Complexity: Scientific Perspectives on Divine Action*, ed. Robert J. Russell et al. (Vatican City: Center for Theology and Natural Sciences, 1995), 242.

[6] Stoeger, "Describing God's Action in the World in the Light of Scientific Knowledge of Reality," 247.

[7] One could say "quasi autonomous" in order to uphold the insight of creation theology that all things are absolutely dependent on God's creating power that sustains their being. But God's ongoing creating Presence is not finite causality; the phrase "autonomous nature" stresses the integrity of secondary causality. This simply stated distinction represents an intrinsically subtle and tensive understanding of things.

One can speak of God's Presence to all reality as creative causality, not generally, but in a manner that completely encompasses every individual thing that exists. That distinctive Presence to each being represents the "special acts" of God in history. In reality, every act of every creature is special because of God's noninterventionist Presence sustaining the existence of each single being and action. God's embrace renders all of reality special. "The presence of God in each entity constitutes the direct, the immediate, relationship of that entity with God, and therefore is the channel of divine influence in secondary causality."[8] This conception, refined and tensive as it is, allows us to appreciate the way science describes the dynamism of our reality on the macroscopic and microscopic levels and, at the same time, to recognize God present and at work in that process.

Direction

Attention needs to be given to a third dimension of evolution referred to as direction or directionality. The evolution of life and its antecedents clearly manifest a movement toward increased complexity of beings. The long process of the evolution of Homo sapiens embodies a steady building across vast phases of cosmic, prebiotic, and biotic development and complexity. Before more intricate molecular structures of life that sustain increasingly elaborate forms of sensitivity and response to environment could take off, the elements from which they are constructed had to emerge. It should be clear from earlier discussion that in scientific usage this does not constitute the ordinary meaning of teleology: a conscious or intentional direction of a process toward a specific goal or a range of them. Because of the enormous density of interrelationships of every form of being and the massive arena of independent and purely functional experiments in evolution that are continuously going on, science cannot grasp a unified purpose at work in the universe. Ultimately, sensible or empirical perception cannot generate such a metaphysical insight and conviction. As Stoeger bluntly states: "It is not possible to specify from the natural sciences and philosophy alone the ultimate end or goal of the universe."[9]

This inability of science to affirm conscious purpose in the universe reinforces the distinction between scientific knowledge and faith commitments of a metaphysical kind. On the one hand, Christians spontaneously think that God creating entails God's frequent intervention into the currents of our planetary life. On the other hand, science cannot, by definition, provide evidence of God's

---

[8] Stoeger, *Chaos and Complexity*, 257.

[9] William R. Stoeger, "The Immanent Directionality of the Evolutionary Process, and Its Relationship to Teleology," in *Evolutionary and Molecular Biology: Scientific Perspectives on Divine Action*, ed. Robert John Russell et al. (Vatican City: Center for Theology and the Natural Sciences, 2006), 189. For Pope's brief recapitulation of Stoeger's sweeping vision of emergence and evolution, see "Does Evolution Have a Purpose?" 464–66.

overt action in the world. But it would be a great mistake for the religious imagination to leave the discussion there, because, in fact, evolutionary science evokes more than it can affirm.

More positively and constructively, it would be embarrassing if there were no signal or intimation of transcendence in the empirical sphere. Science provides data that can evoke a genuine religious sensibility. We can count some ways. First, we can look upon the universe as filled with relatively independent evolutionary processes. Everywhere we look, we find a world in motion producing unintended results that fall within a range of possibilities continually modified by randomness. This means that the universe is riddled with a functional kind of teleology: new things have been fitting in for billions of years.[10]

Second, evolutionary science thus opens up to human consciousness a directedness of reality itself that is not an empirical substance or an isolatable particle or wave, but a quality of the whole universe. Appealing again to Stoeger, this directedness "resides in the totality of ordered and coordinated processes, systems, and entities, and not in any one interaction, relationship, or condition."[11] An active openness to complexity is a quality of reality itself. The bond of time holds reality together; past, present, and future are continuous and depend on one another. The future consists of possibilities released by the past and present. "This togetherness is fundamentally what space and time, and the laws of nature operating within them, do for us—at a very basic level—bringing disparate entities into relationship. And the fundamental interactions provide a dynamics to that togetherness, enriching it, and moving it forward to realize new possibilities and new entities situated in new environments."[12]

Third, the interconnected universe, bonded by space-time and open to new complexities, constantly moves into the future. The universe and we who are part of it possess an openness to newness in the future.[13] That openness appears

---

[10] Pope appropriates the distinction between two forms of teleology, external, directed by an outside intentional or purposeful agent, and internal, referring to the spontaneous, objective, functional mechanisms of things (see "Does Evolution Have a Purpose?" 273–75).

[11] Stoeger, "The Immanent Directionality of the Evolutionary Process, and Its Relationship to Teleology," 169.

[12] Stoeger, "The Immanent Directionality of the Evolutionary Process, and Its Relationship to Teleology," 170.

[13] "Though its actual course is indeterminate, its general course towards complexity, self-organization, and even the emergence of self-replicating molecules and systems, given the hierarchies of global and local conditions which are given, can be interpreted as inevitable in the universe in which we live" (Stoeger, "The Immanent Directionality of the Evolutionary Process, and Its Relationship to Teleology," 180). Stoeger thus joins John Haught in reading the universe temporally as moving toward the future, rather than reductionistically in terms of antecedent causality. See, for example, John Haught, "Destiny: From Individual to Cosmic," *Resting on the Future: Catholic Theology for an Unfinished Universe* (New York: Bloomsbury, 2015), 115–26. We will return to Haught's views.

within the margins of order and the patterns of nature, but it describes creativity that constantly produces the new.

And fourth, it does not seem plausible in an evolutionary context to try to understand the whole of reality without factoring in the phenomenon of human consciousness. True, a scientific perspective has not been able to explain exactly what intelligent human consciousness is. But that mystery provides no ground for effectively ignoring its meaningfulness. Given its existence, the universal human trade in teleology bears penetrating witness to the structure of the reality of which it is a part.[14]

These qualities of evolution, process, integrity, directedness, and the appearance of intelligence in no way threaten a theistic view of the created universe. Evolution does not close down but opens up a spiritual imagination and even lends credibility in the sense of connectedness to theological language.

Theology: God as Source and Goal

Science presents reality as a grand narrative in which our planetary world took shape, and it knows how it will end. Theology does not propose the beginning and the end of that story but a grounding source and a goal formulated from the perspective of human consciousness. Theology is not science, but it has to work along with the descriptive understanding of ourselves that science provides. This section recapitulates a theology of creation and then opens the topic of eschatology; the two together represent the large metaphysical framework of the Christian vision. Within this framework, revelation, manifested in the story of Jesus Christ, guides the Christian theological imagination.

Creation

Most scientists are preoccupied with the focused areas of their research and the principles that govern their own disciplines. Regarding the big picture of a worldview, physicists, especially astrophysicists and cosmologists, have synthesized the algorithms of particular laws to form the scientific worldview that is currently in place. It deals with the universe or universes. What better place to enter into dialogue with science than the Christian view of the whole

---

[14] "The great advances in the physical and biological sciences were made possible by excluding the mind from the physical world. This has permitted a quantitative understanding of that world, expressed in timeless, mathematically formulated physical laws. But at some point it will be necessary to make a new start on a more comprehensive understanding that includes the mind" (Thomas Nagel, *Mind and Cosmos: Why the Materialist Neo-Darwinian Conception of Nature Is Almost Certainly False* [Oxford: University Press, 2012], 8).

contained in its doctrine of creation out of nothing by God? Same subject matter: the whole. But the approaches differ so deeply that failure to recognize the difference leaves only confusion.

Christian theology says that God creates all that is and does so out of nothing. One must begin understanding this with the premise that it cannot be understood; the very idea of creating something out of nothing is unimaginable, because nothing is there to be imagined. The ground for the assertion, then, does not lie with objective evidence, but rather with the human experience that we and the world, which embraces us as its own and of which we are a part, do not have within ourselves the ground of our own being. This inner sensitivity also carries a conviction that such a ground and purpose must exist. Science does not generate this conviction, but it appears to the believer to be as directly connected with reality, as is conscious human existence itself.

We will not rehash in detail what was discussed in Chapter 3 but simply recall two implications that shape the worldview that guides Christian living into the future. The first understands God as the ground of becoming or, in scientific language, emergence and evolution. God transcends empirical reality but supports it. God is not the physical energy of the universe but the creative act that sustains it. God is not a being but an encompassing Presence within the world that cannot be perceived by science because, relative to all the factors and vectors of force in the universe, God is as nothing but the grounding of their being.

The second implication, already implied but here made explicit, posits God as the "within" of the universe.[15] The metaphor of Presence connotes this. Presence suggests unembodied or unidentified attendance, a being there—without substance or particularity—that can still be felt. It suggests, too, in the language of personalism, a "being with" that transcends physicality, as when someone opens up his or her *self* to another. In such encounters one can appreciate the meaning of Presence as something that comes as a gift from a freedom over which one has no leverage or entitlement. Both of these descriptions show that the theological idea of creation enjoys an epistemological realism that runs on a very different track than evolutionary science.

---

[15] The phrase resembles the term used by Pierre Teilhard de Chardin in *The Divine Milieu* (New York: Harper and Row, 1968). Teilhard did not show much interest in the Darwinian mechanics of evolution. He thought rather in terms of an inner principle or reality at the core of all material being. He preferred "not to talk of [it as] consciousness, but rather of the 'within' of things, a sort of subjective pole" (François Euvé, *Darwin et le Christianisme: Vrais et Faux Débats* [Paris: Buchet/Castel, 2009], 118, also 112). I have transposed Teilhard's reference from internal identity to God's Presence within being on the basis of creation theology. This does not replace Teilhard's insight; it simply explains the usage here.

Eschatology

The doctrines about the end of time and the ultimate destiny of human existence fall under the broad name *eschatology*. The Bible has much to say about the end of time, and one has to ask what kind of knowledge it represents, especially since all the messages are not the same. We have thus jumped into the subject matter of this chapter: What can we hope for? What is the character of this hope? This section discusses the grammar of this language, to which we will return in the conclusion of the chapter.

Karl Rahner has succinctly captured the logic of faith statements about the absolute future or end of time when he writes that their meanings "are necessarily conclusions from the experience of the Christian *present*."[16] Rahner writes that we do not project something that we do not know about the future on to our present experience today; we rather project our experience today into the future.[17] Right away, then, before all else is said, we have to realize that the beliefs of Christians about the absolute future represent a conviction that differs intrinsically from statements about what can be experienced here and now. And yet we *have to* think about and make these projections; we cannot abstain from them. This flows from the narrative character of our evolutionary existence. The inner character of reflective consciousness appears in the question: What do I do next? Our being stands poised on the brink of the immediate future. Expanding on this, we are a story that forms part of a larger ontological process. We cannot understand ourselves without asking about our future and implicitly answering by our action. We are moving toward a future that appears absolute for us and implicitly for the world and the universe. The existential dynamism of life itself posits the absolute future as the horizon of conscious existence.[18]

Another quality of this subtle epistemology of the future becomes manifest when we realize how closely the hopes of eschatology resemble the convictions of faith in creation. Although eschatological speech looks toward the absolute future, like the language of creation, it implies transcendent reality. Eschatology points to absolute transcendence and eternity and not time. God's eternal Being

---

[16] Karl Rahner, *Foundations of Christian Faith: An Introduction to the Idea of Christianity* (New York: Crossroad, 1994), 432.

[17] Rahner, *Foundations of Christian Faith*, 432. Yet a certain back and forth can occur here. We can grasp dialectically the way things should be, and that we hope will be, and allow those insights to criticize the present situation and urge reform. Utopia, in other words, is often a critique of sets of relationships or social and environmental structures that are taken for granted but are seen as harmful.

[18] Rahner, *Foundations of Christian Faith*, 432.

encompasses time all at once; the creator of time attends to it but transcends it. The sphere of God does not endure temporality but sustains it.[19] Therefore, this orientation of human consciousness across time to an absolute future resembles the logic of all predicates about transcendence and God. The final things exist as transcendent in God's present; eschatology obeys the logic of creation faith, although it is mentally oriented toward the future.

One more quality of the way we speak about the absolute future has to be underlined. Because the last things refer to transcendent reality, what we are talking about remains entirely hidden from view. Rahner captures this in a phrase: our "absolute future remains incomprehensible mystery to be worshipped in silence."[20] That which we intend lies ineffable and beyond all images on the other side of creation; sensible images, when taken literally and not dialectically, tend to distort our consciousness. We have to respect a strong distinction between the realm of imaginable representations of the end times and the unspeakable reality of an absolute future. We speak apophatically, with primal reserve, into the abyss of Creator God.

To conclude this brief, abstract, and overly dense representation of the logic of statements about our final destiny, we have to ask whether it is possible to step back and describe what is going on here in plain language. Yes, it is. Essentially, envisioning our final destiny follows the path set out by faith in creation. The loving God, who sustains all that is by the radical power of creative Presence, also guarantees creation's meaningfulness.[21] Creative process transforms directionality with divine purpose, which can be asserted but not discerned. The grounding energy of the process of creation implicitly entails a meaningful destiny for the process. We will say more about this faith-hope in the concluding section. For now, it seems completely coherent to say that the creator of an evolutionary universe will be the ground of its meaning at the end of the story in an absolute future.

---

[19] It is important to remain critically alert to the transcendence of God. Neville states this with emphasis on the singularity of God being the act of creation: "The term *God* is indeed legitimately used to refer to the ontological act of creating the world, bearing in mind the need to break the literal application of the model of the person in reference to the ontological act. The ontological act of creating the world is singular. Although not within time or space, it is the one act creating all the determinate things and their changing interactions. Its singularity is eternal and immense. . . . It can be referred to as '*an* act,' singular. Much of what is at stake in theism is the singularity of God, however God is conceived. . . . Thomas's Act of To Be is singular" (Robert Cummings Neville, *Ultimates: Philosophical Theology*, vol. 1 [Albany: State University of New York Press, 2013], 230).

[20] Rahner, *Foundations of Christian Faith*, 434.

[21] The meaning of the word *meaning* or *meaningfulness* itself in some usages runs together with purpose and intent. The absence of purpose creates a sense of incoherence and instability.

Revelation through Jesus Christ

We turn now to the center of the Christian vision provided by historical revelation, placing in clear perspective the revelational role played by Jesus of Nazareth. In some respects this section recapitulates Chapter 6 and Chapter 7, but with new explicit intent: to formulate how Jesus allows Christians to respond to the question: What can we hope for? Three themes in Christology make Jesus directly relevant to this question: another look at how God was present in Jesus's person and ministry and thus a revelation of God; the content of God's self-revelation in Jesus; and how this revelation has existential bearing on human life moving forward.

We begin with the "special" character of God's Presence to Jesus of Nazareth. This issue dominated all premodern Christology; it was *the* christological question. How was God present to Jesus in a way enabling him to mediate salvation from God? We noted earlier that the New Testament contains many different views of how Jesus saves and corresponding Christologies, but in response to the christological question one finds two main formulas. The first, the earliest and most predominate expression of Jesus's divine power and authority, proposed that God as Spirit worked within him. This construction undergirds the narrative in the Synoptic Gospels and can be seen in the letters as well. The other metaphor proposed that the Word of God was incarnate in Jesus as empowerment and especially the vehicle of the divine truth he communicated. Word Christology, formulated most clearly in the Prologue of John's Gospel, predominated in Greek culture, and it provided the language for Nicaea's decisive formula: Jesus was divine because the Word of God incarnate within him was not less than God. Classical Christology was, for the most part, built on the image of the Word of God. Some modern Christologies affirm the doctrine of Nicaea using the image of the Spirit of God. Some Christologies that use both images seem systematically redundant.

We have seen how the dialogue with evolutionary science has changed the context for thinking about how God relates to the world. But two theological moves of earlier chapters resituate the response to the question of God acting in Jesus. Chapter 3 removed the premise for God's intervention in history: God's creative causality amounts to a deep incarnation of God's Presence in an all-encompassing way within all created reality in and according to each being's individuality. And Chapter 4 revisited traditional language of God acting in history as the immanent power of being. God as creating, as Spirit, as *Shekinah,* and as grace, in diverse languages, express the same reality: God's Presence as the power of being. God's Presence so encompassed the individuality of Jesus and his action that he became the medium for new decisive awareness of the self-communicating Presence of God.

Another christological issue bears on the question of what we can hope for, namely, the objective content of Jesus's revelation of God. Can we isolate and name the kernel of what Jesus reveals and makes present without, at the same time, appearing to reduce the expansive character of God's self-revelation and communication? Revelation should not be regarded as a communication of ideas or propositions. Intersubjective encounter, where another's inner self becomes manifest through external word and gesture, offers a better metaphor for revelation. For example, in the gestures of Jesus one can encounter God's goodness. God's self-revelation reflected in Jesus's teaching pertains to the character of God; God is good, friend, and loving, with a love that reaches to each person as though there were no other.

A first reaction to an experience of the goodness of God mediated through Jesus might be a spontaneous desire to respond appropriately, that is, less an immediate response of the moment but more fittingly a deep response that takes the form of a commitment. An encounter with God through Jesus teaches human beings how to live with an ultimate or sacred responsibility. A world embraced by and filled with the intrinsic personal presence and goodness of God differs from a world that exists devoid of ultimate meaning and intentionality. To be caught up in the goodness of God transforms not a single fact or occurrence in the universe, and yet the whole of it is transformed. So, too, does the personal appropriation of this revelation transform a person and his or her actions; it fills them with spiritual and moral resonance.

The rule of God points to a commanding revelation that lay beneath Jesus's teaching and action, so that all he said and did were meant to communicate what this rule of God stood for. The rule of God, we noted, refers to the intention of the Creator, the way God desires creation to be, especially human existence in a community that includes relationship with the wider life of the planet. Jesus exhorted us to pray "God's will be done"; that is, may the rule of God on earth reflect the way the Creator intended it. One has to be careful, however, not to reduce the rule of God to a narrow ethics of normative human behavior. Internalizing the idea of the rule of God means standing before God in one's being and action. The rule of God defines a spiritual and religious relationship that includes the ethical and moral but cannot be reduced to morality.

The rule of God, however, far exceeds personal obligation and draws individual consciousness into community, the immediate community, one's society, the human community, the entire community of life. The rule of God represents no small insight. It belongs to the sphere of transcendent teleology; it symbolizes being drawn into the mystery of God's intention for the universe. The rule of God, as Jesus presented it in parables and actions, opens up a framework of how human beings should live and what they should live for in this world. As Presence, it encompasses, in the sense of being interior or within, the world and human life but with moral impetus and direction. This provides not quite a program for each one's life, even though theological ethicists like Dietrich Bonhoeffer coherently make such a claim,[22] but it solicits a fundamental commitment that needs to be in conversation with other human beings in careful moral discernment. Freedom in the rule of God does not mean moral limpness but self-actualization within a community of life.

Jesus also reveals the resurrection of the dead, partly but not decisively during his ministry, but more importantly in the mediation to the disciples' Easter experience after his death. Jesus did not initiate belief in resurrection, and it is reasonable to believe that all that Jesus taught was learned from his Jewish tradition,[23] not to the exclusion of the personal touch he put on whatever he taught. But for the Christian community these testimonies to resurrection came together in the encounter with God involved in Jesus's resurrection. Ideally, Christian faith includes an Easter experience analogous to that of Jesus's original followers. When, in the final section of this chapter, we turn to the question of what we can hope for, the resurrection of Jesus will provide the deepest and most audacious of spiritual hopes.

Internalization of the meaning of Jesus Christ into one's life today entails faith-hope in resurrection as the inner law or pattern of human existence and perhaps of life itself. Saint Paul represents this most directly and forcefully in the New Testament: death to sin, resurrection in the Spirit to new life, and finally eternal life. Nature offers many symbolic patterns of life, death, and new life in this world, from evolution itself to the cycles of nature on our planet. But Paul reads eternal life as the message of God's revelation in Jesus Christ.[24] "If Christ has not been raised, then our proclamation has been in vain and your faith has been in vain" (1 Cor 15:14).

In preparing the groundwork for a response to the question of what we can hope for, Christian theology brings a wealth of experience, insight, and conviction. It comes from a source other than evolutionary science, respects its awesome accomplishments, but rests on its own autonomous set of experiences. The revelation of God through Jesus Christ, positioned within the parameters

---

[22] Bonhoeffer wrote: "God's commandment is the speech of God to man. Both in its contents and in its form it is concrete speech to the concrete man. God's commandment leaves man no room for application or interpretation. It leaves room only for obedience or disobedience" (Dietrich Bonhoeffer, *Ethics* [New York: Macmillan, 1955], 278). This makes little sense if one thinks of God's command as an objective proposition. Bonhoeffer is writing within the context of a personal encounter with God's Word in faith.

[23] See the development of Pinchas Lapide, *The Resurrection of Jesus: A Jewish Perspective* (Minneapolis: Augsburg, 1983).

[24] Paul's formula had special relevance for ethics. Wayne Meeks writes: "Paul's most profound bequest to subsequent Christian discourse was his transformation of the reported crucifixion and resurrection of Jesus Christ into a multipurpose metaphor with vast generative and transformative power—not least for moral perception" (*The Origins of Christian Morality: The First Two Centuries* [New Haven, CT: Yale University Press, 1993], 196).

of creation and eschatology, opens a transcendent vision that draws scientific knowledge into itself even as it is shaped by a scientific culture. But before passing to a formal theological answer to the question of our destiny that this stimulates, we need to examine briefly one more area of Christian discourse: spirituality. This refers to the kind of life generated by Christian faith in an evolutionary context.

Spirituality

We are setting out theological suppositions for Christian hope. At the end of Chapter 3 we addressed some resonances of creation theology with Christian life. We return now to a larger conception of spirituality as it appears in the framework of an evolutionary interpretation of Christianity. Many threads are woven into the following conception, but it may be helpful to single out Teilhard de Chardin, Juan Luis Segundo, and Ignatius of Loyola, who provide the drift.[25] An outline of spirituality in the context of evolution places another plank on the bridge between the theological vision that has emerged out of an evolutionary worldview and a realistic formulation of hope. What follows draws out the activist character of evolutionary Christian spirituality, its essential character as narrative, how it bears a decidedly social dimension corresponding to the thick integrity of the elements of nature, its inner character as an undertaking or project, and its goal of union with what is ultimate.

Spirituality refers to the way persons and groups lead their lives in relation to what is ultimate. This conception also refers to reflection on existential spirituality and the body of knowledge that accrues from it. This conception of human spirituality directly entails its activist character. Spirituality shares in the dynamic character of reality itself: being is becoming; life is a narrative; the action of each person through time constitutes the character if not the identity of each person. We are part of the process of becoming; without forgetting God's Presence, self-formation by self-actualization places some measure of responsibility for ourselves into our hands as free persons.

The active character of human life commands the attention of Teilhard de Chardin but does not blind him to the passivities of existence. He defines these passivities as what is done to us as distinct from that which is done by us.

---

[25] Teilhard de Chardin, *The Divine Milieu*; Juan Luis Segundo, *The Christ of the Ignatian Exercises* (Maryknoll, NY: Orbis Books, 1987), 41–124; Juan Luis Segundo, "Ignatius Loyola: Trial or Project?" *Signs of the Times: Theological Reflections* (Maryknoll, NY: Orbis Books, 1993), 149–75; Ignatius Loyola, *The Spiritual Exercises of Saint Ignatius*, ed. and comm. George E. Ganss (Chicago: Loyola Press, 1992).

The range of determinisms by far constitutes the largest dimension of human existence, the sea out of which our singular freedom surfaces.[26] These passivities are like the darkness of night in which the light of liberty and reflection sheds a small radius of illumination. These passivities appear as both friendly and hostile to our existence and growth. Some operate from inside us, as biological mechanisms, and others operate upon us through our natural and social environment. The internal processes of growth move us to maturity and creativity, while those of decline and diminishment move us toward death.[27] Nature and evolution serve up this situation as a given. But within it, the inner spirit of reflective consciousness and freedom that define human existence possesses some power of self-actualization, some measure of decision making and commitment.[28]

The substance of spirituality consists of personal history and should be understood in narrative terms. This existential language takes on new interrelatedness and social meaning within the context of evolution. Evolution plays out a metaphysics of becoming; motion defines reality. We have seen how human existence, which evolved within the matter of the universe, remains part of it, even as intentionality adds something to it. In an overt way Homo sapiens injects into the natural world a reflective consciousness and freedom that as far as we know is distinctive. In the human species evolution has become reflectively conscious activity, even though it rarely feels like it. It may seem odd to say that human beings collectively have become responsible for the movement of evolution, even in this tiny niche of the universe. But we are learning this through tragic mismanagement of our world. The responsibility inherent in human life before the personal creator God that Jesus represents cannot be individualist, only for oneself; it shares in something large that expands beyond self, family, nation, and even the species.

This metaphysical structure comes to the surface of everyday life in an ethics of communion of being and an ecological ethics. The dangers to the planet, known for some time by scientists, are pressing in on global consciousness. Pope Francis has raised awareness of a spiritual and a religious dimension to the issue in his encyclical letter *Laudato Si'*. We will not develop a theological

---

[26] "Passivities" in Teilhard are not unlike what Tillich calls "destiny" in polar tension with freedom. See Paul Tillich, *Systematic Theology*, vol. 1 (Chicago: University of Chicago Press, 1951), 182–86, 200–201.

[27] Teilhard de Chardin, *The Divine Milieu*, 46–47.

[28] So deep is the reverence of some theologians for the freedom of the human spirit that they think of death itself as a human act. Often this runs counter to overt evidence, but it gains plausibility when one thinks of the whole of life as shaped by nature's pattern of life and death. Karl Rahner writes that death is "an active consummation, worked out through the whole of life, and, therefore, it is an act of man" (*On the Theology of Death* [New York: Herder and Herder, 1961], 58).

base for an ecological ethics,[29] but rather call attention to how such an ethics finds its grounding in the evolution of the human species out of the stuff of the universe.[30] Ethics, almost by definition, has an intrinsic role in an activist spirituality. The fact that human existence cannot be understood any longer as an independent species on the alien stage of the planet has altered the foundations of our responsibility; human existence carries the conscious, intentional momentum of evolution on the planet.

Without losing this wide perspective we have to attend to personal spirituality and develop further how internalization of evolution entails an activist spirituality. Because of the history of Western Christian spirituality especially, a first step in making this case requires clarification of changes in the premises of the Christian life that are reflected in this work. Two shifts can be illustrated in relationship to the legacy of Augustine. First, Augustine presumed that the actual world in which he lived was not filled with God's grace. His theology of grace functions in response to the pervasive effects of original sin. But, second, when he considered the operation of grace, he was decidedly more positive.[31] He developed the category of cooperative grace, that *auxilium Dei* working within freedom, not against it, but precisely as a transforming and empowering agency within human freedom.[32] Chapter 4 of this work shows how the premises of evolution and the emergence of human existence into a sphere of God's creating love, or Spirit, or grace radically alter the foundations of Christian spirituality.

---

[29] In *Ask the Beasts* Elizabeth Johnson shifts human intentionality away from domination and exploitation of global resource to a sense of community in being with other species. She works from evolution to communicate a sense of being a part of the material of our particular home in the universe. See Elizabeth Johnson, *Ask the Beasts: Darwin and the God of Love* (London: Bloomsbury, 2014).

[30] For a full-scale development of Christian ethics in an evolutionary context, see Stephen J. Pope, *Human Evolution and Christian Ethics* (New York: Cambridge University Press, 2007).

[31] Augustine's picture of the world is a massive work in chiaroscuro where light only pierces the shadows in a very small place. But when his imagination was focused on the light, his portrait of God at work in human freedom was brilliant, transcendent, and classic. H. Richard Niebuhr captures Augustine's positive view of the transforming power of God's grace in *Christ and Culture* (New York: Harper and Row, 1951), 206–18.

[32] I cannot help citing again the classic text of the contemplative activist Bernard of Clairvaux, who cuts through the anthropomorphism implied in so much of the debate over the relationship between nature and grace. How are we to understand God's work within human freedom after first awakening and inspiring it? "What was begun by grace alone, is completed by grace and free choice together, in such a way that they contribute to each new achievement not as if grace did one half of the work and free choice the other; but each does the whole work, according to its own peculiar contribution. Grace does the whole work, and so does free choice—with this one qualification: that whereas the whole is done *in* free choice, so is the whole done *of grace*" (Bernard of Clairvaux, "On Grace and Free Choice," in *Bernard of Clairvaux: Treatises III* (Kalamazoo, MI: Cistercian Publications, 1977), no. 47, p. 106.

The writings of many theologians and spiritual directors today illustrate these new premises. But a category of Juan Luis Segundo puts them in dramatic relief. Much of traditional Christian spirituality unfolded in a framework that envisioned human life in this world as a test, and one passed or failed to pass it on the basis of human choices measured by law and by God as right or wrong. In contrast to this anthropomorphic field Segundo looks upon human life and the use of freedom as a project. This project essentially consists in participating in Jesus's own project of being an agent of God's cause of the rule of God for human flourishing. The point of this distinction does not consist of laying the burden of making the world a better place on each person, but of dramatizing a shift to an evolutionary perspective on reality.

One further question needs to be addressed before turning to the object of Christian hope. A basic issue in all spirituality, and so too in Christian spirituality, lies in the relation of the person to ultimacy. How does spirituality bind a person to what is ultimate? In Christian spirituality this takes the form of union with God. How does Christian spirituality unite a person with God?

Given the dynamism of God's creative energy, given the a priori condition of God's Presence as grace, and considering the activism implied in Jesus's ministry, beneath the level of conscious awareness and religious experience, it seems that personal action itself unites persons more or less closely with God.[33] While this may happen apart from an explicit consciousness, Teilhard appropriates this construction into a foundational conception of Christian life. Our union with God can be read as a function of our action within God's creation in the construction of the world as God intends it. As for personal sanctification, he writes: "In action I adhere to the creative power of God; I coincide with it; I become not only its instrument but its living extension. And as there is nothing more personal in a being than his will, I merge myself, in a sense, through my heart, with the very heart of God."[34] Teilhard describes how the whole of human life becomes united with God and sanctified on the basis and in the measure in which it contributes to the ongoing evolutionary project of God creating the world. This, of course, draws upon the rule of God that Jesus preached. What are we here for? To participate in God's project of creation, which is moving toward completion in an absolute future.[35]

---

[33] I'm responding here not to the ontological unity of a person with God, which is established uniquely by God's creativity, but to the character and degree of human response to this a priori unity.

[34] Teilhard de Chardin, *The Divine Milieu*, 62–63.

[35] In Teilhard's thinking we live within a cosmic drama, and we are part of it. Without this, life takes on a character of futility, of "killing" time. His spirituality trusts that we actually contribute to the end times, a "trust that our efforts can have a *lasting* impact on the whole of things" (John F. Haught, *Christianity and Science: Toward a Theology of Nature* [Maryknoll, NY: Orbis Books, 2007], 81).

But let us conclude this section with a caveat: the activist view proposed here cannot be associated with anything that is "blind"; it is deeply reflective. Such a position burrows down into contemplation and even mysticism. The polarity of active spirituality does not lie in contrast with mindfulness but with a passivity that surrenders freedom. Ignatius of Loyola, an active mystic, represents this tradition in his life and writings. The final contemplation of his *Spiritual Exercises* beautifully illustrates it: "The Contemplation to Attain Divine Love."[36] This contemplation operates within a breathtaking panorama of the work of God creating into which the exercise imaginatively inserts the person considering it. It draws forth the response of love, in action rather than words, Ignatius says, driven by an inner gratitude and a cooperative spirit. This contemplation finalizes a four-week journey of following with a contemplative imagination the activist ministry of Jesus in service of the rule of God.[37]

An even more profound psychological and metaphysical spiritual response to the question of how contemplation can integrate activity into itself was supplied by Meister Eckhart. Bernard McGinn poses the following question to Eckhart: "How does someone actually live who has attained indistinct union in the ground [that is, God]?"[38] How does one who has achieved union with God behave? The response of Eckhart calls for total abandonment of the self to God and living according to what is perceived to be God's will. This is best and most concretely explained in Eckhart's sermon on Mary and Martha, in which Eckhart takes up the tension between contemplation and action.[39] In the gospel story Eckhart "not only abandoned the notion of tension-filled oscillation between action and contemplation but also asserted that a new kind of activity performed out of 'a well-exercised ground' was superior to contemplation, at least as ordinarily conceived."[40] In effect, Eckhart develops a mysticism of participation in history as he elevates Martha to one who has so developed her mystical sense that her activity lives within it, and her union with God becomes actualized by engagement with worldly concerns. For Eckhart, Martha's activity was not a distraction from her contemplation but the fulfillment of it.

---

[36] Ignatius, "Contemplation to Attain Love," nos. 230–37, in Ganss, *The Spiritual Exercises of Saint Ignatius*.

[37] I offer an activist interpretation of the *Spiritual Exercises* in *Christian Spirituality for Seekers: Reflections on the Spiritual Exercises of Ignatius Loyola* (Maryknoll, NY: Orbis Books, 2010).

[38] Bernard McGinn, *The Presence of God: A History of Western Christian Mysticism*, vol. 4, *The Harvest of Mysticism in Medieval Germany (1300–1500)* (New York: Crossroad, 2005), 104–5.

[39] This sermon on Luke 10:38ff. is found in *Meister Eckhart: Teacher and Preacher*, ed. Bernard McGinn (New York: Paulist Press, 1986), 338–45. In Christian literature Mary symbolizes contemplation and Martha activity.

[40] McGinn, *The Presence of God*, 190.

This sets up our final question: Where does life in the sphere of a grace-filled evolutionary world lead?

What Can We Hope For?

The question is phrased in an uneasily defensive way. Should we not ask: For what can we not hope? If God is God, "even though [we] walk through the darkest valley" (Ps 23:4), what should we fear? And yet scientific culture has placed religion on the defensive; pluralism has eroded confidence in the realism of resurrection, and our imaginations fail when we attempt any description of eternal life. The question penetrates deeply into the logic of human life itself and, upon reflection, resolutely refuses to yield to Christian cliché. What can we really hope for?

The Christian conviction about resurrection has been received from the mediation of Jesus Christ as a light that illumines the whole course of one's own life, brightens human existence itself, and even retrieves a holistic worldview from the shadows of incompleteness. But that answer to the question must have roots in the character and identity of human existence as we know it. It cannot be a belief that one picks up; it must spring from a hope and a faith that rises from the depths of nature and self-consciousness.

This conviction, which in many respects shares the same fundamental importance as a belief in creation, requires explanation, if not argument. The following discussion uses a series of propositions to control what might expand indefinitely. We begin with a dynamic metaphysics of human subjectivity derived from two theological accounts of the human person. This will set the conversation within the framework of evolution. From there, we can render in specific but abstract rather than descriptive terms what we should be encouraged to hope for. This discussion forms the conclusion of this work by showing that, far from being a peculiar disposition, realist hope and faith in resurrection correlates with an evolutionary universe.

Hope

Hope arises out of a deep structure of human existence. This appraisal of what we can hope for has roots in a deeper description of the meaning of hope than an expectation of things to come. It consists of more than looking forward to imagine, for example, where we might be after a number of years. We are looking toward an absolute future, something that both includes our personal destiny and infinitely transcends it. Two somewhat different but complementary resources inspire a portrait of hope: Karl Rahner conceives of hope as arising out of the intrinsic makeup of the human person; Edward Schillebeeckx appeals to a constant pattern of historical existence that testifies to hope as a basic human trait.

Rahner views the human spirit as dynamic energy in the world of matter. It is driven by an inner implicit desire to achieve its destiny. The very entrance of the human person "into the world and its destiny, shows itself to be only the coming to be of a spirit which is striving towards the absolute."[41] From an analysis of the dynamics of human subjectivity, he defines the human person as a basic openness to reality. The human person is "by its very nature pure openness for absolutely everything, for being as such."[42] This fundamental openness to existence, reality, the world, or to being itself constitutes hope as a basic structure of the human. Hope refers to "the enduring attitude of 'outwards from the self' into the uncontrollability of God."[43] Hope orients the human person; it positively fixes the human spirit in a direction toward the unknown, the absolute mystery of being itself.

The basis for hope does not lie in faith. Rather, faith finds its roots in hope. Hope structures the human spirit as a quality of its being; it opens a person outward toward the creator God as the ground of being that is subtly entailed in one's commitment to existence. Hope implicitly joins three factors: the indecipherability of the future, the absolute incomprehensibility and mystery of God, and a basic openness and trust that shape deep down the dynamics of human existence. Acts of hope mark the coming together of these elements. The intrinsic character of hope makes it prior to faith and love as an a priori structure of the human.[44] In its primal form hope longs for fulfillment of personal existence and the final validation of the world.

Schillebeeckx's reflection on hope stems from a spiritual and religious concern in an increasingly secular environment. He is far from hostile to secular scientific

---

[41] Karl Rahner, *Spirit in the World* (New York: Herder and Herder, 1968), 407. "Human spirit" in Rahner does not refer to a substance but to the object of self-consciousness. I expect that Rahner would have respected science's unknowing of exactly what the human self is, but he would have insisted that this mystery is something real.

[42] Rahner, *Foundations of Christian Faith*, 20. When Karl Rahner uses the word *freedom* in a sense that defines the human, his meaning transcends "ability to choose" and approaches this basic view of the human spirit as "openness." The human person is incarnate spirit, or spirit-in-matter, or, in our context, the freedom of matter.

[43] Karl Rahner, "On the Theology of Hope," *Theological Investigations* 10, 242–59 (New York: Herder and Herder, 1973), 250. See also Karl Rahner, *A Rahner Reader*, ed. Gerald A. McCool (New York: Seabury Press, 1975), 226–39, corresponding to 245–59 in *Theological Investigations* 10.

[44] The act of hope is "the acceptance of this orientation towards the incalculability and uncontrollability of God. This act comprehends and unifies all these divisions even though, in order to be realized in the concrete, it has itself to be distinguished into faith and love" (Rahner, "On the Theology of Hope," 256). Hope spawns faith and love; it should not be viewed as a parallel virtue. This analysis does not describe overt consciousness; Rahner, here, is constructing a metaphysical view.

reasoning, but it requires a new take on how we understand our relation with God. Hope and, more deeply, basic trust play a major role here. Christians today should seek God within the material world and not outside it. He finds a basis for Christianity within this secular situation in various manifestations of basic trust in existence and life. This basic trust manifests itself in everyday historical social life, not just in special occasions, but in moments everyone can relate to.

To schematize a comprehensive historical anthropology in a few words, we begin with the idea of being in contact with reality rather than in possession of our opinions about it. Schillebeeckx was convinced that we know that we are engaging the real when we meet an impasse. When everything conforms to our thinking, we may be suffering from myopia; when reality does not fit our expectation, we know we are connected. Often an impasse does not just challenge but appears as intrinsically negative. When we confront something that we intuitively know is wrong, we implicitly intuit the positive values that supply leverage for the feelings of revulsion. This negative contrast experience also feeds the wish or even the urge to right the wrong, to seek redress, and to make things whole.[45] This represents a first step in a shift from an intellectual approach to the relevance of Christianity in a secular material world to a practical interest in acting and doing something in the direction of a better future.[46]

Against the impasse of negativity and within the dynamics of moral response, Schillebeeckx discovers what he calls basic trust in existence, life, and history. Basic trust undergirds everyday life. In and against all difficulties and frustrations, from massive social dehumanization to death itself, it urges the meaningful character human existence and its future. This trust in existence is *basic*. The idea of creation and faith in God build on and support it. They form "the reflective justification, made afterwards, of the conviction that this unconditional trust in the gift of a meaningful human future is not an illusion, not a projection of frustrated wishful thinking."[47] The Christian interprets this as a hope for salvation. No proof exists for anything here. But this descriptive analysis uncovers a basis within the project of the universe for the meaningfulness of the idea of God and an absolute human future.[48]

In this view God appears as guarantor of the human project. God does not undermine basic trust in life in the world and history. "Acceptance of God is the ultimate, precise name which must be given to the deepest meaning of commitment to this world."[49] Faith in God really makes its appearance in the

---

[45] Edward Schillebeeckx, *God the Future of Man* (New York: Sheed and Ward, 1968), 154–55.

[46] Schillebeeckx, *God the Future of Man*, 57.

[47] Schillebeeckx, *God the Future of Man*, 75.

[48] This fundamental trust is also exemplified in those who approach death in hope (Schillebeeckx, *God the Future of Man*, 90n19).

[49] Schillebeeckx, *God the Future of Man*, 76.

commitment to the human project; God supplies the ultimacy. "Not to lose faith in man in all his activities, despite all evil experiences, reveals itself, on closer analysis, as a latent, unconditional trust in God, as faith that human existence is a promise of salvation."[50] Christian faith, therefore, is ultimate commitment to the world and its future.

Evolution

Evolution does not obstruct but encourages hope and faith in a creator-finisher God who injects Presence and purpose into the process of the universe. Science sets the premise: a holistic appreciation of emergence and evolution describes the intrinsic form of the finite being of our universe. It manifests a directionality toward complexity and higher forms of life. This seems to be a genial framework for Christian faith in creation having a goal and an end time. John Haught convincingly argues that meaning in an unfinished narrative must include the end of the story, the future or goal of the process.[51] We cannot consciously and logically reduce the universe to matter and motion; we cannot look at generativity without considering the intelligence by which we think. We also have to accept the traditional recognition that faith cannot be reduced to demonstrative reason but must involve a "leap." But that leap has to stay close to the astonishing discoveries of science and cannot jump over them in contradiction. Science rules out the plausibility of God as a "big person in the sky." Anthropomorphism offends religious sensibility as much as it does science. God is not a part of the universe or apart from it but is its ground of being.

Many writers, rather than fighting with science about how things work, have shown that science uncovers dimensions in the story of existence that are deep, lofty, beautiful, and mysterious.[52] Hope and faith are spontaneous human

---

[50] Schillebeeckx, *God the Future of Man*, 77.

[51] We can see a fundamental difference in apperceptive supposition at this point: the perspective of a scientist looking at the past to understand the present and a theologian looking forward. Sean Carroll says that everything of import about our world today can be traced to its causes in the past: "Our progress through time is pushed from behind, not pulled from ahead" (*The Big Picture: On the Origins of Life, Meaning, and the Universe Itself* [New York: Dutton, 2016], 66). By contrast, John Haught says that in a universe in motion and unfinished to determine the nature of reality by looking backwards spells death. "Nature is not simply and solely the outcome of a past series of mechanical causes, but also the *anticipation* and *promise* of an indeterminate cosmic future" (John F. Haught, "Science, Death, and Resurrection," in *Christianity and Science: Toward a Theology of Nature* [Maryknoll, NY: Orbis Books, 2007], 172). I don't see why these two perspectives cannot be conjoined.

[52] John Haught develops a concise argument from the narrative of ongoing creation of higher forms of complexity and beauty for hope in an absolute future in *Christianity and*

responses: hope opens one to some future, and human life always lives by some faith. But, more specifically, faith in God fills the cosmos with intentionality and purpose, however elusive their contours. Hope in a finisher God offers a possibility of meaning that seems impossible without it. Faith in a creator God holds out a divine Presence within the material, the scientific, and the secular that guarantees their value. It confirms the value of truth and the sin of falsifying evidence, the value of penetrating deeper into the mechanisms of the universe and the sin of using this intelligence for killing others or defacing creation. Invisible to sight, unimaginably transcendent, God is the within of things. God as finisher communicates meaning right down to the individual actions of an individual person here and now and allows for hope for ultimate meaning.

Values

One should hope for a cosmic preservation of the value and integrity of being. From its objective empirical viewpoint science extrapolates different possibilities for the end of our world. It is not in the business of providing a transcendent object of faith. And because science constantly confronts opinion and conviction gained from the surface of things, it has to possess a critical edge. Question and demonstrative proof, by reworking the epistemological path of experiment, define the logic of a body of knowledge that grows by a slow increment of solid evidence. And justly so. But there are other forms of knowledge. One of these works through the internal reflective conviction that the quest for truth constitutes a value so important that it must have a ground or status that preserves its inviolable character. It is hard to commit to research into cognitive truth without endowing true knowledge with some status in being. Reflection on value gives this conversation a new dimension.

Hope can be cultivated as a moral disposition, and faith can be seen as including reflective consciousness that brings focus to hope through more specific objects, at least on the formal level. The world of values and the process of perceiving and affirming values bring some clarity to the operation of hope and faith and its relation to the epistemology of science.

We regard something that is considered important as valuable; value is a quality that establishes importance. Realism in value theory means that, although values are perceived by a certain resonance between the value and human value response, value defines a quality of reality and dictates the response; human interest does not constitute it but is drawn to it. The perception of values and commitment to them sheds light on the function of hope and faith, how they

---

Science (59–64). He summarizes it in this way: "There has to be a permanence in the depths of the world process that redresses the fact that nothing lasts" (63).

operate in contrast to a narrow view of scientific method and yet are complementary to it, especially evolutionary understanding.[53]

An epistemological position that affirms God on the basis of value perception and the objectivity of values says "that 'God exists' is simply true. Such a truth can be independent of what we might construe as good for us or in our long term best interest, as is the case with all objective truth applied to values."[54] It is not the affirmation of a fiction but a reality on the basis of value. Affirmations are grounded in "seeing as" or on the basis of objective and commanding values.

Faith, when it takes the form of belief, transpires within a consciousness that is sensitive to value. It gives more definite shape to basic trust. "Faith then becomes a form of life which *sees* the source of human good (events of grace) *as God*. This statement may be reversed as well: faith sees *God* as the source of human good."[55] This fills out basic trust, the intrinsic moral disposition of openness to the future. Existentially, as a form of life defined as openness to the future, faith provides the valuational matrix that makes it appropriate to see God as the ground of being and as Presence.[56]

Hope for a cosmic preservation of value and for the integrity of being appears natural within the sphere of values. Of course, the questions of whether values are real and how they are to be measured will always be there. Those questions remain an internal and ongoing issue in the dialogue between science and theology.

Innocent Suffering

One should hope for a restoration of meaning relative to innocent suffering. The human person and meaningful existence possess values that are known by an intuition more stable than empirical evidence. Most people affirm these values, humanists and scientists alike. But history tells another story. We turn now to a

---

[53] The logic of value perception can be seen at work in the negative experience of contrast that was described earlier relative to the thought of Schillebeeckx; it recurs, below, in the thinking of Johann Baptist Metz. Negative and positive resonance with an event or situation correlates with the sphere of value perception. This is not the place to digress into the epistemology of values; the point is to differentiate this sphere of perception from scientific knowledge narrowly conceived and then show their congruity. For a short defense of realism in value perception, see Wesley J. Wildman, *Science and Religious Anthropology: A Spiritually Evocative Naturalist Interpretation of Human Life* (Surrey, UK: Ashgate, 2009), 194–95.

[54] Charley D. Hardwick, *Events of Grace: Naturalism, Existentialism, and Theology* (Cambridge: Cambridge University Press, 1996), 67.

[55] Hardwick, *Events of Grace*, 179.

[56] "Once we see the linkages among 'God exists' as a seeing-as, a valuational matrix, and a form of life, then the content of the gospel need not be non-cognitive, though the cognitivity issue will be settled in a valuational . . . context" (Hardwick, *Events of Grace*, 179).

combination of a desire for cosmic justice and an interpretation of Jesus Christ that addresses innocent human suffering, a quest for comprehensive meaning, and the role of resurrection in contemporary life. Few theologians have discussed these issues more incisively than Johann Baptist Metz. Compressing his thought into two points does not do justice to his penetrating insight.

Metz establishes a basis of his thinking in a fusion of a negative experience of contrast and the essential meaning of the message of Jesus Christ. He formulates negative experience concisely: "The essential dynamics of history consist of the (1) memory of suffering as a negative consciousness of (2) future freedom and (3) as a stimulus to overcome suffering within the framework of that freedom."[57] This is the same experience to which Schillebeeckx appealed, but Metz offers it as an account of the dynamics of history, not in a philosophical idealist sense, but as descriptive of what we encounter. Metz sees this pattern within the Christian memory of Jesus's suffering, death, and resurrection. In a christomorphic imagination Jesus Christ provides the archetype of innocent suffering and a tortured death, something utterly shocking in its contrast to the rule of God that Jesus stood for and actualized in his ministry. Yet Jesus's resurrection reverses that negation and absolutizes the rule of God. In other words, resurrection breaks the impasse of innocent suffering. Nothing else can do it. The formula reveals the large canvas upon which Metz displays the logic of faith, science, history, and eternal life. It remains to highlight the practical directives of life that flow from it.

Metz underlines the value of human life, and this leads him to a somewhat negative view of the physical sciences.[58] In contrast to all objectification of the human, the rule of God and resurrection honor human life absolutely. But the resurrection of Jesus also represents a "dangerous memory," because it entails responsibility and moral reckoning of one's own freedom in an absolute future.[59] The memory of Jesus's suffering and all innocent suffering makes demands on us. Attending to innocent suffering is subversive; it breaks the moral plausibility of prevailing structures or ideologies that say things are all right. The memory of suffering thus constitutes an iconoclastic tradition that "resists any attempt

---

[57] J. B. Metz, *Faith in History and Society: Toward a Practical Fundamental Theology* (New York: Seabury Press, 1980), 108.

[58] In Metz, *science* and *evolution* tend to represent naturalism, scientism, evolutionism, and the reduction by instrumental reason of the human and its future to what can be rationally planned by ideologies and bureaucratic systems. Humanity is being threatened by human beings themselves; subjectivity is treated objectively. Metz saw "the processes of technological civilization" turning human existence into their product. In Metz's language the "political" stands for human transcendence and freedom morally managing nature and not being reduced to a product of nature (Metz, *Faith in History and Society*, 102, 107–8.) Admittedly, these are dangers. I turn to Metz for his theological views rather than his critique of science.

[59] Metz, *Faith in History and Society*, 90.

to do away with it by means of a purely affirmative attitude to the past."[60] And, finally, only resurrection, or something functionally analogous to it, can ultimately bestow meaning on innocent human suffering. "No improvement of the condition of freedom in the world is able to do justice to the dead or effect a transformation of the injustice and the non-sense of past suffering."[61] Human existence craves meaning and justice; without resurrection, Metz is saying, nothing makes any ultimate sense.[62]

The Easter Experience

One may hope for the preservation of the human person and personal resurrection. This statement utterly transcends the scope of science. Evolution may show directionality, but it cannot find any sign of resurrection. Resurrection completely transcends the pattern of nature's seasonal rebirth or metamorphosis into other forms of being. Here, we are moving into the sphere of hope shaped by a faith mediated by the Easter experience that Jesus died into life within the sphere of God. John Haught expresses commitment to resurrection in terms of an act of faith; it can be formulated in terms of Pascal's wager on ultimate meaning—no faith or faith. On the one hand: "Apart from God's preservative remembrance of the whole series of events that make up the cosmic story, the world would amount to nothing in the end." On the other hand: "It is only through faith and not sight that we gain at present any sense of this destiny."[63] The alternatives are stated in a way that recommends faith on both sides, but the contrast shows what is at stake. But more has to be said about the plausibility of resurrection.

A first premise for thinking about the possibility of resurrection, prior to its assertion by faith, resides in a holistic appreciation of reality that was discussed earlier: being is dynamic becoming, a history of reality qualified as space-time in movement that remains incomplete. Its final intelligibility as a narrative will be determined by its end or completion. Haught calls attention to time, moving forward, building ever more complex forms of life and levels of meaning; he stresses the still unfinished character of the process. Instead of thinking of all

---

[60] Metz, *Faith in History and Society*, 110. This seems to be an accurate appraisal of most institutional histories.

[61] Metz, *Faith in History and Society*, 128. The doctrine of original sin was based on the premise that God created a perfect world in the beginning. Emergence and evolution show creation of a world unfinished and still being created. This relieves some pressure, not all, on the problem of theodicy. Salvation and completion are up ahead. See John Haught, *Christianity and Science: Toward a Theology of Nature* (Maryknoll, NY: Orbis Books, 2007), 82–107.

[62] The stoic says, "So be it." The Buddhist says, "Craving must yield to detachment." The Christian says, "Craving for justice is a realistic testimony of nature itself."

[63] John Haught, *Resting on the Future: Catholic Theology for an Unfinished Universe* (New York: Bloomsbury, 2015), 126.

reality as finally disintegrating into chaos, it makes more sense to hope that a final meaning of the narrative lies out in front of the universe.[64] "Cosmic hope reads the world of becoming as a universal stream into which we may confidently insert our own lives and particular callings. The living God is to be sought not so much beneath, above, or behind the flux of time as up ahead, calling the temporal world into being from out of the future."[65] Haught thinks narratively in terms of events that accumulate over time, so that temporal linkage and constructive building allow one to hope in a future that is absolute and that draws the past into itself. "It is hard to fathom how such imperishability would not also include the survival and renewal of our own subjective consciousness."[66]

But problems plague the very idea of resurrection of individuals in a formal sense: it is unimaginable. Recall the critique of Steven Pinker of the ghost in the machine. Given our scientific culture and the evidence of how closely mind and consciousness are linked with the organic brain, we cannot conceive of a spiritual self that is independent of bodily existence. The question of the relation of mind and brain raises questions all around. One cannot reduce human consciousness to physical interactions, even though one cannot separate them; and one cannot imaginatively envision what resurrection looks like, either of a soul or of a body. Whatever we can concretely imagine does not really work. Thinking imaginatively of personal resurrection in objective terms of body or soul is intrinsically problematic.

The problem begins with the question of what accounts for our individual identity. What carries our identity across the temporal material changes of ourselves? Are we not the same person? In the classical thought of Thomas Aquinas, the human soul defines what *kind* (species) of being we are, and soul shaping matter defines our continuous personal identity. Given the attack on the ghost in the machine, John Polkinghorne takes "information" from biological science and uses it to interpret "soul." "Soul" is not an individual something; it becomes the "immensely complex 'information-bearing pattern' in which . . . matter is organized. This pattern is not static; it is modified as we acquire new experiences, insights and memories, in accordance with the dynamic of

---

[64] This has long been the framework of Haught's thinking. It stands in contrast to finding an adequate explanation of things exclusively through the vectors of the past that produced what is given. These are not necessarily hostile perspectives, unless either claims to be an exclusive source of intelligibility.

[65] Haught, *Resting on the Future,* 121. I do not think of God being beneath, above, behind, or in front of the finite universe as alternatives. God can be simultaneously thought of non-spatially in all of those modes at the same time.

[66] Haught, *Resting on the Future,* 125. I cannot accept any reasoning that says resurrection is impossible. The simplest regard for the universe and the intricacies of evolution should dispel any doubt about the power of a creator God.

our living history. It is this information-bearing pattern that is the soul."[67] In the end, however, this shift of language amounts to classic projection. We do not have the equipment to form an objective conception of God, let alone the constitution of resurrected life within God's sphere. The ultimate ground for hope in personal resurrection ultimately comes down to faith in the creator God who is also the lover and the finisher of finite existence.

A better approach to resurrection, therefore, leaves attempts at objective conceptualization aside and focuses on the dynamic formal conceptions of God presented in Chapter 3. Can God as pure act, ground of being, absolute mystery, serendipitous creativity, or Presence refocus an approach to resurrection? John Haught uses the phrase, "God's preservative remembrance of the whole series of events that make up the cosmic story."[68] The problem with the idea of God's memory lies in anthropomorphism. The metaphor readily suggests an association with human memory of things that no longer exist; memory represents what was, a replica of the nonexistence of the past. The potential of the metaphor can only work if it is critically reconceived in terms of the transcendent formal concepts of God. For example, God as pure act bears no limitations of time, space, or finitude. God as ground of being bestows being. The "memory" of *God* is "God acting" to both preserve the reality of the past earthly narrative and to continue to actualize it. God's memory is God simultaneously conserving identity forged in a lifetime and generating actual being within God's sphere.[69] The memory of God refers to God acting, and God's acting in this case accomplishes two things: it preserves identity created in time, and it actualizes it as finite being, or as continued becoming, in God's eternal present.[70] Resurrection into eternal life does not repeat history but preserves and actualizes it within God's eternal and encompassing self-presence or actuality. If God is God, why cannot one hope for the preservation of the human person and personal resurrection? We revert

---

[67] John Polkinghorne, *The God of Hope and the End of the World* (New Haven, CT: Yale University Press, 2002), 105–6. He adds: "I believe that we can follow Thomas Aquinas in adopting, in appropriately modern phrasing and understanding, the concept of the soul as the form, or information-bearing pattern, of the body" (106).

[68] Haught, *Resting on the Future*, 126. Haught is not alone in looking to the "memory of God" as a way of finding a language to talk about this faith conviction.

[69] Using the philosophies of Pierce and especially Whitehead, Joseph Bracken develops a theology in which the mutual entailment of body and human spirit as a single reality is preserved objectively in the reality of God from the beginning of each being's existence; at death the total subjective existence of human beings is preserved in the consequent nature of God. Joseph A. Bracken, "Bodily Resurrection and the Dialectic of Spirit and Matter," *Theological Studies* 66 (2005): 770–82. One has to be particularly careful about an anthropomorphic imagination in conceiving and responding to questions about a "bodily" resurrection.

[70] Gregory of Nyssa taught that resurrection was universal, the intrinsic destiny of creation. But not all are resurrected at once to union with God. He thought of continued "becoming" in terms of purification. *An Address on Religious Instruction*, in *Christology of the Later Fathers*, ed. Edward R. Hardy (Philadelphia: Westminster Press, 1954), no. 35, p. 317.

to a primal creation-consciousness: God loves and does not forget or cease to love what God creates.[71]

✦ ✦ ✦

In summary, the evolutionary character of reality commands subtle but real adjustments in a human consciousness that values place and stability. These values have to be retrieved within a new framework of movement toward an ever-receding historical horizon. The Christian theological vision, centered by the revelation mediated by Jesus of Nazareth, within the metaphysical framework of creation and eschatology, can appropriate into itself emergent cosmology and the evolution of life. This appropriation does no violence to the picture presented by science; it gives the world as science describes it metaphysical depth and lasting value. But more importantly here, this appropriation injects new vitality into the Christian vision.

The shift of meaning can be described in many ways, but this chapter has highlighted two distinctive features. First, evolution reinforces an active spirituality. The movement of time takes on distinctive dimensions in reflectively conscious Homo sapiens. In human consciousness, self-presence, deliberation, and will, within the broad framework of intentionality, explicitly shape human activity. And we are always responding to the world: the environment, culture, and immediately pressing demands. Our form of being becomes "more" intensely human by degrees in the mix of self-knowledge and agency together. Human life requires a form of meaning and purpose.

Second, to have a specific horizon for living that can in some measure be clarified fills individual and group with a sense of identity. Grounded in hope and faith, a conception of an absolute future gives meaning that has grounding, direction that supplies a rationale for living, and a motive for living actively in an unfinished world that continually challenges that faith. The response to the challenges subsists in activity that promotes the values of the rule of God. That activity unites one to God and, in the end, who one is and what one does will be drawn into God's sphere. This hope includes personal resurrection but transcends individualism: it cannot be less incarnational and social than is actual human existence. In this way Christian faith offers something truly worthy of one's hope.

.

---

[71] John Polkinghorne, in the end, agrees. He writes that death is real, and resurrection is a further act of God that preserves the psychosomatic unity of the person in another sphere of life or environment. "The only ground for this hope—and the sufficient ground for this hope, as we have already emphasized—lies in the faithfulness of the Creator, in the unrelenting divine love for all creatures" (*God of Hope and the End of the World*, 108).

Conclusion

We can summarize this book in terms of creation, revelation, and the goal of human life. These three spheres of reflection offer a lean but energetic conception of the content of Christian faith—energetic because a full Christian life, including prayer and devotion, are animated by it. The ways of approaching this core Christianity are many, but a dialogue with science, and especially evolution, highlights the logic.

Creation

The idea of creation encapsulates Christian faith's conception of the grounding of reality. It provides a place where theology almost spontaneously encounters science and descriptions of an evolutionary world. Evolution has an impact on almost every phase of human self-understanding. How could one think of God as creator and not summon up the pictures of the universe with which science now feeds our imaginations? God created our universe. To understand what that means, we have to attend to the creation that God created. All the disciplines dedicated to understanding the human have been revolutionized by the dynamics of evolution.

The dialogue with science, and particularly evolution, as with no other partner, helps theology become aware of its inner inclination toward anthropomorphism. Science forcefully asks us to take reflective responsibility for our language about God and what God does in this world.[1] The large concepts of God offered here, with an accent on Presence, help to revise interventionist images of how God acts. They supply comprehensive intellectual metaphors that actually bring God closer to our world and envision God as being entirely

---

[1] I distinguish theology from preaching. Theology should have some influence on preaching, but preaching ordinarily should not be a lecture in theology. This has been a work in theology, but occasionally I have turned to the implications of theology for spirituality. Spirituality provides a testing ground for theological language.

more accessible than interventionist language implies. God as the "within" of reality virtually overcomes the baffling enmity that arose between science and faith and challenges the overt violations of method that unnecessarily separate these two worlds of human response and understanding.[2]

The dynamics of creation theology allow the theological imagination to enter the world of science, to learn from it, and to rethink certain conceptions that simply do not communicate in a present-day, scientifically influenced linguistic framework. Creation theology positively encourages building coalitions between frequently competitive or uncoordinated systems of understanding that refer to the same thing. More specifically, creation theology clarifies God at work in the world not by a concrete imaginative construction but by not confusing it with such conceptions. God's action cannot adequately be imagined in sensible terms. The running together of God's continuous creative action with Spirit, grace, and God's active love is not a tour de force but an easy alliance based on religious experience and insight into the all-pervasive Presence of God.

Jesus Christ Revealer

The doctrine of creation does not enjoy rational or philosophical autonomy but appears within a Christian imagination. An evangelical theologian would begin a synthesis with the revelation of Jesus Christ. But having begun with a conversation between creation and evolution, creation together with evolution still leaves basic questions unanswered. Two major ones concern the character of God, as distinct from the idea of "what" God is, and the intention or goal of creation. Jesus as revealer of God responds to these questions. The answers lie embedded in the overarching Jewish metaphor that guided Jesus's ministry: the rule of God. In Jesus's teaching the rule of God refers to God's will or intention for creation with special focus on human existence. Jesus's teaching about the rule of God and his symbolic actions that dramatized it represent to the human imagination some specific impressions about the character of the creator God. The present and the future dimensions of the rule of God in Jesus's usage amount to exegetical and theological commonplaces. But each of these mutually intertwined dimensions bears important meaning for Christian faith.

In theological terms relative to human life on earth, Christians almost take for granted that God as ideal Father realistically characterizes the creator. Parent

---

[2] The theology of creation remains underestimated in its power to offer comprehensive theological intelligibility and positively thwart the misunderstanding occasioned by anthropomorphic language. The dialogue with science and evolution goes a long way toward reestablishing the extensive all-pervasive character of the theology of creation for understanding the other doctrines and for mediating concepts of faith to a wider public audience.

language presents God as personal and loving all, as Father or Mother, but attending especially to those on the edges of life. God loves everything that God creates. Much of practical theology orients its language toward those who cannot come to this place for any of many possible reasons. Jesus's ministry presents a God whose character intrinsically consists of drawing people into the community and making up for every disadvantage. The metaphor of the rule of God is too expansive in Jesus's teaching and too rich in its tradition to be reduced to obeying particular ordinances. The idea of a sphere of God's intention for a just and harmonious society comes closer to Jesus's meaning than a narrow focus on laws. The rule of God is spiritual rather than moralistic; individual but personal and communitarian and not individualist; governing relations with God and other human beings. The rule of God carries transcendence, always with the twist of the chasm between God's loving intent and self-serving human inclination.

The rule of God also looks forward to completion of creative intent in an absolute future. As various philosophical and scientific reductionists have precipitously concluded, this looks like a mere projection of the self-fulfillment of the human. The Christian counterview resonates with faith's realism. Granted that we have no conclusive or self-evident material evidence that the revelation of the rule of God mediated through Jesus represents a real promise of God. But human beings can do no other than live by faith. And a phenomenology of the expansive and transformative experience that underlies this vision proposed by Jesus, when anthropomorphic language is shorn from revelatory encounter, makes this faith more plausible and generative than its alternatives.

Eschatology

Filling in the content of the promised rule of God involves more work than simple openness to the idea. We know nothing "in fact" about the condition of creation within the sphere of God's memory. The primary burden of the doctrine consists in accepting that God the author of finite reality is its finisher. This allows the dialectical transfer of meaning from the present to the future; dialectical because it is stripped of all empirical detail. This perspective gives the resurrection of Jesus Christ a specific relevance for Christian faith, not its idea, but the reality to which it points. It signifies transformation into a new form of being that is both discontinuous and continuous with created this-worldly identity. The reality of Jesus's resurrection promises the rule of God in the future and eternal life.

This theological study has consistently rejected an anthropomorphic imaging of the sphere of God because of the long-term damage it causes. But critique of this language should not minimize the experience of God's Presence to which Christian language refers. That Presence of God, experienced within, draws all finite reality into itself and transcends the boundaries of finitude. Experience of union with that God promises a future.

In conclusion, the dialogue between Christian faith and science, in particular with evolution, should not be defensive but positive and constructive. This work takes the notion of evolution from science and gives it a theological context, one that recognizes how deeply anthropomorphism has confused our spiritual and religious options. That theological context avoids those misrepresentations that appear to be scientific but are also anthropomorphic, and it clarifies the meaning of Christian faith in a way that speaks to our scientifically influenced critical culture. Its intention aims at enriching Christian life for those who internalize the questions that a secular scientific culture legitimately raises. More and more, these questions press in on all of us. They are good questions, and they stimulate a deeper faith. If our world is evolutionary, we have to incorporate its reality in our faith vision. My hope is that this book may help some people in doing that.

Index